PURE DESSERT

PURE DESSERT

■

ALICE MEDRICH

artisan/new york

Published by Artisan
A Division of Workman Publishing Company, Inc.
225 Varick Street
New York, NY 10014-4381
www.artisanbooks.com

Library of Congress Cataloging-in-Publication Data

Medrich, Alice.
Pure dessert / Alice Medrich.
p. cm
ISBN-13: 978-1-57965-211-1
1. Desserts.   I. Title

TX773.   M4276 2007
641.8'6—dc22
2006050411

Design by Jan Derevjanik
Photographic styling by Sara Slavin
Food styling of ice cream and sorbet photographs by Sandra Cook

Printed in Singapore
First printing, August 2007

10 9 8 7 6 5 4 3 2 1

for lucy

contents

■

in pursuit of pleasure

Faced with an overly sweet, complicated dessert or one made with mundane ingredients, I sometimes long instead for a bowl of good plain yogurt drizzled with honey and sprinkled with walnuts or pistachios, a piece of bittersweet chocolate, or some ripe figs.

I haven't given up dessert, but when I eat it, I want it to taste as good as that bowl of yogurt or piece of chocolate. I want the soul satisfaction and the sensual pleasure of real flavors. The best chefs cook savory food simply, with the best ingredients. That's how I like to eat. Why don't we make more desserts that way?

The dessert repertoire needs an infusion of new and better ingredients and new approaches to working with them. High-quality ingredients of all sorts are available now. Fresh, delicate cheeses (cow, goat, and sheep) can redefine cheesecake. Interesting grains should not be reserved for heavy loaves and health food: their toasty, nutty flavors can bring nuance and depth to indulgent buttery cookies, delicate wafers, and moist, tender cakes. Organic yogurts, milks, and creams can transform ice creams and sherbets. Great chocolates and cocoas can elevate simple desserts, as will flavors captured from fresh flowers and herbs, coffee beans, and tea leaves.

Pure Dessert is a collection of simple, ingredient-driven recipes for cakes, cookies, tarts, ice creams, and other desserts, made from fresh, artisanal, organic, natural, or otherwise distinguished "real" ingredients. Such ingredients are increasingly abundant in better supermarkets as well as in the obvious places: farmers' markets, cheese shops, gourmet and natural food shops online, and a growing number of urban and suburban gardens.

Authentic ingredients are important because they taste good. Simple recipes are essential because they allow us to savor that goodness. The emphasis on flavor means desserts that are often (but not always) less sweet and/or less rich than mainstream desserts. If they *are* less sweet and rich, it is primarily in pursuit of pleasure. Incidental health benefits are just bonuses.

My pure desserts are simple, relaxed, convenient, and elegant. These accessible, home-kitchen–friendly recipes include tips to ensure success and notes that reveal the method to my madness. Pure desserts are for busy people who love food and care about what they eat, for people who are curious and open to new tastes, and for those who appreciate the details that make the difference between a good dessert and a great one.

Pure desserts can stand alone or be mixed and matched for special occasions. Sour Cream Ice Cream, Tropical Lace Cookies, and strawberries is worthy of a dinner party, but each component is delicious on its own. Pure dessert recipes are brief and inviting, and they welcome improvisation.

The media proclaim the message: organic, natural, local, "slow," hand-crafted, and authentic. So what more could we ask for? Here are recipes and techniques that are simple, and as easy for the home cook as the chef. That's the cherry on the top.

before you start

No two cooks do things in exactly the same way, whether it is measuring flour or preparing a cookie sheet. If you have a passion for cookbooks, you already know that the pages before and after the recipes—where the impatient never stray—hold valuable keys to producing the best each recipe has to offer. Although seemingly mundane, the equipment and ingredient information and tips on technique are a personal introduction to the author-as-cook in her kitchen—a real piece of her mind. How does she think and move and solve problems? What does she love or hate? And how can she help you succeed?

details make a difference

Although the recipes in *Pure Dessert* are relatively relaxed and easygoing, small, simple, often nonintuitive details can alter the results. Unlike the savory cook, the baker can rarely taste and adjust or repair as he or she mixes batters. Knowing which details are important sets you free to be as creative and playful as you like, without sad surprises.

mise en place

Mise en place is a French phrase that means "put in place" or "set up." Professional chefs could not survive in a busy kitchen without their "mise." When you see TV chefs with all their ingredients measured in little dishes before any cooking begins, that's mise en place!

The ritual of setting out and measuring ingredients focuses your attention and promotes a calm connection to the task at hand. It allows you to be sure, before you start a recipe, that you have all of the ingredients and equipment you need. You are less likely to measure incorrectly or forget to include an ingredient, regardless of any distractions.

Most dessert recipes turn out best when the recipe steps are performed without interruption. Mise en place ensures that once you begin the recipe, you will not have to run to the store, search the sandbox for your sifter, or rummage through the pantry for a particular pan while your chocolate hardens, your eggs curdle, or your batter deflates. Mise en place makes baking and dessert making both more enjoyable and more successful.

measuring

Many experts emphasize the importance of accuracy in baking without making a distinction between the critical ingredients, which make or break the recipe and must be measured accurately, and those that may be adjusted to your taste. You can use a liberal hand with, or instead omit, inclusions such as raisins, nuts, chocolate chips, or even vanilla to your taste. You can normally substitute dried fruits and nuts in equal measure one for another, and experiment with flavor ingredients. You can substitute one liquor or liqueur for another, or even omit it without affecting the result.

But, for tender cakes with a perfect crumb, delicate cookies, or perfect panna cotta, you must carefully measure the baking soda, baking powder, salt, gelatin, and particularly the flour and cocoa powder. Even in, or especially in, the simplest recipes, baking is not as forgiving as cooking. If cakes or cookies are tough, dry, doughy, or leaden, chances are your flour measurement is at fault.

A cup of all-purpose flour can weigh anywhere from 4 to 6 ounces, depending on whether or not it is sifted before measuring or packed firmly into the cup. That 2-ounce (50 percent!) discrepancy can make the difference between a moist, light, poem of a cake and a highly effective doorstop. Cooks and cookbook authors do not all measure flour the same way, so it is best to read any instructions about how to measure in each book that you use (or get a scale—see page 9).

HOW TO MEASURE FLOUR

When a recipe in this book calls for 1 cup all-purpose flour, this means 1 cup flour measured without first sifting, as follows: Loosen the flour in the sack or canister with a spoon if it is compacted. Spoon the flour lightly into a 1-cup dry measure until it heaps above the rim. Do not shake or tap the cup to settle the flour! Sweep a straight edged knife or a spatula across the rim of the cup to level the flour. A cup of unsifted all-purpose flour measured this way weighs 4.5 ounces; a cup of unsifted cake flour weighs 4 ounces.

If a recipe calls for 1 cup sifted flour, sift the flour before measuring. (Ignore the "presifted" label on flour sacks. Presifting eliminates any stones and foreign matter, but the flour gets compacted again en route to your grocer's shelf.) Set the measuring cup on a sheet of wax paper. Use a medium fine-mesh strainer (my preference) or sifter to sift the flour over the cup until it is heaped above t he rim. Do not shake or tap the cup to settle the flour! Sweep a straight-edged knife or a spatula across the rim of the cup to level the flour. One cup of sifted all-purpose flour measured this way weighs 4 ounces; 1 cup of sifted cake flour weighs 3.5 ounces.

Especially in baking, you will get better results if you measure flour on a scale rather than with measuring cups.

HOW TO MEASURE COCOA POWDER

Normally my recipes call for unsifted cocoa. If your cocoa is very lumpy and compacted, press out most of the lumps with the back of a spoon then stir it a little to loosen it before measuring it as you would unsifted flour (see above). A cup of unsifted cocoa measured this way weighs 3.25 ounces. If sifted cocoa is called for, use a medium fine strainer to sift and measure it as for sifted flour (see above)

Dry measures are measuring cups used for measuring dry ingredients such as flour, sugar, and salt. Dry measures are filled level with the rim of the cup: use a 1-cup measure to measure 1 cup flour, for example, and ½-cup measure to measure ½ cup, rather than filling a 1-cup measure halfway. (The same is true for measuring spoons.) Unless a recipe calls for a packed or lightly packed measure, as in the case of brown sugar or shredded mint leaves, dry ingredients should be heaped above the rim of the cup without tapping or shaking, then leveled by sweeping a straight-edged knife or a spatula across the rim.

Liquid measures are clear plastic or glass cups used for measuring liquids. They have pouring spouts and lines up the sides to indicate measurements. To measure accurately with a standard liquid measure, set the cup on the counter before pouring in the liquid—you can't hold it completely level in the air. Lower your head so that you can read the measurement at eye level as you pour in the liquid. A newer type of liquid measure is designed to be read accurately without bending to check at eye level.

mixing

For best results, use the specific type of mixing utensil suggested in each recipe. Mixing with a rubber spatula results in a different texture in the finished dessert than mixing with a wire whisk does. Folding, stirring, beating, and whisking all produce different results. When a recipe calls for mixing (or folding, or stirring) in an ingredient "just until incorporated," this signals that overmixing may deflate the batter, result in a tough cake, or cause other problems.

Add and mix ingredients in the order called for. The order in which key ingredients are mixed can be critical. If a recipe calls for stirring A into B, it is safest to assume, especially when working with chocolaty batters or mixing liquid ingredients with dry ones, that stirring B into A may not produce as good a result.

In order to blend flour and other dry ingredients into batters without excessive mixing, many recipes call first for whisking the flour thoroughly with the other dry ingredients (such as leavening, spices, and salt). In very delicate cakes such as sponge cakes, the dry ingredients may be sifted together two or three times as well. Whisking and/or sifting fluffs and aerates dry ingredients so they blend easily into a batter or dough with minimal mixing and without lumps.

To prevent overmixing and to prevent the flour from flying, turn off the mixer before adding the flour to a dough or batter. Then restart the mixer on the slowest speed.

hot and cold

The texture of cakes and other desserts can be critically affected by the temperature of the individual ingredients called for in the recipe. Mixing cool or cold ingredients into tepid chocolate can cause a batter to harden precipitously. When a recipe calls for butter, milk, eggs, or any usually refrigerated ingredient to be at room temperature, the ingredient should be at 65° to 70°F, which is still cool, but not cold. Remove such items from the fridge early, or bring them to room temperature more quickly as follows:

- Put eggs still in the shell in a bowl of warm water and let stand a few minutes. Or crack them into a stainless steel bowl (transferring heat faster than a glass bowl) set in a larger bowl of hot tap water and stir until they are no longer cold to the touch.

- Microwave milk or other liquids in a glass measure or other container on low power or on the defrost setting for just a few seconds. Or set the container in a bowl of hot water and stir occasionally just until no longer cold.

- Cut butter into chunks and microwave on low power or on the defrost setting, a few seconds at a time, until pliable but *not* melted.

baking

Always preheat the oven for 15 to 20 minutes so that it reaches the correct temperature before you bake. Follow the instructions for rack placement in each recipe—baking higher or lower in the oven can over- or under-brown the top or bottom of your dessert or affect the baking time. For most cakes, I position a rack in the lower third of the oven so that when placed on the rack, the cake actually sits only slightly below the center of the oven. When I bake a thin sheet cake or a single pan of cookies, I position the oven rack in the center.

Set a timer for the shorter time indicated in the recipe so you can check for doneness. Cookies, for example, are so small that just an extra minute or two in the oven can make the difference between perfection and overbaking.

The recipes in this book were developed and tested in a conventional gas oven, without convection. For convection baking, make adjustments according to the oven manufacturer's instructions. Generally this means baking at a lower temperature and for less time than the recipe specifies.

Unless otherwise instructed, cool baked items on a rack, and let them cool completely before covering or wrapping. Wrapping cakes and cookies before they are completely cool produces damp soggy textures and invites mold and bacteria.

equipment

BOWLS

I use stainless steel and glass mixing bowls for different purposes. Stainless bowls are best for improvising a water bath, or a double boiler, over or directly in a saucepan of water; I use them this way for melting chocolate, making sabayon, and rewarming sauces, among other tasks. Glass bowls are necessary for melting or warming ingredients in the microwave. Their weight also prevents them from flying across the room when you must whisk with one hand while pouring in an ingredient with the other. Bowls that are nearly as deep as they are wide keep dry ingredients from flying out when using a hand mixer and are best for beating egg whites. One- and 2-quart glass measuring cups with handles also make wonderful mixing bowls and are perfect for melting chocolate in a microwave.

CAKE PANS

For even baking and moist, tender cakes, I like medium- to heavy-weight aluminum or professional-quality steel (not stainless steel) cake pans. There are also newer, but quite expensive, heavy-duty stainless pans with aluminum cores, for even heating (otherwise stainless heats unevenly). For light-textured cakes or for heavy, gooey batters such as for rich brownies, avoid glass pans and pans with dark finishes, even if they are nonstick. These tend to overbake the edges and bottom of cakes, sometimes even before the inside is done. Richer, heavier loaf cakes, pound cakes, and Bundt cakes are different—the deep golden-brown crust produced by heavy (often decorative) tube and loaf pans is both delicious and beautiful to see. Always read the information that comes with these pans; you may be advised to lower the baking temperature by 25 degrees—which is also the standard advice if you must bake in a glass pan.

I also use 8- and 9-inch round and square cake pans and 9 by 13-inch baking pans, all 2 inches deep. Instead of traditional springform pans, I prefer the 8- or 9-inch Magic Line "cheesecake pans" with removable push-up bottoms; these are 2 or 3 inches deep. Except for tube pans, I prefer cake pans with straight rather than sloped sides.

To prepare baking pans, follow the individual recipes. When a recipe says to line the bottom and all sides of a pan with foil, turn the pan upside down. Over the pan center a sheet of foil about two inches wider than the pan on all sides. Press the foil over the sides of the pan, folding the corners neatly as though wrapping a package.

Slip the foil off of the pan. Turn the pan right side up and fit the foil into it, pressing the corners and edges in place.

BAKING SHEETS AND JELLY-ROLL PANS

Medium- to heavy-weight aluminum baking sheets and jelly-roll pans will not warp or bend and they cook evenly, without hot spots. I avoid dark or nonstick surfaces, which can toughen and overbake tender sheet cakes and cookies; nor do I like cushioned pans, because they yield uninterestingly uniform cookie textures. Professional aluminum "half sheet pans," which measure 12 by 16 inches by 1 inch deep, fit in most home ovens and perform much better than lighter-weight 11 by 17-inch standard jelly-roll pans. You can buy these pans at specialty cookware stores, restaurant supply stores, and warehouse grocery discount stores.

To prepare baking sheets, follow the individual recipes. Even for cookies, there is no one treatment fits all. Depending on the cookie, I line the pan with parchment or foil or leave it bare or grease it.

SILICONE BAKING MATS

For some, but not all, cookies, I use a silicone mat. Reusable silicone baking mats for lining baking sheets prevent cookies from sticking and make cleanup simple. They are especially superb (but not essential) for making thin crisp cookies such as lace cookies and tuiles. That being said, silicone is not the ultimate answer for everything. For cookies meant to be soft inside and crunchy on the outside, for example, parchment paper or a bare baking sheet may produce better results than silicone, depending on the type of batter involved.

COOLING RACKS

Racks for cooling cakes and cookies speed the cooling process and can keep some baked goods from getting soggy. To save counter space, I use an inexpensive 4-tiered rack from King Arthur Flour (see Resources, page 249), which folds up for storage.

FOOD PROCESSOR

The food processor is invaluable for pulverizing nuts or chocolate, grating piloncillo sugar, making fruit purees, and mixing some tart and cookie doughs. I keep a mini processor on hand too, for small quantities.

BLENDER OR IMMERSION BLENDER

Although less versatile than a food processor, a blender or immersion (stick) blender is actually more effective than the processor for making super-smooth chocolate pudding, some ice cream bases, and ganache for chocolate truffles.

MEASURING CUPS AND SPOONS

For measuring liquids, I have 1-cup, 2-cup, 4-cup, and 8-cup glass measures. I also have a 4-quart glass measure, which doubles as a heavy mixing bowl. For measuring dry ingredients, I keep at least one set of metal or plastic measuring cups including ⅛-cup (2 tablespoons), ¼-, ⅓-, ½-, and 1-cup measures. I keep at least one set of metal or plastic measuring spoons. I do not use measuring spoons that purport to measure a pinch or a smidge.

MICROWAVE OVEN

The microwave is handy for melting chocolate, reheating sauces, liquefying crystallized honey, and toasting small quantities of nuts. It thaws frozen ingredients and transforms cold eggs, butter, cheese, and milk (ever so carefully) into room-temperature (70°F) ingredients that are ready to use. And I use the microwave to prepare Summer Apple Carpaccio (page 112).

MIXERS

I use a KitchenAid 5-quart mixer for larger jobs and a hand-held mixer for smaller jobs. I keep extra sets of beaters for both mixers and an extra bowl for the stand mixer so that I do not have to wash these between mixing a batter and beating egg whites, etc.

PARCHMENT PAPER AND WAX PAPER

Baker's parchment is cleaner and more reliable than butter or oil on the bottom of cakes pans, and it is often my liner of choice on cookie sheets too. Everything from crisp meringues to sticky macaroons releases easily from parchment paper. Wax paper is cheaper than parchment and thus useful for tasks that do not require the special characteristics and expense of parchment: providing a landing place for sifted flour or freshly dipped chocolates, separating layers of cookies, and so forth.

PASTRY BAGS AND TIPS

Choose pastry bags made of nylon or polypropylene rather than cloth, because they wash easily, remain supple, and do not become sour smelling. Whipped cream doesn't weep through these bags either. Disposable plastic pastry bags eliminate the need to wash the bags at all. A large 16- to 18-inch bag is handy for piping a batch of meringue. A 10- to 12-inch bag is good for smaller quantities. Since pastry bags should not be filled more than half full, bigger bags are more versatile than small ones.

Pastry Tips ▪ Ateco is the universal brand. A useful assortment of tips might include plain round tips varying in diameter from ⅜ to ¾ inch as well as closed star tips that range in the same diameter (Ateco numbers 842 to 849). The occasional baker may want only a large closed star tip (number 848 or 849) for whipped cream, if that.

PASTRY BRUSHES

Natural boar's-bristle brushes, despite their tendency to hold odors, are better than nylon or other sythetic bristles. I was hopeful about the new silicone brushes, because they clean up so perfectly, but so far I find them useless for pastry applications, which often require control: thin, but thorough, coverage (with egg wash, melted butter, milk, cream, or what have you) without excess dripping. Keep separate natural-bristle brushes for pastry and savory cooking, or your desserts may taste of garlic or barbecue sauce.

ROLLING PIN

Choose a pin that is comfortable for you: with or without handles, heavy or light-weight. I find that a straight rather than a tapered pin works best for beginners. Absent a rolling pin, you can improvise with a length of thick dowel or pipe or a tall bottle.

SCALE

A scale is the cleanest, simplest, and most accurate way to measure everything, but especially flour and nuts. Unlike with volume measure, an ounce is an ounce, whether the flour is compacted or loose and light in the canister, or the nuts are whole or chopped. If flour must be sifted anyway, it's easier to weigh out exactly what you need first, before sifting it. Instead of setting a cup on wax paper, sifting over it until heaped, leveling, returning excess flour to the canister, and cleaning up the mess, you simply weigh the flour and sift it. Similarly, if a recipe gives a weight for chopped or ground nuts, it's much easier to weigh first and then chop or grind exactly what you need rather than guessing how much to grind or grate before measuring with a cup.

Many fine chocolates do not come in premeasured squares, so a scale is a must when using these. Using a scale is also the easiest way to divide a batch of tart dough or brioche, for example, into equal pieces to line tartlet pans or into individual brioches. And with a scale, you can measure ingredients in any bowl or container you like, without dirtying a drawer-full of measuring cups. Cookware stores sell a variety of scales at all prices. A battery-operated digital scale will last and remain more accurate longer than a spring scale. The recipes in this book give weights for ingredients such as flour, nuts, and chocolate.

SCISSORS

Keep a good pair in the kitchen for cutting parchment paper and for other tasks.

SERRATED BREAD KNIFE

A knife with a 12-inch blade is ideal for cutting cakes into horizontal layers, but a shorter blade will also do.

SKEWERS AND TOOTHPICKS

For testing cakes, slim wooden (barbecue) skewers are cleaner than broom straws and longer than toothpicks. Moist batter and crumbs stick to a wood skewer or toothpick much better than to a metal cake tester, so that you can see exactly how gooey or dry your cake is within.

SPATULAS

Rubber and Heatproof Silicone Spatulas ▪ Three sizes will cover every contingency: The largest can be used for folding beaten egg whites into delicate batters and scraping large bowls. A mini spatula teases tiny quantities from small containers. Medium handles everything in between. Rubber spatulas melt if used over heat, but silicone spatulas are miraculous for cooking everything from custards and ice cream bases to caramel. They can sweep the sides, corners, and bottom of pots without missing a square inch of territory where ingredients may stick or burn. After trying multiple brands and designs, however, I have despaired of the spatulas with removable wooden handles that fall off at odd times and allow bacteria to grow if they are not taken apart for cleaning and those with metal handles that get hot. I like the silicone spatulas with integral hard plastic handles. If only they came in more sizes.

Metal Spatulas ▪ For frosting cakes, I like a narrow stainless steel spatula with a straight 8-inch-long blade that is rounded at the end. For spreading cake batter in a thin, even layer in a jelly-roll pan, I like an offset spatula (the blade has a bend in it right after the handle) at least 8 inches long. A small offset spatula with a 4-inch blade is useful for smoothing cake batter in round and square pans, among other tasks.

STRAINERS

Sifters are cumbersome to clean and store. I prefer to use a large medium-fine-mesh strainer to sift flour and other dry ingredients. It requires only one hand and it shakes out and cleans easily. Fine-mesh strainers are best for dusting desserts with powdered sugar or cocoa. I have a couple of good fine-mesh stainless steel strainers and several inexpensive medium-mesh plastic strainers in a variety of sizes.

TART AND TARTLET PANS

I use round tart pans with fluted edges and removable bottoms in several sizes: 9½ inches, 6½ to 7 inches, and 4½ inches; I also use an oblong 13½ by 4¼ inch pan. I prefer pans with a shiny reflective surface rather than those made of darkened steel.

I also keep several sizes of shiny metal tartlet pans. Those that measure 3½ to 4 inches across the top are most useful for making a single serving. It takes 1 ounce of dough to line a 3½-inch pan and about 1½ ounces or a little less to line a 4-inch pan.

THERMOMETERS

Instant-Read Thermometer ▪ An inexpensive instant read thermometer is useful for cooking custards and ice cream bases, working with chocolate, taking the internal temperature of a yeast bread, and determining when eggs, butter, milk, etc., for baking are at room temperature (70°F). Digital thermometers cost a bit more, but they are easier to read. The usual range for instant-read thermometers is 0 to 220°F, which covers everything in this book except caramel; if you have only one of these thermometers, you will need a separate candy thermometer to measure temperatures exceeding 220°F. I cover all bases with a digital combination timer/thermometer made by Polder, with a range of 32° to 392°F (0° to 200°C). It has a probe attached to a wire than can be inserted into a loaf of bread or roast chicken in the oven or into a pot of caramel on top of the stove. The temperature registers on an easy-to-read digital display that sits on the counter, and it can be set to beep when the desired temperature is reached. This is the best thermometer for recipes that require heating and stirring eggs to a particular temperature: just hold the probe in the bowl with one hand and stir with the other until the beeper sounds. Digital candy thermometers with the same range are also available without the timer.

Oven Thermometer ▪ You can roast a tasty chicken at almost any temperature, but cookies and cakes suffer when baked in an oven that is too hot or too slow. Use an oven thermometer to check your oven every now and again to see that it is accurate. If necessary, have it calibrated professionally, or compensate for any discrepancy yourself until you can have the oven adjusted.

TIMER

Whether it's an old-fashioned windup or a sleek digital, a timer is essential in the kitchen.

WIRE WHISKS

A whisk is an essential hand tool, and not just for beating. Whisks are better than kitchen forks for thoroughly mixing dry ingredients together or fluffing up flour before it is added to a batter.

ZESTER

A Microplane zester transforms the usually tedious task of removing the thin colored top layer of citrus peels. This simple tool lifts off the thinnest shreds of zest effortlessly, and without any bitter white pith or scraped knuckles. You can also use one to grate whole nutmeg faster and more easily than with your little-bitty nutmeg grater, and you won't believe how delicious cinnamon from a freshly grated stick is compared with ground cinnamon from a jar!

how and where to shop for ingredients

Most of the ingredients called for in *Pure Dessert* can be found in a good supermarket. In a great supermarket, you will even find specialty sugars such as muscovado and piloncillo; flours such as buckwheat, kamut, and corn flour; and even fresh cheeses such as fromage blanc, labneh, or kefir! The baking aisle of my (admittedly fantastic) supermarket partly inspired this book. One day I stopped ignoring all of those packages of interesting grains and sugars—I started buying and tasting. Supermarkets in metropolitan areas have organic fruit, handmade cheeses, all kinds of honey, and great selections of wines and spirits. If yours does not, reach out beyond the supermarket aisles to specialty cheese shops, farmers' markets, and gourmet shops, or use mail-order sources (see Resources, page 249). I also shop in ethnic markets such as Mexican, Indian, Asian, and Middle Eastern groceries.

BAKING POWDER AND BAKING SODA

Cakes are sometimes leavened with baking powder or with baking soda, or both. Baking powder has an expiration date because it loses its oomph if not fresh and kept stored in a tightly sealed container. To check to see if baking powder is still good, add about a teaspoon to ¼ cup hot water. If it bubbles vigorously, use it. If in doubt, toss out the old tin and buy a new one.

BUTTER

The recipes in this book use regular unsalted butter. Salted butter contains ¼ teaspoon of salt per stick, and it will make many butter-rich desserts taste too salty. If using salted butter in a recipe where the butter is a relatively minor ingredient, subtract ¼ teaspoon of salt from the quantity in the recipe for each stick of salted butter. If you must use margarine or shortening instead of butter, avoid tub margarine and butter substitutes and spreads, which may contain a very high percentage of water. These ingredients are not made for baking, and results will be unpredictable. Do not expect predictable results from substituting vegetable oils for solid fats either.

French or European-Style Butter ▪ A variety of imported and domestic "European-style" butters are now available in the best supermarkets and in specialty shops. These butters are higher in fat than standard American butter: they contain a minimum of 82 percent (and up to 87 percent) fat compared with the standard 80 percent. They are also lower in moisture than standard American butter. Some of the European-style butters are made from milk that is cultured (like cheese) before it is churned. Cultured or not, the flavor of European-style butters varies considerably from brand to brand. Some have such magnificent flavor that you may want to spread them as lavishly as cheese on your bread. However, with the exception of a few recipes, such as puff pastry and croissants (of which there are none in this book), the exquisite characteristics of these butters are largely lost in baking. I love this type of butter spread on my bread, but I don't usually bake with it. (Even my brioche and shortbread recipes—made with loads of butter—did not taste better or have a nicer texture when tested with European-style butter!) If you do bake with European-style butter, its higher fat and lower moisture content may affect some recipes: cakes may come out more dense but with more butter flavor, cookies may spread too much on the baking sheet and seem too buttery or greasy, pie crusts may be crisper but less flaky. Using 5 to 10 percent less butter in the recipe may correct some of these effects if they are unwanted.

FRESH CHEESES

Fresh cheeses (and here I include their cousins, cultured milk products) are unaged and unripened cheeses. They are made with fresh milk coagulated with enzymes or cultured with bacteria so that they last a little longer than the fresh milk they are made from. In the words of Paula Lambert, author of *The Cheese Lover's Cookbook and Guide*, fresh cheeses are "just a step away from milk." By their nature, fresh cheeses are meant to be consumed shortly after they are made. Of course, food science has lengthened that window of freshness, usually at the expense of flavor, and with the effect of creating a more stable and uniform texture. Everyone is familiar with some fresh cheeses: supermarket cartons of cottage cheese, ricotta, and packages of cream cheese. Some are quite acceptable, though most have at least some added preservatives to keep them "fresh" beyond their natural life, as well as stabilizers or starches to keep the curds from continuing to separate from the whey. (Commercial cream cheese is an extreme example of a fresh cheese reinvented by science: stabilizers and gums have transformed it into a neutral-tasting platform for smoked salmon and glue for bagel halves. Even if you enjoy it, there isn't much "cheese" about it.)

The most exquisite fresh cheeses are free of preservatives, gums, and starches; their textures are idiosyncratic and ever changing, and they capture all of the authentic flavors of the milk they were made from. They are smooth and creamy, or gently curdy;

they are tart and tangy or sweet and milky. A connoisseur might taste the difference between milks from different seasons, different kinds of cows, or the flavor of different pastures! You might at first think fresh cheeses are "bland" or lacking in character. But slow down and taste again, and you will pick up delicate flavors of real milk: sweet nutty cow's milk, tangy, grassy goat's milk, and slightly gamy, herbal sheep's milk.

Fresh cheeses from small producers have never been so available in such glorious variety. Visit an urban cheese shop, a farmers' market, or a top supermarket and you will find them, served up from bulk containers or prepackaged in cartons. They include fromage blanc, fromage frais, quark, and lebni or yogurt cheese, as well as cottage cheese, ricotta, even cream cheese. Look for producers who use the fewest ingredients, no stabilizers, and no preservatives. Considering the world of processed foods that we live in, the sheer quantity of exquisite handmade, often organic cheeses is indeed a miracle. If you are a cheese lover, these pure products will leave you breathless. Rich or lean, any one of them can be dessert, scooped into a bowl with fruit, drizzled with honey, or sprinkled with sugar. Or make the luscious Lebni Tart (page 39), Quark Soufflés (page 52), Ricotta and Lace (page 41), or Caramelized Crepes Filled with Fresh Cheese (page 50).

Ricotta ▪ Ricotta is a mild-flavored fresh cheese usually made in this country with cow's milk, but also made with ewe's milk in Italy. The best ricotta has a very delicate, slightly sweet, fresh milk flavor. Depending on the producer, it may have moist creamy curds or drier, grainy, almost gritty curds. Some are a tad saltier or tangier, with less of the prized fresh milk flavor. It is worth your while to shop for ricotta in a good cheese store, to seek out a local producer, or to go online and buy from a specialist (see Resources, page 249).

Fromage Blanc/Fromage Frais ▪ Similar to quark (see below), fromage blanc, or fromage frais, is a soft, creamy fresh cheese that varies in richness from producer to producer.

Lebni/Kefir Cheese/Yogurt Cheese ▪ Lebni— variously transliterated from Arabic as labneh, labne, lebna, etc.— is also called kefir cheese or yogurt cheese. Lebni can be purchased in Middle Eastern groceries, some cheese shops, and some very comprehensive supermarkets. Like yogurt, lebni is made by culturing milk with a bacteria and then draining the whey to produce a creamy cheese that resembles extra-thick sour cream with tart yeasty or nutty flavor, depending on the brand. The Byblos brand of lebni (imported by Kradjian in Glendale, California) that I use to make the Lebni Tart on page 39 is also labeled kefir cheese (not to be confused with the kefir drink); and both "lebni" and "kefir cheese" also appear on Abali and Sadaf brands of lebni. All three brands are made with milk and cream and thus moderately rich at 6 grams of fat per 30 grams of cheese. Although commercial producers enrich their product with cream or extra milk solids, you can make your own lebni by scooping your favorite (nonstabilized) yogurt, adding cream if you like, into a cheesecloth-lined strainer set over a bowl and refrigerated for several hours or overnight to drain the whey.

Quark ▪ Quark is a cultured milk (or cream), similar to sour cream, that is common in Germany and Austria, where it is enjoyed on bread at breakfast, used as a garnish on savory soup, and as an ingredient in sweet recipes such as cheesecakes, mousses, and frozen desserts. Quark varies in richness, depending on whether it is made with skimmed or whole milk or cream or any combination thereof. See Quark Soufflés, page 52.

CHESTNUTS

If you don't roast or steam your own, the best whole cooked chestnuts are the ones in vacuum packages, available in better supermarkets and in gourmet stores. Those in jars are not quite as good, but they are still acceptable. In either case, do not confuse them with chestnuts in syrup. You can also use Faugier chestnut puree (ingredients are listed in this order: chestnut puree, water, corn syrup), which is essentially unsweetened, except for the tiny amount of corn syrup. Do not confuse this with the sweetened chestnut puree, also called chestnut spread, that comes in cans or jars (see Resources, page 249).

CHOCOLATE

Buy chocolate that you like and choose the best you can afford. The recipes in this book will work and will taste fine made with ordinary supermarket brands, as long as they are the type of chocolate called for in the recipes. However, better chocolate makes better desserts, especially when the recipe is very simple, as the ones in this book are. Note that not all of the better brands of chocolate are conveniently divided into 1- or 2-ounce portions, so you may need a scale for measuring.

Unless you are very experienced, use the type of chocolate called for in the recipe. Do not try to substitute bittersweet for unsweetened chocolate or milk chocolate for bittersweet. Even substituting one semisweet or bittersweet chocolate for another may be problematic if the cacao content of each is very different (see below).

For a comprehensive discussion and guide to chocolate, types of chocolate, and working with chocolate, consult my book *BitterSweet: Recipes and Tales from a Life in Chocolates.*

Cacao (or Cocoa) Nibs ▪ Cacao (or cocoa) nibs are the essence of chocolate: pieces of roasted and hulled cocoa beans—100 percent pure cacao. Nibs are comprised of slightly more than 50 percent cocoa butter and slightly less than 50 percent dry cocoa solids. Normally nibs are ground to a molten paste (chocolate liquor), then rehardened to become unsweetened chocolate or further processed into all of the sweetened kinds of chocolate. However, recently nibs have appeared as an ingredient on their own. Crunchy and relatively bitter, nibs have all of the flavors and nuances that may be found in chocolate—toasted nuts, wine, berries, tropical fruit, citrus, grass, or spice, to name just a few—as well as some of the (frankly) rougher, earthier, more tannic flavors that are normally eliminated in the processing that would transform them into chocolate. Crushed, ground, chopped, or left in their natural form, or infused in cream, nibs add an incomparable and unique chocolate flavor and texture to baked goods, desserts, and ice creams.

Unsweetened Chocolate ▪ Technically called chocolate liquor (though it contains no alcohol), unsweetened chocolate is pure ground cacao nibs, often with a fraction of a percent of lecithin as an emulsifier. Some companies include a little vanilla, but most do not. Like cacao nibs, unsweetened chocolate contains a little more than 50 percent fat (cocoa butter) and a little less than 50 percent dry cocoa solids; it is sometimes labeled "99% cacao." High-quality unsweetened chocolate is palatable enough to use chopped or ground up in recipes as well as melted and blended into batters. There is now a range of unsweetened chocolate to choose from, rather than only two or three brands. Try different brands before settling on a regular choice.

Semisweet and Bittersweet Chocolate ▪ Both bittersweet and semisweet chocolates are sweetened chocolates, usually with a little extra cocoa butter added to them and usually, but not necessarily, containing no milk solids. Technically the two terms are interchangeable. Standard domestic bittersweet and semisweet chocolates usually contain 50 to 60 percent chocolate cacao (though the legal minimum is 35 percent) and thus 40 to 50 percent sugar. Generally bittersweet is less sweet than semisweet, but the industry does not make an official distinction between them, so one brand of semisweet may be sweeter than a bittersweet made by a different company. The percentage of cacao in the chocolate is a better predictor of relative sweetness than the name, but the cacao percentage does not yet appear on all domestic chocolate labels, although many manufacturers are now adding it.

Imported bittersweet and semisweet chocolates and the best American brands often have a higher cacao content (and less sugar) than the standard domestic brands, and usually the percentage is marked on the wrapper. (Cacao content may also be referred to as chocolate liquor, percentage of cocoa beans, cacao, cocoa solids, or cocoa *masse.*) The higher the cacao content, the lower the percentage of sugar and the stronger and more intense the chocolate.

Cooks, confectioners, and bakers should be aware that cacao percentage affects both the flavor and the texture of desserts and that substituting chocolate with a significantly higher percentage of cacao than what is suggested in the recipe may not simply result in a more deliciously chocolaty dessert. A few recipes are instantly improved with extra chocolate intensity, but more often, unless adjustments are made, substituting chocolates with high cacao content produces dry, overbaked cakes, curdled sauces, grainy ganache, or bitter, gummy mousse. (Appropriate recipe modifications would include reducing the amount of chocolate, adding a bit more sugar, and adding liquid or reducing the flour.) To simplify matters for the cook, where necessary, the recipes in this book call for chocolates with a specific cacao percentage or range, and they may also include tips for using other types of chocolates.

Milk Chocolate ▪ Milk chocolate is sweetened chocolate with a minimum cacao content of 10 percent and a minimum of 12 percent milk solids, plus milk fat. Milk chocolate is mild, sweet, and creamy tasting in comparison to semisweet and bittersweet chocolates. The most flavorful milk chocolates exceed the minimum cacao requirement, resulting in chocolate with more chocolate flavor and less sweetness.

Gianduja ▪ Gianduja is sweetened chocolate, usually milk chocolate, containing toasted hazelnuts ground to a perfectly smooth, unctuous paste. A few companies, such as Scharffen Berger, make gianduja with a base of semisweet chocolate instead of milk chocolate.

White Chocolate ▪ White chocolate is made of cocoa butter (but no dry cocoa solids) combined with sugar, dry milk solids, milk fat, lecithin, and vanilla. White chocolate (only recently recognized and defined by the FDA as a form of chocolate) should not be confused with "white confectionery coating," which contains other tropical vegetable fats instead of cocoa butter.

Chocolate Chips, Morsels, and Chunks ▪ Chocolate chips, morsels, and chunks, whether semisweet, bittersweet, milk, or white, are formulated with less cocoa butter than bar chocolate so that they hold their shape when baked. They are usually less smooth on the palate and relatively sweet compared with a fine bar of chocolate. For that reason and because I love to have as many choices as possible, I often chop up plain chocolate bars to use in place of ordinary chocolate chips and chunks in cookies and cakes. The reverse, however, is not true: I never use chocolate chips in place of bar chocolate for melting and mixing into batters, mousses, ice creams, or other desserts because they are much sweeter than I like and because they are formulated to hold their shape, so they do not melt well.

Chocolate Pastilles, Buttons, Pistols, Callets, and Ribbons ▪ Not to be confused with chips and chunks, these small chocolate pieces are formulated like regular chocolate but are made into small ready-to-melt pieces for chefs, commercial bakers, and chocolatiers. They are wonderfully convenient, but, like chocolate bars, they vary in quality from excellent to ordinary, depending on the manufacturer.

CINNAMON

True Ceylon cinnamon has a complex, almost citrusy flavor; the more familiar cassia cinnamon that Americans know best is strong and sweet. Either way, consider grating it yourself with a Microplane zester, rather than pulling out the jar of ground spice. The flavor is far more intense when fresh. Cassia cinnamon sticks are reddish brown and very hard, like wood, but they are miraculously easy to grate with the Microplane. Ceylon cinnamon sticks are buff-colored rolls of papery bark, which are easy to crumble between your fingers and can be chopped with a heavy knife or ground in a spice or coffee grinder. You can buy Ceylon cinnamon in some specialty food stores and in Mexican markets, where it is called *canela*. Or, order it by mail (see Resources, page 249).

COCOA POWDER: NATURAL AND DUTCH-PROCESS

Cocoa powder is made by removing 75 to 85 percent of the fat (cocoa butter) from chocolate liquor, then pulverizing the partially defatted mass that remains. The result is natural, or nonalkalized, cocoa. To produce Dutch-process, or alkalized, cocoa, the beans (or powder) are chemically treated with an alkali to reduce both their natural acidity and any harshness that may be a result of poor-quality beans or under- or over-fermentation. Alkalizing darkens the color of cocoa and alters its flavor. Chefs, and consumers, vary in their preferences for these two styles of cocoa. Of course, quality makes a difference, but it is worth tasting different cocoas to learn your own preferences. Fans of Dutch-process cocoa extol its rich color, toasted nutty flavor, and coffee notes, while others find the taste dull, dusty, chemical, uniform, and lacking in fruitiness. Natural cocoa tastes vibrant, fruity, and complex to its admirers (including me) and harsh, bitter, and sour to its detractors. Generally, in recipes that include leavenings such as baking powder or baking soda, stick with the type of cocoa called for to avoid bad results. But absent any leavening in the recipes (such as those for brownies, puddings, sauces, sorbets and ice creams, and hot chocolate), it is usually safe to use the type of cocoa that tastes best to you.

COCONUT

Sweetened desiccated (dried) shredded coconut is easily found in the baking aisle of the supermarket. It contains preservatives and ingredients to keep it moist, in addition to lots of sugar. The recipes in this book call instead for unsweetened shredded dried coconut, which can be found in better supermarkets, in specialty markets that sell nuts and dried fruit in bulk, in natural foods stores, and online (see Resources, page 249).

COFFEE AND ESPRESSO POWDER

If a recipe calls for freshly ground coffee beans, use freshly roasted beans from a specialty coffee purveyor, and grind or crush them yourself if possible. Bypass the vacuum-packed can of ground coffee from the supermarket. For recipes that call for espresso powder, use Medaglio D'Oro instant espresso powder rather than freeze-dried crystals, if possible. If you must use freeze-dried crystals or regular powdered coffee, increase the amount by about 25 percent.

CREAM

The freshest, best-tasting cream is simply pasteurized, rather than ultra pasteurized or sterilized (for longer shelf life), and contains no ingredients other than cream. Cream stabilized with carrageenan makes smoother whipped cream, but I still prefer natural unstabilized cream.

DRIED FRUITS

Dried fruit should be moist, plump, and flavorful. Whole pieces are always better, fresher, and moister than prechopped or extruded pellets. If the fruit is sticky, chop it with an oiled knife or use oiled scissors.

EGGS

Use Grade AA large eggs for the recipes in this book. Buy eggs from a source that keeps them refrigerated, and do likewise in your home. When a recipe calls for eggs at room temperature, remove the eggs from the refrigerator at least an hour or so early. Or warm cold eggs quickly in a bowl of warm water, or break them into a bowl and set the bowl into a larger bowl of hot tap water, and stir until they are no longer cold to the touch.

EXTRACTS

Always use pure extracts. Artificial flavorings are not worthy of the time and other good ingredients that you put into your favorite recipes.

FLOUR

Wheat Flours ▪ Most of the recipes in this book were developed and tested with Gold Medal or King Arthur unbleached all-purpose flour or Gold Medal bleached all-purpose flour, or, when cake flour is used, Soft as Silk cake flour.

Technically, unbleached rather than bleached flour fits the *Pure Dessert* concept, but this presents a quandary. Bleached flour makes marvelously tender cookies and cakes because it usually has a slightly lower protein level than unbleached flour, it is more finely milled, and the bleaching process acidifies the flour, which also has a tenderizing effect.

When my recipes call simply for all-purpose flour, you can use either bleached (I often do) or unbleached flour, and expect excellent but slightly less delicate results. Or you can create a lower-protein unbleached flour by blending 5 parts unbleached all-purpose flour with 1 part unbleached pastry flour.

Whole Wheat Flour ▪ The best whole wheat flour is stone-ground from the whole wheat kernel and still includes both the germ and the bran. Long a staple of health and natural foods proponents, whole wheat flour is typecast in robust and delicious breads and nutritious morning cereals. Indeed, the flavor of whole wheat is appealingly nutty, but there is no need to assume that everything made with it must be hearty and heavy, or chewy and down to earth. Raspberry–Chocolate Chunk Muffins (page 160) raise the grain to elegant heights, as do the meltingly tender and exquisitely flavored Whole Wheat Sablés and variations with cacao nibs, hempseed, or hazelnuts (pages 88–89). As with all whole grains, whole wheat flour should be kept in the refrigerator or frozen to preserve its flavor and prevent rancidity.

Graham flour is whole wheat flour without the germ (as such, it is less perishable), and sometimes with added rye flour. It may be substituted for whole wheat flour.

Buckwheat Flour ▪ Buckwheat is not really a grain, but an herb. Its seeds are ground into the dark flavorful flour that many Americans may know only, if at all, in hearty pancakes and, possibly (and not always favorably), in buckwheat groats or kasha. Buckwheat has a nutritional profile similar to wheat's but it is unrelated, and thus can often be tolerated by those with wheat allergies. The flavor is malty, earthy, and pleasantly bitter—some would say strong. However, used with a light hand, buckwheat flour adds elegant nutty flavor and complexity to Buckwheat Strawberry Shortcakes (page 61), Cornmeal-Buckwheat Scones with Walnuts (page 63), and tender Nibby Buckwheat Butter Cookies (page 93). Buckwheat flour is available in light and dark varieties, which may be used interchangeably in recipes, though the latter has a stronger flavor. Like other specialty flours, it should be stored in the refrigerator or freezer to prevent it from becoming rancid. Buckwheat flour is available in some supermarkets, from health food and specialty food purveyors, and online (see Resources, page 249).

Chestnut Flour ▪ Used widely in traditional northern Italian baked goods, chestnut flour is 100 percent pure pulverized dried chestnuts. The flour (about 78 percent carbohydrates and only 1 percent fat) has the sweet slightly nutty flavor and starchy characteristics appreciated by those of us who love chestnuts in any form. It makes a delicate crisp tuile, an irresistible meringue with walnuts (page 70), and a rich buttery pound cake, plain or laced with nuts and dried fruit. Imported Italian and domestic chestnut flour are available in better supermarkets and specialty stores and online (see Resources, page 249).

Corn Flour ▪ Corn flour is finely ground cornmeal from the whole kernel, not to be confused with cornstarch, which comes from the endosperm only. Corn flour adds the flavor of cornmeal without the gritty texture of cornmeal. Use it to make divine Corn Tuiles with Salt and Pepper (page 90) or add it to pancakes, muffins, waffles, or corn bread. As with other whole-grain flours, keep corn flour refrigerated or freeze it to preserve flavor and prevent rancidity.

Kamut and Spelt Flours ▪ Kamut and spelt are nutritionally superior ancestors of modern wheat. Spelt was cultivated in Europe more than nine thousand years ago, and kamut (the Egyptian word for "wheat" and once called the grain of pharaohs) was a dominant crop from 4000 B.C. to the late Roman Empire, until an early form of durum wheat succeeded it. Both kamut and spelt contain a unique type of gluten that is more digestible than common wheat gluten. Like quinoa, amaranth, and chia, kamut and spelt have gained attention from the natural foods community, home bread bakers, and those allergic to wheat. They can be substituted for whole wheat flour in breads or for a portion of the white flour in cakes and pastries. Kamut and spelt impart a rich nutty flavor, and kamut adds a fragrant buttery flavor and lovely yellow color to baked goods made with them.

Anyone familiar with the dense, heavy texture of whole-grain breads and "healthy" recipes made with spelt or kamut will be astonished at the delicate, tender texture and sensational flavor of Golden Kamut Shortbread (page 67), Whole Wheat Sablés made with spelt (page 88), or Kamut Pound Cake (page 65) made with either spelt or kamut. Like all whole grains, kamut and spelt should be stored in the refrigerator or kept frozen (for up to 8 months) to preserve their flavor and prevent rancidity.

GINGER

Ginger adds a hot, fresh, palate-tingling flavor to savory dishes and desserts. It comes in several forms, which may be used separately, or in combination.

Dried Ground Ginger ▪ Buy this familiar yellow powder in a jar from the spice section of the supermarket or from a purveyor of bulk spices. It is very pungent and earthy, and it has a slightly peppery flavor, more muted than fresh ginger.

Fresh Ginger ▪ Available in the produce section of many supermarkets, fresh ginger looks like a knobby root or stem (it is actually a rhizome or tuberlike stem) with a brown, papery skin. Buy fresh ginger that feels heavy for its size, rather than light or shriveled (which would suggest that it has lost a lot of its natural moisture). Look for taut, smooth skin with a slight sheen. Young or baby ginger looks fresh and moist with a yellowish green color and even more delicate thin skin.

Fresh ginger keeps for at least a week, unwrapped in a cool dry place. It will keep refrigerated for several weeks as long as you wrap it first in a paper towel (to absorb moisture that might produce mold) and then enclose it in a plastic bag.

Peel ginger with a vegetable peeler before slicing, grating, or pureeing. To avoid long, stringy fibers, slice ginger thinly across the grain before chopping, mincing, or pureeing. When fresh ginger is added to recipes that call for ground dried ginger, it imparts pungency and tartness to the flavor.

Crystallized Ginger ▪ This is candied ginger coated with sugar. The Australian variety is exquisitely tender and somewhat milder than ginger from other sources (such as Thailand). Crystallized ginger is delicious when eaten like candy (also dipped in chocolate) or when chopped and included, like raisins or chocolate chips, in cookies or cakes, where it adds tiny bursts of intense flavor and heat. Ginger chips (crystallized ginger that is already diced) are available in the baking aisle of some supermarkets or from specialty stores, but I usually like to dice my own.

HEMPSEED

Although no longer a mainstream ingredient, hempseed was cultivated more than six thousand years ago in China, where it predated soy as an important food source. The seeds are is exceedingly high in protein and rich in iron, omega-3 fatty acids, and vitamin E (they have three times the vitamin E contained in flaxseed). And hempseed is delicious; it has a light, slightly fluffy texture and delightful nutty flavor, similar to but more delicate than that of sunflower seeds. I use hempseed in Hempseed Whole Wheat Sablés (page 89), sometimes with pecans and sesame seeds. Look for hempseed, either in packages or in bulk, in markets that sell natural and whole foods. Keep it in a sealed container in a cool, dark place or in the refrigerator to prevent rancidity. Hempseed does not contain psychoactive substances, by the way.

JASMINE TEA

The jasmine teas I use in my recipes are looseleaf teas (not tea bags) purchased from purveyors who specialize in tea. They are fine green teas that have been infused with the flavor of fresh jasmine blossoms: the tea leaves are layered with the blossoms until the flavor and scent of the blossoms have fully permeated the tea. Then the blossoms are removed, to prevent decay or spoilage, and the tea leaves are dried again. The presence of jasmine blossoms in tea may mislead the uninitiated buyer into thinking he or she is buying the finest quality, an easy mistake to make. In fact, blossoms are left in only lesser-quality green teas, to cut labor costs—to the detriment of the tea's flavor. If you can, try a top-grade jasmine tea such as Jasmine Downy Pearls or Yin Hao. Good purveyors also sell more moderately priced teas. Ask for a jasmine tea that was flavored with blossoms rather than with essential oils or extracts. If you purchase medium-priced jasmine teas in boxes, look at the ingredients label and take the following advice from the late tea guru Helen Gustafson, from her book *The Green Tea User's Manual:* "Remember that the term 'natural flavors' is a dumping ground for any kind of flavor, including chemically produced ones. A good rule of thumb for medium-priced jasmines is to buy the one with the fewest additives." Only small amounts of tea are used in my recipes, so why not learn to brew and steep the tea properly for drinking? Use less-than-boiling water and steep only 2 to 3 minutes, to avoid bitterness. Consult your tea purveyor for more details. The most seemingly expensive teas cost very little per cup.

LAVENDER

Dried culinary lavender is available in the spice section of better supermarkets. If you want to grow your own lavender for culinary uses, select the variety *L. x intermedia,* also called Provence lavender, which, according to Sharon Shipley, California chef and author of *The Lavender Cookbook,* has a lower camphor and resin content than other varieties.

LIQUEURS AND SPIRITS

When recipes call for spirits, such as brandy or rum, it is not necessary to use the finest and most expensive brand, but choose one that you can sip without grimacing—or omit it altogether. If you omit the liquor or liqueur used as a flavoring, there is usually no need to substitute another liquid in its place. Omitting the small quantity of liquor called for in some frozen desserts is acceptable, but it may affect the creaminess of ice cream or sorbet. Omitting the liquor used to flavor truffle centers will make the centers firmer; this can be corrected with a little extra cream or by using a little less chocolate. I never use liquor flavorings or extracts because they taste artificial.

Eaux-de-Vie • Eaux-de-vie are high-proof, usually colorless, unaged fruit brandies, the finest of which are distilled from fresh fruit. The classics are raspberry (framboise), cherry (kirsch), and pear (poire), but you will also find eaux-de-vie made from quinces, apples, plums, and any other fruit that catches the distiller's eye. This type of fruit brandy should not be confused with sweet, syrupy "fruit brandies" or with sweet fruit liqueurs, such as Chambord. My favorite eaux-de-vie are made in California by St. George Spirits (see Resources, page 249).

NUTS

For freshness and flavor, buy nuts raw, not toasted, and in bulk from stores that have lots of turnover, rather than packaged from the supermarket. Larger halves and pieces stay fresher longer; it's better to chop them yourself. Packaged airtight, nuts keep well in the freezer.

Fresh nuts are delicious raw, but toasting brings out such rich new flavors that almonds and hazelnuts are virtually transformed. Toasted nuts are also crunchier.

To toast nuts, spread them in a single layer on a baking sheet. Bake in a preheated oven—350°F for almonds and hazelnuts; 325°F for pecans and walnuts—for 10 to 20 minutes, depending on the type of nut (soft nuts such as walnuts and pecans and tiny nuts such as pine nuts take less time than almonds and hazelnuts) and whether they are whole, sliced, or slivered. Check the color and flavor of the nuts frequently, and stir to redistribute them. Almonds and hazelnuts are done when they are golden brown when you bite or cut them in half; pecans and walnuts are done when fragrant and lightly colored and pine nuts when they are golden brown. Pine nuts can also be toasted in a skillet like sesame seeds (see below).

To rub the bitter skins from toasted hazelnuts, cool them and then rub the nuts together until most of the skins flake off. When chopped toasted nuts are called for, toast them whole or in large pieces and chop them once cool.

To pulverize or grind nuts in a food processor, without making nut butter or paste, start with a perfectly dry processor bowl and blade and nuts that are at room temperature. (Frozen or cold nuts will produce moisture that will turn the nuts to paste, as will nuts still hot from the oven.) Use short pulses, stopping from time to time to scrape the corners of the processor bowl with a skewer or chopstick. If you observe these rules, there is no need to add some of the flour or sugar from the recipe to the nuts to keep them dry, as some cookbooks suggest, although you may do so as a precaution.

SESAME SEEDS

Sesame seeds are used in sweet and savory dishes in Asian, African, and Middle Eastern cuisines. In North America, we most often encounter them sprinkled on breads and bagels. But we taste their nutty flavor in the toasted oil used in Chinese cooking, in the Middle Eastern confection known as halvah, and in dips and dressings made with the ground sesame seed paste called tahini. I add their nutty rich flavor to Sesame Coins (page 97), Sesame Brittle Ice Cream (page 80), and Sesame Seed Cake (page 82). Hulled sesame seeds are off-white or cream; natural, or unhulled, seeds are tan, black, or red (very rare in this country). I use them interchangeably. Sesame seeds turn rancid quickly. Buy them in small quantities from a reliable source and store in the refrigerator up to 3 months or freeze.

To toast sesame seeds, spread the seeds in a dry wide skillet and stir constantly over medium heat until they just begin to color. Turn the heat down (seeds burn quickly once they get hot) and continue to stir until the seeds are fragrant and medium golden brown, with a nice toasted flavor. I usually take the pan off the heat early and continue to stir—the hot pan finishes the toasting gently and evenly. The whole process takes less than 5 minutes. Immediately scrape the seeds onto a plate to cool completely before using.

Sesame Tahini ▪ Sesame tahini is 100 percent pure hulled (roasted or unroasted and usually unsalted), ground sesame seeds. Its texture resembles very runny natural peanut butter and its color ranges from a creamy tan to a color like pale peanut butter. Because it does not contain emulsifiers or thickeners, the oil from the sesame seeds separates from the solids—just as all natural nut butters do—so that you must stir the contents of the container each time before using it. Tahini has the flavor of sesame seeds, sometimes including a slight bitterness. However, excessive bitterness or a pronounced metallic flavor is an indication that caustic chemicals were used in hulling the seeds and or that the seeds were rancid or of poor quality. Do not confuse tahini with dips or sauces or products that contain ingredients in addition to ground sesame seeds, including the Israeli product Tahineh, which contains chickpeas. Tahini may be imported from the Middle East or domestic. I prefer the richer flavor of tahini from roasted seeds over that made with raw seeds. Tahini made with roasted seeds may or may not be so labeled. However, raw tahini is always labeled "raw," so you should not have any problem identifying the type you want. Tahini packed in jars usually tastes better than tahini from cans. I especially like the family-owned Tarazi Brand Sesame Tahini (Tarazi Specialty Foods of Chino, California), made with seeds hulled with a water process rather than caustic chemicals; it is made from roasted seeds, although the label makes no mention of that.

SPICES

For the best and brightest flavors, use ground spices that still smell potent in the jar. Grinding one's own spices may seem extreme to many American cooks, but nutmeg and cinnamon are easy to grate on the spot using a Microplane zester. The rewards are significant in terms of flavor and aroma, especially considering the small effort involved.

SUGAR

Granulated White Sugar ▪ Processed white sugar is a staple of Western baking. It has been so completely cleansed, bleached, and freed of any impurity that it is hard to remember it is a product of agriculture to begin with. Exactly for this reason, regardless of any other issues, refined white sugar is the perfect neutral sweetener because it does not compete with the flavor of other ingredients. For example, in the finest chocolates, white sugar sweetens the cacao without altering its flavor.

I use cane sugar rather than beet sugar for baking and dessert making. Chemically, the two substances are the same, yet many bakers and pastry chefs have reported differences and disappointments with beet sugar. After having several cakes fall, I now avoid sugar that contains added fructose. (Granulated sugar is, by definition, a combination of sucrose and fructose, but when fructose is on the ingredients list, it means that extra fructose has been added.) The recipes in this book were tested with C&H granulated cane sugar purchased in the supermarket.

Sugars can vary in coarseness in different parts of the country. Fine sugar makes velvety cakes and tender cookies (notwithstanding the fact that a little coarse sugar mixed into cookie dough can also increase tenderness!). If your sugar is coarser than regular table salt and/or your cookies are tough or your cakes are falling, switch to a finer granulated sugar or even superfine sugar (sometimes called bar sugar) or simply process your regular granulated sugar briefly in the food processor before using it. (Or look for C&H bakers' sugar.)

Brown Sugar ▪ The original brown sugars were semirefined, with some of the natural molasses left in them (see Raw Sugars, below). Today commercial brown sugar is retrofitted; that is, it is refined white sugar with added molasses. The resulting light (or golden) brown and dark brown sugars impart pleasing caramel or butterscotch flavors to desserts. Some recipes may specify a preference for light or dark brown sugar, but you can use them interchangeably to your taste. Brown sugar hardens with exposure to the air; store it in an airtight container or tightly sealed in the bag it came in. The sugar should be lump-free before it is added to a batter or dough since it is unlikely to smooth out once it is added. Soft lumps can be squeezed with your fingers or mashed with a fork before adding. *To soften hardened brown sugar,* sprinkle it with a little water, put it in a tightly covered container (or wrap tightly in foil), and place it in a 250°F oven for a few minutes. Allow it to cool before using it. Brown sugar is measured by packing it fairly firmly into a measuring cup. My recipes are based on 7 ounces of brown sugar per cup.

Raw Sugars ▪ Raw sugars are semirefined, with varying amounts of natural molasses left in them. Unlike processed white sugar, raw—or specialty—sugars are not only sweeteners, but also bona-fide flavor ingredients. They add to a chef's arsenal of flavors to play with or play off, or even to showcase. Some resemble commercial brown sugars in texture and appearance, but the best of these sugars burst with complex tastes and aromas. They vary in color and consistency from coarse crunchy grains with a light caramel hue (and flavor to match) to amber and russet sugars with the moist consistency of familiar brown sugar. At the top of the color and flavor spectrum, dark muscovado is deep mahogany brown, almost black, with dark flavors of molasses, ripe tropical fruits, and smoke.

Turbinado is a coarse raw crystal sugar, rather than a moist brown sugar. The best turbinado is semirefined: most but not all of the molasses has been removed, leaving the sugar with a delicate caramel-molasses flavor. But some turbinado sugars are made similarly to commercial brown sugars, by adding molasses to refined sugar for flavor and color. Turbinado is popular as a table sugar for use in coffee or tea, or it may be sprinkled on the top of baked goods. Similar in process, color, and crunch, Demerara sugar is a little more flavorful than turbinado sugar. I like to mix a little of these coarse sugars into shortbread and butter cookie doughs to add crunch and tenderness—subtract a little of the regular sugar from the recipe to compensate for the added sugar.

Muscovado Sugar (Light and Dark) ▪ From Barbados or Mauritius, muscovado sugar is semirefined or raw sugar, with lots of the natural molasses left in it. Soft and moist rather than a crunchy crystal sugar, it has an earthy, tropical fruit aroma and flavor with a touch of smoke. Light muscovado has the relative intensity and sweetness of commercial dark brown sugar with far more flavor and complexity. Almost black, dark muscovado has deep aromatic molasses notes without the bitter pungency of the latter. Dark or light muscovado can be simply eaten on bread and butter or substituted for brown sugars in traditional spice cakes and cookies, but they are most exciting when their flavor is contrasted with other elements in a dessert, as in Muscovado Bread Pudding (page 182) or laced into a buttery brioche (see Tropical Swirl Babka, page 196), or made into a sauce (see page 185) for ice cream or a filling for tea cakes (page 193).

Palm Sugar/Coconut Sugar/Jaggery/Gur ▪ Palm sugar is made from the sugar palm and coconut sugar comes from the coconut palm. However, you may find, as I did, a package of "Pure Palm Sugar" that also says "fresh natural juice from coconut flower." Jaggery and gur are also names for unrefined palm or cane sugars, although in some parts of the world *jaggery* is the term for cane and *gur* the word for palm sugars. Regardless, each is made from the sweet sap that drips from cut flower buds. I used the "Pure Palm Sugar" to make Coconut Palm Cream Cake (page 191) and Tropical Lace Cookies (page 189). The sugar (Double Horses Brand from J & A Importers, Inc., in Vernon, California) is the color of pale maple sugar and comes molded into round pillow shapes that are rock hard. The flavor is delicate, with notes of maple and coffee and a nuance of coconut, and it is quite sweet. I also bought a can of coconut sugar (the ingredient list read, "100% coconut sugar") that contained seemingly hard sugar, which liquefied into a dense sticky paste when I scraped it out of the can and mashed it to remove the lumps.

Palm and coconut sugars are used in sweet and savory Thai and other Southeast Asian cuisines. Because these are not refined sugars, they vary in color and flavor, from pale beige to dark caramel and from delicate to very flavorful but less sweet;

textures range from soft and sticky to rock hard. If the latter, you can make the sugar user friendly by placing it in a bag and smashing with a hammer. Or grate it (more than you need at one time) with the coarse grating disk of your food processor. Press very lightly on the pusher for the feed tube, and use the pulse button so that you can stop at a moment's notice if the sugar jams in the blade—which it tends to do once the pieces become small. Remove small pieces and finely chop them by hand. Do not attempt to process these sugars with the metal processor blade, as this may damage the motor. Once grated, the sugar will be soft, like brown sugar. Store it in an airtight jar and measure it as you would brown sugar, lightly packing it in the cup.

I solved the problem of measuring sugars of different consistencies by equating 1 cup of any sugar that is the consistency of regular brown sugar (after it is grated) with ⅔ cup of any sugar that is the consistency of a thick sticky paste. Both measures weigh 7 ounces.

Piloncillo ▪ This raw sugar, also called *panela* or *panocha,* is a traditional Mexican sugar made from boiled sugarcane juice and molded into cone shapes. Brown and hard as a rock, piloncillo doesn't invite the regular use that it deserves. To remedy that problem, grate piloncillo cones as you would palm sugar, or put a cone in a bag and smash it with a hammer.

In color and relative sweetness and intensity, piloncillo is similar to dark brown sugar, but the flavor is brighter and more interesting, with caramel and molasses notes and a slight flavor of smoke. Grate it and store it in an airtight jar, and you will use it regularly in place of brown sugar in recipes or on your oatmeal. Although their flavors are different, piloncillo and light muscovado can be used interchangeably.

Golden Syrup ▪ Golden syrup is an amber-colored cane sugar syrup similar physically and chemically to honey. It tastes like vanilla butterscotch honey, and it is delicious enough to drizzle on pancakes, spread on bread and butter, or eat with a spoon. Generally, you may use golden syrup as you use honey, corn syrup, or molasses. The English brand Lyle's Golden Syrup is the most well-known brand in the United States. It is found easily in good supermarkets, specialty stores, or online (see Resources, page 249). I use it to make sensational Golden Vanilla Bean Caramels (page 226).

VANILLA

Vanilla Extract ▪ I use only pure vanilla extract—Tahitian, Mexican, or Bourbon, depending on what flavor I want. Tahitian has the most floral aroma, like exotic tropical flowers, with flavor notes of cherry, licorice, and raisins. It is a lovely flavor to feature rather than use as a background flavor in cookies or custard or ice cream. Mexican vanilla has some aromas of rum and caramel and very ripe fruit. Bourbon vanilla (also called Madagascar), the type most familiar to North Americans, is most difficult to describe because it smells and tastes like . . . well, vanilla.

Vanilla Beans ▪ Vanilla beans are luxurious to use, though a bit more time-consuming than opening a bottle of extract. Split the bean lengthwise and use the point of a paring knife to scrape the seeds into a batter, dough, or custard. In the latter case, or wherever there is a liquid to be flavored, steep the split pod as well as the seeds. After steeping, retrieve and scrape any remaining seeds from the pod into the liquid; then discard the pod.

Ground Vanilla ▪ I also use ground-up whole vanilla beans in cookie dough, cheesecake batter, and ice creams. If you can't find jars of ground vanilla beans (not to be confused with vanilla powder or vanilla paste), you can chop a whole bean and grind it as fine as possible in a coffee or spice grinder. As a rule of thumb, you can use ¼ teaspoon ground whole vanilla beans to replace 1 teaspoon vanilla extract, but I often use more.

The focused attention that must be given to tasting and to understanding how elements of sweetness, richness, texture, and flavor act together is one of the great pleasures of working on a new cookbook. When I explore new ingredients or combinations, the learning curve is steep and quietly exciting, often with unexpected results, as I figure out which things go with what and begin to develop my own quirky explanations for why.

Sometimes I feel like Sherlock Holmes. Take the case of the Vin Santo Chiffon Cake (page 237) and the Olive Oil and Sherry Pound Cake (page 86). Both have a bit of orange zest and olive oil, but their flavors and textures are different. When I tasted each cake with fresh orange segments, the chiffon was delicious and melted in my mouth. But the pound cake flavor was overwhelmed by the oranges, and its texture suddenly felt damp and coarse in my mouth. I can recommend the chiffon with oranges, but not the pound cake!

Richness affects both flavor and texture. Nutella Bread Pudding (page 154) is sinfully delicious with a relatively rich egg mixture, but Muscovado Bread Pudding (page 182) needs less egg and cream in the mix in order to support the subtler tropical flavors of the raw sugar. Intense fruit flavors sing in lean sorbets and sherbets, rather than in cream- or custard-based ice creams. Guinness Ice Cream (page 235) wants a custard base to bring out its flavor, while honey wants only milk and cream (without eggs) to carry its delicate varietal flavor into ice cream (see page 177).

Because I am fascinated with the effects of small changes, I sometimes test a recipe more than anyone in her right mind would. But there are some shortcuts. If a cake tastes flat or seems lacking in some flavor, I leave it out on the counter for a few days and taste it from time to time with another flavor, or even with just a few extra grains of salt or sugar sprinkled on top. It was in that way that I learned that the Walnut Sponge Cake (page 77) needed extra salt and lemon zest, while the Olive Oil and Sherry Pound Cake wanted orange (definitely not lemon) zest. Finding the right balance or flavor combination feels like a light suddenly switched on.

Blending flavors is not always the best way to enjoy them together. I love spices and I love chocolate, but mixing them does not always please me: often the clarity of the chocolate flavor is muddied by the spice. Fortuitously, I discovered that dusting the surface of a warm brownie with spice (page 139) gives it an enticing, aromatic "nose" (think glass of wine) that enhances rather than blurs the chocolate flavor. Dusting with spices, rather than blending them into the batter, can play on the intimate relationship of aroma and taste. In the case of the brownie, it offers the best of the spice and the best of the chocolate.

As a child, I learned that eating vanilla ice cream with chocolate sauce made the chocolate taste more chocolaty by contrast. I sometimes extend the vanilla ice cream rule beyond usefulness, assuming that almost anything good will taste even better with vanilla ice cream. Sauces made with raw sugars such as piloncillo and muscovado were so instantly compelling, I automatically reached for the carton of vanilla ice cream, expecting greatness. The light muscovado and piloncillo sauces were divine, but in the confrontation with vanilla ice cream, the dark muscovado lost its lovely complexity, and its ripe, dusky tropical flavors suddenly tasted like bitter molasses. The sauce needed a softer contrast, or complementary flavors, or both. It was glorious in a sundae with Sour Cream Ice Cream (page 49) and the (related!) flavors of grilled ripe pineapple and bananas.

Strawberry sorbet (see page 128) provided a lesson in flavor as well. With dozens of simple strawberry sorbet recipes easily available, I wondered what I could contribute. So I began testing. I made one sorbet with raw berries and one with cooked berries (despite my prejudices). As expected, the raw sorbet had a brighter, cleaner, fresher fruit flavor. Again as expected, the cooked sorbet tasted too cooked. But it also had some deeper rounded strawberry flavors that were missing in the raw sorbet, and a smoother texture. Obviously, to get all of the possible strawberry flavors and the best texture into my sorbet, I need raw and cooked fruit. Using both raw and cooked berries is the key to greatness again in the Really Raspberry Coconut Tart (page 104).

Cooks have many choices and tricks for getting the best flavors from ingredients. A few years ago, I experimented with fresh mint leaves, rose petals, rose geranium leaves, and jasmine green tea infused in cream, with my then-assistant Maya Klein. We were completely fascinated at the differences in flavor caused by infusing these aromatic ingredients in hot cream versus cold cream. Each sample was good in the hot infusion, but spectacular in the cold. Cold cream coaxed forth the high notes and the floral flavors; hot cream produced more earthy vegetal notes, including the bitter tannins in the green tea. We were captivated by our results and promptly concocted stunning whipped cream toppings and ice creams and even chocolate truffles. We also discovered that once the infused materials (leaves, petals, etc.) were spent and discarded, the infused cream could *then*, if necessary, be heated (to make ganache, for example) without damaging its exquisite flavor. The learning experience pleased me as much as the recipes that resulted!

the flavors of milk

In a book devoted to ingredient-inspired desserts, I begin with milk—and a celebration of the butter, cream, and fresh cheeses that are made from it. This is a quiet, subtle start.

Along with white flour and eggs, we call them staples and we take them for granted: aren't they just a backdrop for fancy flavors like chocolate, lemon, raspberry, or spice? Yet, without them, the classic dessert repertoire—custards, puddings, ice creams, cookies, and cakes—would not exist.

Each recipe in this chapter is an eloquent expression of its defining ingredient. You could call them plain. I call them pristine, even sumptuous. Tasting them will remind you that milk, butter, and cream are primal flavors on their own. And, if you're not yet tasting and comparing the milks, creams, and butters available to you, it's time to begin. Golden brioche and crunchy shortbread speak butter. Butter is responsible for the tender crumb and soul-satisfying flavor of the best cakes. Good milk and cream make silky custards and divine ice creams—even without other flavors. The gamut of available fresh cheeses, several of which were new to me—with sweet, yeasty, nutty, tart, or tangy flavors—was so compelling that I wanted to preserve the character of each one. The result is soulfully simple recipes: cheese is contrasted with sweet lace cookies; nuts and candied citrus peel are wrapped in caramelized crepes, puffed into a soufflé, or used to fill a buttery tart shell.

For the passionate cook, these recipes not only set the stage for an emphasis on ingredients but are also a starting point from which to create new desserts, by adding flavors, substituting ingredients, or following whatever inspiration comes. All sorts of variations are possible, some of which will be found in the chapters to come.

twice-baked shortbread

There are a couple of secrets to this tender, buttery, crunchy shortbread. For the best flavor and texture, let the dough rest in the pan for at least 2 hours, or overnight, before baking. A second short bake toasts each piece ever so slightly, adding extra flavor and resulting in a light, crunchier texture through and through. If you don't have a pan with a removable bottom, line the pan with foil to facilitate removal. Shortbread keeps for many weeks in a sealed container, and it makes a wonderful gift.

makes fourteen to sixteen 2-inch squares or 16 wedges

12 tablespoons (1½ sticks) unsalted butter, melted and still warm

5 tablespoons granulated sugar

1 teaspoon pure vanilla extract

¼ teaspoon salt

1½ cups (6.75 ounces) all-purpose flour

Turbinado, Demerara, or granulated sugar for sprinkling

EQUIPMENT

A baking pan with a removable bottom, such as a 9½-inch round or a 4 by 14-inch rectangular fluted tart pan, or a one-piece 8-inch square pan

IF USING A PAN with a removable bottom, grease the pan; if using the one-piece 8-inch pan, line it with aluminum foil, leaving an overhang on two opposite sides.

In a medium bowl, combine the melted butter with the sugar, vanilla, and salt. Add the flour and mix just until incorporated. Pat and spread the dough evenly in the pan. Let rest for at least 2 hours, or overnight (no need to refrigerate).

Position a rack in the lower third of the oven and preheat the oven to 300°F.

Bake the shortbread for 45 minutes.

Remove the pan from the oven, leaving the oven on. Lightly sprinkle the surface of the shortbread with sugar. Let the shortbread cool for 10 minutes.

Remove the shortbread from the pan, being careful to avoid breaking it. Use a thin sharp knife to cut it into oblong "fingers," wedges, or squares. Place the pieces slightly apart on a parchment-lined baking sheet and put it in the oven for 15 minutes. Cool on a rack.

lebni tart

PHOTOGRAPH ON PAGE 40

Lebni is a creamy smooth and tangy cheese, like sour cream with soul. If there were such a thing as "the little white dress," this would be the dessert equivalent: a pristine, delicately set ivory filling in a sweet buttery crust. Although it needs nothing else, it welcomes accessories such as ripe strawberries (served alongside or sliced and arranged on top *à la française*), or roasted figs or plums, or shards of caramelized walnuts or pine nuts (see page 81). The only secret for success is *not to overbake it,* for, as with all custards and cheesecakes, the filling continues to cook after it emerges from the oven.   serves 8

FOR THE CRUST

8 tablespoons (1 stick) unsalted butter, melted

¼ cup granulated sugar

¾ teaspoon pure vanilla extract

¼ teaspoon salt

1 cup (4.5 ounces) all-purpose flour

FILLING

3 large eggs

¼ cup plus 2 tablespoons sugar

⅛ teaspoon salt

½ teaspoon pure vanilla extract

1½ cups (12 ounces) lebni (kefir cheese; see Note)

1 egg yolk, lightly beaten with a pinch of salt

EQUIPMENT

A 9½-inch fluted tart pan with a removable bottom

TO MAKE THE CRUST, position a rack in the lower third of the oven and preheat the oven to 350°F.

In a medium bowl, combine the butter with the sugar, vanilla, and salt. Add the flour and mix just until well blended. If the dough seems too soft and gooey, let it stand for a few minutes to firm up.

Press the dough evenly over the bottom and up the sides of the tart pan to make a very thin, even layer. This takes a little patience, as there is just enough dough; to avoid ending up with extra-thick edges, press the dough squarely into the corners of the pan. Place the pan on a cookie sheet.

Bake until the crust is a deep, golden brown, 20 to 25 minutes, checking after about 15 minutes or so to see if the dough has puffed up from the bottom of the pan. If it has, lift and gently slam the cookie sheet down to settle the dough, or press the dough down with the back of a fork and prick it a few times.

Meanwhile, make the filling (somewhat surprisingly the order in which the ingredients are mixed makes a big difference in the smoothness of the tart, so proceed without deviation): In a medium bowl whisk the eggs with the sugar, salt, and vanilla. Whisk in the cheese.

(CONTINUED)

When the crust is ready, remove it from the oven and turn the temperature down to 300°F. Brush the bottom of the crust with a thin layer of the beaten egg yolk to moistureproof it. Return the crust to the oven for 1 minute to set the yolk.

Pour the filling into the hot crust and spread it evenly. Return the tart to the oven and bake until the filling is set around the edges but, when the pan is nudged, quivers like very soft Jell-O in the center, about 15 to 20 minutes. Check often in the last few minutes, as overbaking will destroy the silky-smooth texture of the filling. Cool the tart completely on a rack. Refrigerate if not serving within 3 hours.

NOTE: I use Byblos brand lebni (kefir cheese), made with both milk and cream, so it is moderately rich (with 6 grams of fat per 30 grams of cheese).

ricotta and lace

In Italy ricotta cheese is made from cow's or sheep's milk: every ricotta I tasted was divine. To find good ricotta closer to home, sample those from the best cheese vendors in town (or see Resources, page 249).

Good ricotta tastes of sweet fresh milk—a flavor so delicate and satisfying you may be tempted to eat it all up plain. Even for dessert I hesitate to sweeten the cheese itself with sugar, preferring to add contrasting sweet elements separately to accentuate the flavor of the ricotta. Here, with candied orange peel and caramelized lace cookies, ricotta becomes a simple and pretty dessert.

As an alternative to shaping cookie cornets or cups, you can leave the cookies flat and assemble little napoleons (at the last minute to keep the cookies crisp) by stacking three cookies with creamy ricotta between them. No time to assemble anything? Sometimes I just open the carton of ricotta and dip the cookies in! serves 4 to 6

1 pound (2 cups) fresh ricotta

2 to 3 tablespoons chopped Candied Orange Peel (page 131) or Quick Orange Zest Garnish (page 133)

¼ cup (1 ounce) toasted pine nuts or toasted slivered almonds (see page 25; optional)

6 extra-large Tropical Lace Cookies (page 189), shaped into cornets or cups

Cocoa powder or grated chocolate for sprinkling

WHISK THE RICOTTA until fluffy. Stir in the candied peel and toasted nuts. Just before serving, spoon the ricotta onto the lace cookies, and sprinkle a little sifted cocoa powder or grated chocolate on top. Serve immediately.

Desiré's brioche

This is the very best brioche I know. When I was twenty-five, I watched Desiré Valentin make fifty pounds of it at three in the morning in the cathedral city of Rheims. Chilling the flour and the creamed butter allows you to beat oodles of butter into the dough without its melting or separating. My recent addition of sour cream—suggested by Portland cooking teacher Maya Klein—heightens the flavor of the butter. The result is luxuriously old school: the richest brioche, with a featherlight texture and golden crust. Serve with more butter or a fresh artisan cheese, such as fromage blanc, and a little honey, or your best preserves. Or lace the dough with raw sugar and turn it into Tropical Swirl Babka (page 196). (Would a Frenchman approve?) Don't forget to allow for resting the dough overnight.

makes 10 individual brioches

3 cups (15 ounces) bread flour

20 tablespoons (2½ sticks) cold unsalted butter

1 envelope active dry yeast

⅓ cup plus 1 teaspoon sugar

¼ cup warm water (105° to 115°F)

5 large cold eggs

1 tablespoon sour cream or yogurt

1½ teaspoons salt

1 egg

EQUIPMENT

Heavy-duty stand mixer with a paddle attachment and a dough hook

Ten 4-inch individual brioche pans

Instant-read thermometer (optional)

PLACE THE FLOUR in a shallow pan, cover, and freeze for 30 minutes. Put the cold butter in the mixer bowl and use the paddle attachment to beat it only until it is creamy and smooth; there should be no small hard lumps when you pinch it between your fingers. Scrape the butter into a mound on a piece of wax paper and refrigerate. (Proceed with the recipe right away; a long delay will reharden the butter.)

In the clean mixer bowl, dissolve the yeast and 1 teaspoon of the sugar in the warm water just until dissolved. Attach the dough hook. Add the remaining ⅓ cup sugar, the eggs, sour cream or yogurt, salt, and flour and mix on low speed until the ingredients are blended, scraping the bowl as necessary. Knead the dough on medium speed for 5 minutes. At the end of the kneading period, the dough will be very soft, moist and sticky, and very elastic; it will be wrapped around the dough hook.

Add the cold creamed butter in several pieces, pushing it into the dough and beating thoroughly until it is incorporated. This will require stopping several times to scrape the dough from the sides of the bowl and off the hook. Scrape the dough into a bowl, cover, and refrigerate overnight, or for as long as 24 hours.

Generously butter the brioche pans. Scrape the dough out onto a floured surface and deflate it with your hands. Divide it into 10 equal pieces (each weighing 4 ounces).

(CONTINUED)

You can shape these into the classic brioche à tête shape, with a topknot, or skip down to the equally lovely free-form twisted knot, which is much easier for beginners.

To form traditional brioches with topknots, first round each piece of dough as follows: Place a piece of dough cut side down on the lightly floured counter. Cup your floured hand over the dough, palm facing downward and with your thumb and pinky touching the counter—your hand should be like a loose cage over the dough. Press the dough down gently as you rotate your hand counterclockwise (if you are right-handed) in a small circle. Your hand must stay dry while the counter becomes slightly tacky from contact with the cut side of the dough. Between your dry hand and the tacky counter, the dough will begin to form a tight ball with a seam at the bottom. (If the dough rips on top, you are pressing too firmly or your hand is not dry. If the dough slides on the counter, you are not pressing firmly enough or the counter is too dry.) Continue to press down and rotate until you feel a firm ball taking shape in your hand. This takes practice, so do the best you can if you are a beginner. Set the ball of dough aside seam side down and repeat until all the dough pieces are rounded.

Now form each round into a fat snowman shape: Cup your hands around the top third of a dough ball and squeeze gently with the sides of your hands while you shimmy them back and forth to form a narrow neck with a little head on top. Place the snowman in a buttered brioche pan. Grasp the head from the top with your fingertips at the neck, and simultaneously pinch and twist the neck, then jam it deep into the dough in the pan. To secure the topknot and prevent it from popping out during proofing and baking, flour your index finger and poke it deep into the seam on one side of the topknot. Rotate the pan and poke your floured finger two or three more times around the seam of the topknot to secure it. Repeat until all of the brioches are formed.

To form simple twists, on a lightly floured surface, roll a piece of dough into a fat rope about 8 or 9 inches long. Make a loop at one end of the rope and insert the other end through it, as though tying a knot. Nestle the knot into a buttered brioche pan with the inserted tail of the dough facing upward (like a topknot!). Repeat until all of the brioches are formed.

Place the pans on a baking sheet and cover loosely with plastic wrap. Let rise in a warm place until almost doubled, about 2 hours.

Preheat the oven to 350°F. Thoroughly whisk the egg with 1 teaspoon water and strain it to remove any large bits of white. Brush the egg wash gently over the surface of each brioche, taking care not to get it on the pans. Bake until the tops are deeply browned and the bottom of the pans sound hollow when tapped, or an instant-read thermometer registers 200°F when inserted in the center of the bread, 20 to 25 minutes. Cool on a rack.

Serve warm or at room temperature. Even stale brioches are magnificent sliced and toasted.

Why bother to make ice creams or sorbets when the supermarket is packed with them? Because home-made is exponentially better than store-bought and because ice cream making is so easy and fun that the avid beginner achieves mastery in very short order—and then often moves on to create new ice cream flavors.

The newest, most exciting approach to ice creams emphasizes flavor rather than butterfat content as the paramount criterion for quality. Thus milk or yogurt or water can be as important as cream, and tastes are derived from real ingredients and simple infusions rather than from extracts or prepared goop from jars and cans. The newest gelato shop in my town, for example, features gelato made exclusively with local organic milk and yogurt (not cream). Home cooks can do likewise, if they desire.

Anyone who acquires a new ice cream machine experiences a phase where any and every food, if only for a moment, is considered a potential ice cream flavor. In my case, I also could not wait to address my biggest complaint about commercial ice creams: they are uniformly, boringly too sweet and too rich. I wondered why ice creams never have tart and tangy ripples, why there aren't some pleasingly bitter as well as sweet flavors in ice creams, why sorbets melt like snow cones into sweet syrup. I don't want kitschy flavors: I simply want ice creams and sorbets that do not bombard the senses with fat or sugar.

Officially, commercial ice creams, sherbets, ice milks, and sorbets are defined by the ingredients they include and their fat content, though regulations are not consistent from state to state (or country to country). The home cook is free of regulation. I have used the term "ice cream" for all recipes that are creamy like ice cream, regardless of the butterfat percentage, if they include at least some cream, or a cream-like ingredient (such as sour cream), whether or not eggs are included. I call fruit ices that do not include any dairy ingredients "sorbet," and those made with milk or buttermilk "sherbet." Gianduja Sorbet (page 152) and Milk Chocolate Sorbet (page 151) are named whimsically: these are made with water, rather than milk, but there is plenty of milk or cream in the chocolate and gianduja itself. Coarse icy mixtures that are frozen without agitation, and usually but not always made with liquid or juice rather than fruit pulp, are "granitas."

Ice creams, sorbets, sherbets, and granitas each highlight flavors in a very different way, and they feel different on the palate as well. And even among ice creams, there is no one-base-fits-all: eggy custard bases complement some flavors perfectly, while other flavors are more vibrant with a base of cream and milk.

In general, leaner frozen desserts—sorbets and sherbets and even lower-fat ice creams—feel colder, taste more refreshing, and have brighter flavors. Fruit sorbets and sherbets have truer fruit flavor than do fruit ice creams. Richer mixtures taste and feel creamier, smoother, and more luxurious on the palate. Sometime a choice must be made. To insist that the richest is always the best is to miss both bright *and* nuanced flavors. When I make ice cream with an infusion of cacao nibs or with a raw sugar, I use a relatively lean mixture of milk and cream, because the delicate flavors of the cacao infusion or the sugar would otherwise be lost. I also happen to like the more refreshing quality of these ice creams, so I do not mind that they are not ultra-smooth and creamy. In trade-offs such as this, I often lean toward best flavor over smoothest texture. If I love the flavor, I may also appreciate the rusticity of ice cream that is not perfectly smooth. But every palate is different. In Rome, I visited the six or seven "best" gelato shops. The media darling of the moment turned out not to be my favorite. The setting was stylish and the ingredients were of the highest quality, but to my taste, the gelatos were all just a tad too rich—I was missing clear flavors. (Of course, it took me several visits to be sure!)

Back in my own kitchen, I discovered that the flavors and textures of sorbets could be affected by the use of raw versus cooked fruit. I experimented with Sicilian gelatos made with only milk and a little starch for creaminess and with neither eggs nor cream. I compared the results of ice cream machines that churn at different rates of speed, and I made some sherbets and sorbets using a food processor. And, of course, I tried rich creamy bases, custard mixes, and just plain water or milk in order to decide which best expressed the flavor of bananas, or honey, or beer, for example.

In the end, I concluded that ice cream making at home is not an exact science, nor can the details be set in stone, because there are so many variables: machines differ, fruit varies in sweetness and ripeness, milk and cream are not the same at all times of year or in every location, and every cook's palate is different. This very inex-actitude is an invitation. If you like a certain ice cream but wish it were creamier, substitute more cream for the same amount of milk or add an extra egg yolk to the custard base. If your machine churns faster than mine, your results may be more aerated, and thus less intense in flavor. Next time, try the recipe with less liquid, or increase the flavoring ingredient, or stop the churning early.

True to my initial intention, some of the best ice creams include ingredients that are inherently tart or tangy, even appealingly bitter: beer, buttermilk, and sour cream. Beer (Guinness, in particular) makes a surprisingly delicious ice cream, and one that answered my craving for the simultaneous sensation of cold and creamy, bitter and sweet. I started with a beer granita, which was delightful. But beer ice cream was both a revelation and an education. I began gently, with a bottle of Sierra Nevada Pale Ale from California and a Czech favorite, Pilsner Urquel. The beer-and-custard base instantly reminded me of sabayon, but with an elusive and compelling edge of bitterness. The addition of another egg yolk produced an even more delicious ice cream. Then, scavenging in the fridge, I found a lonely bottle of Guinness left over from a bout of making Christmas puddings, and I turned that into a sensational ice cream with a creamy dark caramel and malt flavor. It was especially fine with tiny ripe strawberries from my farmers' market. With supreme confidence, I tried a super hoppy India pale ale—one of those deliciously bitter IPAs that I love to drink. Ouch! The IPA had a bitter, nasty bite to it. Even more cream (with less milk) didn't tame the beast. Thanks to my beer-loving brother Albert, I learned to select more delicate beers or those with a rich malty rather than hoppy flavor. Delicious ice cream can be made with pale ales, pilsners, lagers, and wheat beers.

Buttermilk—somewhat less unusual than beer—is also a delicious ice cream ingredient. It add superb body and creaminess to a rustic berry sherbet, along with a wonderful tangy flavor and very little fat. Making lime sherbet one day, I noticed that the lime juice curdled the milk (why was I surprised?) and realized that I was inadvertently getting the advantages of buttermilk, even though I began with fresh sweet milk!

Finally, I love the way the tart and tangy flavor of sour cream ice cream partners with sweet sauces and fresh fruit.

sour cream ice cream

Here is an irresistible new ice cream, gently sweetened so that you can savor the rich nutty flavor and pleasant edge of the sour cream. Nothing more, not even a whisper of vanilla, is needed. A traditional egg-custard ice cream base would have blurred the pristine flavor of the sour cream, so I chose a base of milk with a little (very little) cornstarch instead—like true Sicilian gelato. I adore this ice cream right out of the machine, with nothing but a spoon. It also makes a fabulous sundae with bananas and/or grilled or sautéed pineapple or strawberries and Raw Sugar Toffee Sauce (185) made with muscovado sugar or serve it with Tropical Lace Cookies (189).   makes about 3 cups

2 cups sour cream

⅔ cup sugar

1 tablespoon plus 1 teaspoon cornstarch

⅛ teaspoon salt

1 cup whole milk

EQUIPMENT

Ice cream machine

PUT THE SOUR CREAM in a medium bowl and set aside.

In a small saucepan, combine the sugar, cornstarch, and salt. Whisk in a little of the milk until smooth, then whisk in the remaining milk. Whisk constantly over medium heat until the mixture is warm and foamy. Continue to whisk as the foam subsides and the mixture thickens and begins to boil. Whisking and scraping the bottom and sides of the pan constantly to prevent scorching, boil steadily but not furiously for 1½ to 2 minutes, or until the mixture thins slightly and becomes a bit more translucent. It is important to cook the base adequately, or you will taste and feel the raw cornstarch on your palate and the flavor of the sour cream in the finished ice cream will not be clear and bright.

Remove the pan from the stove and whisk for a few seconds to release some heat. A little at a time, whisk the hot mixture into the sour cream. Let cool, then cover tightly and refrigerate, covered, until thoroughly chilled, at least 4 but preferably 12 hours.

For an extra-cold start, put the mixture in the freezer for 20 minutes, stirring once or twice to prevent freezing.

Freeze the ice cream according to the instructions for your ice cream machine. Serve, or pack into an airtight container and freeze. If the ice cream sits in the freezer for several hours, it will be too hard to scoop. Soften it slightly by transferring the container to the refrigerator for a few minutes before serving; or microwave on low or on the defrost setting for a few seconds at a time until scoopable.

caramelized crepes filled with fresh cheese

Minimalist, revamped cheese blintzes? You bet. Crepes make a tasty wrapper for a variety of fresh artisan cheeses, such as fromage blanc, cottage cheese, yogurt cheese, paneer, and even soft fresh goat cheese. Unlike the cheese filling for classic blintzes, here the cheese stands alone: I don't mix it with egg or even sugar (unless the cheese is especially tart). The cheeses that work best have a little, but not too much, tanginess to them, so they contrast nicely with the lightly caramelized crepes. Very delicate cheeses, such as fresh ricotta, are less interesting here. Cheeses that are quite tart, like sour cream or kefir cheese, can be mixed with a little sugar and vanilla to taste before they are rolled up. If in doubt, roll and sauté a sample and taste it. Grate a little bit of cinnamon stick or nutmeg over the crepes before serving, if you like.   makes about 18 small crepes, to serve 6

FOR THE CREPES

1¾ cups whole milk

2 tablespoons butter, melted

3 large eggs

1 cup (4.5 ounces) all-purpose flour

⅛ teaspoon salt

Butter for cooking the crepes and sautéing the filled crepes

About 1 pound slightly tangy fresh cheese, such as cottage cheese, fromage blanc, mild goat cheese, paneer, or yogurt cheese

Sugar for sprinkling

Sour cream for serving

EQUIPMENT

A crepe pan or 6-inch skillet

TO MAKE THE CREPES, combine the milk, melted butter, and eggs in a pitcher or measuring cup with a pouring spout. Put the flour and salt in a blender or food processor. With the motor running, pour the milk mixture through the feed tube and blend for 5 seconds. Set a medium mesh strainer over a bowl and strain the mixture into the bowl. Press any lumps through the strainer and stir them into the batter. Cover and refrigerate for at least 1 hour, or up to 1 day.

Heat crepe pan or 6-inch skillet over medium-high heat. Brush the pan lightly with butter. Pour 2 tablespoons of the batter into the pan and immediately tilt the pan to coat the entire surface evenly. Cook, on one side only, until the crepe is uniformly translucent and the surface no longer looks wet, 45 seconds to 1 minute. Loosen the edges of the crepe with a spatula and invert it onto a piece of wax paper. If necessary, unfold the crepe. (It is not important that the crepes lie perfectly flat, but try not to make holes in them.) Repeat with the remaining batter, buttering the pan as necessary. (The crepes can be stacked between sheets of wax paper, wrapped airtight, and stored in the refrigerator for up to 2 days.)

To assemble the crepes, place a slightly rounded tablespoon of cheese below the center of the brown side of a crepe. Shape the cheese into a cigar about 3½ inches long. Then roll up the crepes, as you would a rug, around the cheese. Place the filled crepe seam side down on a wax-paper-lined tray. Repeat to fill all of the crepes. Cover tightly with plastic wrap and refrigerate for at least 1 hour, or up to 2 days.

To sauté the crepes, first warm a serving dish or attractive pan in a 300°F oven; it will hold the finished crepes. Heat a large skillet over medium-high heat. When the pan is hot, add 1 tablespoon butter and swirl to coat the pan. Sprinkle 2 to 3 teaspoons sugar over the butter, and add only as many crepes to the pan as will fit comfortably. Cook seam side down only until just browned on the first side, about 30 seconds. Sprinkle the crepes with sugar, turn them carefully, and brown the bottoms. Place on the warm serving plate. Repeat with the remaining crepes. Serve immediately.

quark soufflés

These little puffed, golden soufflés retain the slightly tart cultured flavor of the cheese. Perfect just as they are, they are also a good foil for fresh seasonal fruit or a fruit sauce such as the blackberry. Instead of quark, you could try kefir cheese or fromage blanc.

serves 6

1 cup (8 ounces) quark

3 large eggs, separated

3 tablespoons all-purpose flour

⅛ teaspoon salt

1 teaspoon pure vanilla extract

⅛ teaspoon cream of tartar

¼ cup plus 1 tablespoon sugar, plus additional sugar for sprinkling

Chunky Blackberry Sauce (page 105; optional)

EQUIPMENT

Six 6-ounce ramekins

POSITION A RACK in the center of the oven and preheat the oven to 375°F. Butter and sugar the ramekins and place them on a baking sheet.

In a medium bowl, whisk together the quark, egg yolks, flour, salt, and vanilla.

In a large bowl of a stand mixer or in a small bowl with a hand-held mixer, beat the egg whites with cream of tartar until soft peaks form when the beaters are lifted. Gradually add the sugar, continuing to beat, until the whites are stiff but not dry. Scrape the cheese mixture onto the egg whites and fold together gently.

Divide the batter among the ramekins. Sprinkle the top of each soufflé with sugar. Bake the soufflés until they are puffed and slightly golden brown, about 15 minutes. Serve immediately.

crema ice cream

Americans take vanilla ice cream for granted. Gelato shops in Italy serve a flavor called *crema*, or "cream." It took me a few days without seeing vanilla gelato to realize that basic white ice cream in Italy is all about the cream. If you have marvelous organic cream and milk available to you, honor them with this ice cream. When you cease to consider vanilla a given, you notice and enjoy the flavor of the cream and milk. Then, rather than being the basic recipe, vanilla ice cream is a variation. You may appreciate vanilla even more when you use it consciously rather than automatically. I start with crema when I invent new flavors too; then ask myself if the flavor really needs vanilla.

To further accentuate the fresh cream flavor, you can make this recipe without cooking the cream at all: simply make the custard with milk, strain it as required, and then add the cream before chilling. When I make the vanilla bean variation, however, I prefer the slightly caramelized flavor produced by heating the cream and milk together.   makes 4 cups

2 ¼ cups heavy cream

1 cup whole milk

⅓ cup sugar

Slightly rounded ⅛ teaspoon salt

4 large egg yolks

EQUIPMENT

Instant-read thermometer

Ice cream machine

PLACE A STRAINER over a medium bowl and set it near the stove, for the finished ice cream base.

In a medium saucepan, combine the cream, milk, sugar, and salt and bring to a simmer over medium heat.

Meanwhile, in a medium bowl, whisk the eggs yolks just to combine them. Add the hot cream mixture in a thin stream, whisking constantly. Return the mixture to the pan and cook, stirring constantly, until it thickens slightly and registers between 175° and 180°F. Strain the mixture into a clean bowl, in order to remove any bits of cooked egg. Let cool, then refrigerate, covered, until thoroughly chilled, at least 4 but preferably 12 hours.

For an extra-cold start, put the mixture in the freezer for 20 minutes, stirring once or twice to prevent freezing. Freeze according to the instructions for your ice cream maker.

Serve soft or transfer to an airtight container and freeze until hard enough to scoop, at least 3 to 4 hours. If the ice cream gets too hard, before serving, let it stand for a few minutes, put it in the refrigerator for 15 minutes or longer, or microwave it on low (defrost) for a few seconds at a time until scoopable.

vanilla bean ice cream

Vanilla is versatile. Top a scoop of vanilla ice cream with Beer Granita (page 245) for an unexpected change, or drizzle over a little extra virgin olive oil for a truly sensual experience. Or go for the classic and top with Cocoa Fudge Sauce (page 161).

Cut a vanilla bean lengthwise in half, and use the tip of a paring knife to scrape the tiny seeds out of both pieces into the pan with the cream, milk, sugar, and salt as above. Toss in the pieces of pod and bring to a simmer. Remove from the heat, cover, and steep for 10 minutes. Fish out the pieces of pod and scrape any loose seeds back into the pan. Reserve the pod pieces. Reheat the mixture and proceed as directed, adding the pod pieces back to the finished custard before chilling. Remove and discard the pod pieces before freezing.

the flavors of grain,
nuts,
and seeds

Many grains and seeds unfamiliar to American home cooks are quite commonplace in other parts of the world or in ethnic communities here. Some are already known to avid bread bakers, as well as to those with allergies or who are otherwise interested in healthy "alternative" ingredients. Indeed, "alternative" flours and whole grains have been typecast as hearty, wholesome, and nutritious ingredients suitable mostly for robust dense breads, rather than fancy desserts or pastries. But, in reality, to limit the use of whole grains to "health food" is to miss some of their glory. Used with finesse, whole grains and seeds—like nuts—star in delicate desserts and pastries, indulgent cakes, and tender cookies. Used strategically, they function in recipes just as ground nuts do, adding rich flavor, texture, and tenderness too. Botanically both grains and nuts are seeds. So it stands to reason that the flavor of whole grains is often described as nutty, and that nuts, seeds, and whole grain should have an affinity for one another, as much in buttery cookies and rich cakes as gutsy breads. The simple recipes in this chapter celebrate the flavors and textures of seeds, grains, starches, and nuts, alone and together, in recipes old and new. Sampling them you will discover that an ancient form of wheat called kamut tastes amazingly like butter, that corn flour is sweet, that stone-ground whole wheat goes well with bits of roasted cacao beans and chocolate, that buckwheat flour loves strawberries and cream, and that chestnut flour makes the best meringues you may ever have tasted. Whole grains and specialty flours, especially those that include the germ, should be stored in the refrigerator or freezer (six months or more) to preserve their flavor and prevent rancidity.

buckwheat strawberry shortcakes

Not your usual strawberry shortcakes, these cakey little cream scones with a hint of buckwheat for flavor are an inspired partner for strawberries and cream. I seek out the small sweet Seascape strawberries from my local farmers' market whenever possible. And I often substitute blackberries when they are ripe and sweet.

serves 9

FOR THE SHORTCAKES

1 cup plus 2 tablespoons (5 ounces) all-purpose flour

¼ cup plus 2 tablespoons (1.7 ounces) buckwheat flour

¼ cup sugar, plus extra for sprinkling

1¾ teaspoons baking powder, sifted if lumpy

⅜ teaspoon salt

1 cup heavy cream

A little extra cream (dregs left in the bottom of the measuring cup) or milk for brushing the tops

FOR THE FILLING

1¼ cups heavy cream

Sugar to taste

2 to 2½ pints (16 to 20 ounces) fresh ripe strawberries, rinsed, patted dry, and hulled

EQUIPMENT

Baking sheet

POSITION A RACK in the center of the oven and preheat the oven to 425°F. Line a baking sheet with two layers of parchment paper (two layers protect the bottoms of the shortcakes from browning too fast before the top and interior are fully baked).

In a large bowl, thoroughly whisk the flours, sugar, baking powder, and salt. Make a well in the center and pour the cream into it (set the measuring cup aside). Use a rubber spatula to push the dry ingredients from the sides of the bowl into the well, cutting and turning the mixture just until the dry ingredients are almost entirely moistened and the dough looks rough and shaggy. Gather the dough into a ball and knead it gently against the sides of the bowl five or so times, pressing loose pieces into the dough, until it just holds together (it should not be smooth) and the bowl is fairly clean.

Turn the dough out onto a lightly floured board and pat it into a 6-inch square about ¾ inch thick. Trim the edges, using a sharp knife and quick downward (guillotine) strokes, so as not to compress the dough, for the best rise. Cut the dough into 9 squares. Place them at least 1 inch apart on the baking sheet. Brush the tops with the cream left in the bottom of the measuring cup or with a little milk, and sprinkle lightly with sugar.

Bake the shortcakes until the tops are golden brown, 12 to 15 minutes. Cool on a rack.

(CONTINUED)

Meanwhile, in a chilled bowl, whip the cream, sweetening it lightly to taste, if desired (I don't always sweeten the cream if the berries are sweet) as it begins to thicken. Continue beating until it holds a soft shape—not too stiff. (The cream can be covered and refrigerated for up to several hours. If liquid separates from the cream, whisk briefly before using.)

Slice the berries and sweeten them lightly to taste (I use 1 to 2 tablespoons of sugar). For a saucier filling (optional), transfer one quarter of the berries to another bowl and mash them with a fork. Stir them back into the remaining sliced berries. (The berries can be covered and refrigerated for up to 1 hour.)

To assemble the shortcakes, slice each cake horizontally in half. Place the bottom halves on serving plates. Top each with a scoop of the strawberries and a dollop of whipped cream. Cover with the tops of the cakes.

NOTE: You can also serve the shortcakes warm. Reheat the cakes on a cookie sheet in a preheated 325°F oven for 5 to 10 minutes. (Reheating crisps the delicate crust on top of the cakes and accentuates the soft tender interiors.) Whip the cream a little stiffer than usual. Split and fill the warm cakes, and serve immediately.

cornmeal-buckwheat scones with walnuts

These are flaky and flavorful, especially with fresh stone-ground cornmeal and buckwheat flours, such as those from Anson Mills (see Resources, page 249). Add ½ cup raisins or currants if you like them.

makes 8 or 9 scones

1 large egg

½ cup whole milk

¼ cup heavy cream

1⅓ cups (6 ounces) all-purpose flour

⅓ cup (1.5 ounces) buckwheat flour, preferably stone-ground

⅓ cup (1.5 ounces) cornmeal, preferably stone-ground

⅓ cup sugar, plus extra for sprinkling

2½ teaspoons baking powder

½ teaspoon salt

6 tablespoons cold unsalted butter

¾ cup (3 ounces) coarsely chopped walnuts

Extra milk or cream for brushing the tops

EQUIPMENT

Baking sheet

IN A SMALL BOWL, whisk the egg with the milk and cream. Set aside. In a large bowl, thoroughly whisk together the flours, cornmeal, sugar, baking powder, and salt. Cut the butter into several pieces and add it to the flour. Using two knives or a pastry blender, cut the butter into the flour, tossing the pieces to coat them with flour as you work and continuing until the largest butter pieces are the size of fat peas and the rest resemble bread crumbs. Stir in the walnuts. Pour the egg mixture over the dry ingredients and, using a rubber spatula, fold the ingredients together just until all the dry bits are moist and the dough looks shaggy, not smooth.

Gather the dough into a ball and knead it gently against the sides of the bowl five or so times, pressing loose pieces into the dough, until the dough just holds together (it should not be smooth) and the bowl is fairly clean.

Turn the dough out onto a lightly floured board and pat it into a 7-inch square or 8-inch round about ¾ inch thick. Trim the edges of the dough, and cut the dough square into 9 squares or rounds or cut the dough round into 8 wedges. Push any scraps together (without kneading them) to form additional scones. Transfer to a plate. Refrigerate for 30 minutes.

Position a rack in the center of the oven and preheat the oven to 425°F.

Line a baking sheet with two layers of parchment paper. Place the scones at least 1 inch apart on the lined baking sheet. Brush the tops of the scones with milk or cream and sprinkle lightly with sugar. Bake until the tops are golden brown, 12 to 15 minutes. Cool on a rack. Serve warm or at room temperature.

kamut pound cake

Here is a versatile plain pound cake (adapted from the pound cake in Rose Levy Beranbaum's *The Cake Bible*) with several whole-grain options. Stone-ground kamut flour produces pound cake with a buttery flavor, lovely golden color, and sandy texture, almost like cornmeal: serve it plain or toast thick slices and top them with sliced fresh peaches and cream. Or toast slices and sprinkle with coarse salt and pepper, and serve with a cup of black tea. Do not miss the version with kamut and corn.   serves 8 to 10

3 tablespoons whole milk, at room temperature

3 large eggs, at room temperature

1½ teaspoons pure vanilla extract

1 cup (3.5 ounces) sifted (before measuring) cake flour

⅓ cup plus 1 tablespoon (1.75 ounces) whole-grain kamut flour

¾ cup sugar

¾ teaspoon baking powder

¼ teaspoon salt

13 tablespoons unsalted butter, softened

EQUIPMENT

An 8 by 4-inch (4 to 5 cups) loaf pan

POSITION A RACK in the lower third of the oven and preheat the oven to 350°F. Line the loaf pan with parchment paper.

In a medium bowl, whisk the milk, eggs, and vanilla to combine.

Mix together and then sift the flours, sugar, baking powder, and salt into the bowl of a stand mixer or another large bowl; if any bran is left in the sifter, add it to the mixture. Cut the butter into chunks and add it, then pour in half of the egg mixture. Beat on low speed just until the dry ingredients are moistened. Increase the speed to medium (or high if using a hand-held mixer) and beat for 1 minute only. Scrape the sides of the bowl. Add half of the remaining egg mixture and beat for 20 seconds. Scrape the bowl. Add the rest of the egg mixture and beat for 20 seconds.

Scrape the batter into the pan and smooth the surface. Bake until a wooden skewer or toothpick inserted in the center of the cake comes out clean, 55 to 65 minutes. (To prevent excessive browning, cover the loaf loosely with foil after 30 minutes, if necessary.) Cool the cake in the pan for about 10 minutes on a rack, then remove and cool completely on the rack.

bourbon and nutmeg pound cake

The aroma of the spice and spirits as the cake bakes is delicious. Whole wheat or spelt flour adds a subtle nutty flavor.

Substitute 1 tablespoon bourbon for 1 tablespoon of whole milk. Substitute whole wheat or spelt for the kamut flour, and add ½ teaspoon freshly grated nutmeg to the dry ingredients. Bake in a loaf pan, as directed, or bake in a 9 by 2-inch round cake pan, sides greased and bottom lined with parchment paper, for 30 to 35 minutes.

wheat and chocolate pound cake

Substitute whole wheat or spelt for the kamut flour. Add 3½ ounces grated semisweet or bittersweet chocolate with the last addition of eggs. Grate the chocolate on the large holes of a box grater or the large grating disk of food processor, or pulse, using the steel blade, in the processor.

kamut and corn pound cake

Substitute 3 tablespoons stone-ground cornmeal for 3 tablespoons of the kamut.

golden kamut shortbread

PHOTOGRAPH ON PAGE 96

Kamut flour makes exceptional shortbread. The texture is tender, dry, and sandy; the color is golden; and the flavor is delicately sweet from the grain. I often sprinkle it with flaky sea salt and freshly ground pepper as well as sugar.

makes fourteen to sixteen 2-inch squares or 16 wedges

12 tablespoons (1½ sticks) unsalted butter, melted and still warm

5 tablespoons sugar

1 teaspoon pure vanilla extract

¼ teaspoon salt

¾ cup (3.4 ounces) all-purpose flour

¾ cup (3.4 ounces) kamut flour

Turbinado, Demerara, or granulated sugar for sprinkling

Flaky sea salt and freshly ground black pepper (optional)

EQUIPMENT

A baking pan with a removable bottom, such as a 9½-inch round or a 4 by 14-inch rectangular fluted tart pan, or a one-piece 8-inch square pan

IF USING A PAN with a removable bottom, grease the pan; if using the one-piece pan, line it with aluminum foil, leaving an overhang on two opposite sides.

In a medium bowl, combine the melted butter with the sugar, vanilla, and salt. Add the flours and mix just until incorporated. Pat and spread the dough evenly in the pan. Let rest for at least 2 hours, or overnight (no need to refrigerate).

Position a rack in the lower third of the oven and preheat the oven to 300°F.

Bake the shortbread for 45 minutes.

Remove the pan from the oven, leaving the oven on. Lightly sprinkle the surface of the shortbread with sugar. If desired, sprinkle a little flaky sea salt and grind a little black pepper over the shortbread: do this by eye, as though seasoning a salad. Let the shortbread cool for 10 minutes.

Remove the shortbread from the pan, being careful to avoid breaking it. Use a thin sharp knife to cut oblong "fingers," wedges, or squares. Place the pieces slightly apart on a parchment-lined baking sheet, and put it into the oven for 15 minutes. Cool on a rack.

Shortbread keeps for several weeks in an airtight container.

chestnut and vanilla ice cream squares

These are spectularly good just on their own. Period. But you can gild the lily with whipped cream and strawberries. For wedges instead of squares, use a 9-inch spring-form pan.   makes 16 squares

Chestnut-Walnut Meringue batter
(page 70), freshly made

1½ pints (3 cups) vanilla or Vanilla Bean
Ice Cream (page 55), homemade or
purchased

Lightly sweetened whipped cream
(optional)

Strawberries (optional)

EQUIPMENT
An 8-inch square baking pan or a 9-inch
round springform pan

POSITION A RACK in the lower third of the oven and preheat the oven to 325°F. Line the bottom and sides of the square or springform pan with foil.

Spread the meringue evenly in the pan. Bake for 15 minutes. Turn down the oven to 300°F and bake for 3 hours. The meringue will rise and form a dry top crust; the center will remain a little soft.

Remove the meringue and cool completely on a rack.

Soften the ice cream for 15 to 20 minutes in the refrigerator, or with 10-second bursts in the microwave, just until pliable but not melting. Distribute large flat spoon-fuls of ice cream over the meringue. Gently spread the ice cream (don't worry if the meringue crust collapses) evenly over the meringue. Swirl the surface of the ice cream with a spoon.

Wrap airtight and freeze until firm. The dessert can be prepared to this point a week in advance.

To serve, lift the edges of the foil, or remove the sides of the springform, and transfer the dessert to a cutting board. Cut into 16 squares or wedges. Serve plain or with lightly sweetened whipped cream and berries.

chestnut-walnut meringues

Chestnut flour and walnuts transform meringues into a richer, more complex sweet to enjoy as a simple cookie, especially with coffee. But these new meringues are also sensational in a sundae: nestle or sandwich them with a scoop of vanilla ice cream, heap with sliced ripe strawberries, and top with unsweetened whipped cream. Or make Chestnut and Vanilla Ice Cream Squares (page 68). Oooh!   makes 30 to 40 meringues

¼ cup (1 ounce) chestnut flour

⅔ cup (2.6 ounces) coarsely chopped walnuts
(if using a pastry bag, finely chopped)

1 cup sugar

4 large egg whites, at room temperature

⅛ teaspoon cream of tartar

EQUIPMENT

Baking sheets

A large pastry bag fitted with a large star
tip (optional)

POSITION THE RACKS in the lower and upper thirds of the oven and preheat the oven to 200°F. Line the baking sheets with parchment paper.

In a small bowl, mix the chestnut flour and walnuts with ⅓ cup of the sugar. Set aside.

Combine the egg whites and cream of tartar in the clean dry bowl of a stand mixer or another large bowl. Beat at medium-high speed (high speed with a hand mixer) until the egg whites are creamy white, instead of translucent, and hold a soft shape when the beaters are lifted. Continue to beat, adding the remaining sugar a little at a time over 1½ to 2 minutes, until the whites are very stiff and glossy. Pour the chestnut flour mixture over the egg whites and fold in with a rubber spatula just until combined.

Drop heaping tablespoonsful of meringue, or use the pastry bag to pipe any size and shape you like, 1½ inches apart on the lined cookie sheets. Bake for 2 hours.

Remove a test meringue and let it cool completely before taking a bite. (Meringues are never crisp when hot.) If the meringue is completely dry and crisp, turn off the heat and let the remaining meringues cool completely in the oven. If the test meringue is soft or chewy or sticks to your teeth, bake for another 15 to 20 minutes before testing another meringue.

Once they are completely cool, the meringues should be transferred to an airtight container as soon as possible to prevent them from becoming moist and sticky. They can then be stored for weeks.

chestnut pound cake

This is a subtly delicious plain cake for chestnut lovers (that's me), and it is especially nice with walnuts. Sip rum or brandy with it, or a medium sherry, or amontillado (fino is too dry).

serves 16

2 cups (9 ounces) all-purpose flour

1 cup (4.5 ounces) chestnut flour

½ teaspoon baking powder

½ teaspoon baking soda

½ teaspoon salt

4 large eggs, at room temperature

½ pound (2 sticks) unsalted butter, softened

2 cups sugar

⅔ cup buttermilk, at room temperature

⅓ cup dark rum

1½ cups (6 ounces) coarsely chopped walnuts (optional)

EQUIPMENT

A 12-cup plain or fancy tube or Bundt pan or two 8½ by 4½-inch (5 cups) loaf pans

POSITION A RACK in the lower third of the oven and preheat the oven to 325°F. Spray the pan(s) with vegetable oil spray. (Or line the loaf pans with parchment paper.)

In a large bowl, mix the flours, baking powder, soda, and salt together, then sift the mixture three times. In a small bowl, whisk the eggs with a fork to combine the whites and yolks; set aside.

In the bowl of a stand mixer (use the paddle attachment) or another large bowl, beat the butter for a few seconds, until creamy. Add the sugar in a steady stream and beat at medium speed (high speed with a hand-held mixer) until light and fluffy, about 4 minutes. Beating constantly, dribble the eggs into the butter mixture a little bit at a time, taking 2 to 3 minutes to add them all.

Stop the mixer and add one-third of the flour mixture and beat on low speed only until no flour is visible. Stop the mixer and add half of the buttermilk and half of the rum and beat only until the liquid is absorbed. Repeat with half of the remaining flour, then all of the remaining buttermilk and rum, and finally the remaining flour with the walnuts if using. Scrape the batter into the prepared pan(s). Bake until a toothpick inserted in the center of the cake comes out clean, about 40 minutes for a tube pan, 50 to 55 minutes for the loaves. Cool in the pan(s) on a rack for about 10 minutes before unmolding.

If using a tubepan, slide a skewer around the tube. If the sides of the pan are straight, slide a thin knife or spatula around the sides of the pan to release the cake. If using a Bundt or other decorative pan, tap one side of the pan against the counter to release the cake, then tap the other. Invert the cake onto a cooling rack. Turn the preferred side up before cooling the cake completely.

Wrapped airtight, the cake keeps well at room temperature for up to 3 days; or freeze for up to 3 months.

almond cake

This is a classic rich, sweet almond cake reinvented and simplified. It starts with whole almonds in the food processor, and two minutes later, you have batter. The cake is hard to stay away from: it's sophisticated enough to serve for dessert with pureed raspberries or sliced fresh strawberries, plums, or nectarines, but it's difficult not to nibble on it throughout the day if you leave it on the counter. Wrapped in cellophane or presented in a pretty tin, this cake is a fine holiday hostess gift. For the best flavor and texture, make this a day ahead. (The photograph opposite shows the cake with a crunchy almond crust— see page 74)

serves 10 to 12

¾ cup plus 2 tablespoons (4 ounces) unblanched or blanched whole almonds

1 cup plus 2 tablespoons sugar

¼ teaspoon salt

½ teaspoon pure almond extract

3 large eggs

8 tablespoons (1 stick) unsalted butter, cut into several chunks and slightly softened

1 tablespoon kirsch (optional)

⅓ cup (1.5 ounces) all-purpose flour

¼ teaspoon baking powder

Powdered sugar for dusting (optional)

EQUIPMENT

An 8 by 2-inch round cake pan

POSITION A RACK in the lower third of the oven and preheat the oven to 350°F. Butter the sides of the cake pan and line the bottom of it with a round of parchment paper.

Place the almonds, sugar, salt, and almond extract in the bowl of a food processor and process until the nuts are finely pulverized. Add the eggs, butter, and kirsch, if using, and pulse to blend thoroughly. Add the flour and baking powder and pulse just until blended.

Scrape the batter into the prepared pan and spread it evenly. Bake until the cake is golden brown on top and a toothpick plunged into the center comes out clean, 35 to 40 minutes. Cool completely in the pan on the rack.

To unmold, slide a slim knife or spatula around the cake to release the sides. Cover the pan with a plate and invert both. Remove the cake pan, peel off the parchment liner, and turn the cake right side up. Dust lightly with powdered sugar before serving, if desired. Tightly wrapped, the cake keeps well at room temperature for several days.

Serve with fresh berries, a fresh berry puree, or with sliced fresh plums or nectarines.

almond cake with crunchy crust

PHOTOGRAPH ON PAGE 72

Smear the sides and bottom of the pan generously with about 1 tablespoon softened butter; do not line the pan with parchment. Scatter 6 tablespoons sliced almonds over the bottom of the pan and press some of them about 1 inch up the sides; distribute any extra nuts evenly over the bottom. Sprinkle 2 tablespoons sugar over the bottom and sides of the pan. Make the cake batter, scrape it carefully into the prepared pan, and bake as directed. Cool the cake on a rack for 10 minutes before unmolding. To unmold, slide a slim knife or spatula carefully around the inside of the pan, pressing against the pan to release the cake without cracking the crust. Cover the pan with a plate, and invert both. Remove the pan and leave the cake crust side up to serve.

plum and almond tart

This almond lover's dessert is a slightly more sophisticated incarnation of the Rustic Plum Tart on page 106. The sweet, rich almond dough makes an addictive counterpoint for tart juicy plums. Leftovers—although not likely—will make good nibbling for days.

serves 8

½ cup (2.5 ounces) unblanched or blanched whole almonds

¾ cup sugar

¼ teaspoon salt

⅜ teaspoon almond extract

¾ cup (3.4 ounces) all-purpose flour

⅜ teaspoon baking powder

1 large egg

3 tablespoons firm but not hard unsalted butter, cut into a few pieces

4 large or 6 smaller juicy, flavorful plums, such as Santa Rosas, Elephant Hearts, Larodas, Friars, or pluots (see Note)

Powdered sugar for dusting (optional)

EQUIPMENT

A 9½-inch fluted tart pan with a removable bottom

POSITION A RACK in the lower third of the oven and preheat the oven to 375°F. Generously butter the tart pan. Combine the almonds, sugar, salt, and almond extract in the bowl of a food processor and process until the nuts are finely pulverized. Add the flour and baking powder and pulse to mix thoroughly. Add the egg and butter pieces and pulse until the mixture is damp (with no dry flour showing) and begins to clump around the blade. Press the dough evenly over the bottom but not up the sides of the pan.

If the plums are no bigger than 2 inches in diameter, cut them in half and remove the pits. Cut larger plums into quarters or sixths, removing the pits. Leaving a margin of ½ inch around the edge of the pan, arrange halves cut side up over the dough, with a little space between each one. Arrange wedges skin side up (they look beautiful that way after baking), pressing them slightly into the dough to prevent them from turning onto their sides as they bake.

Bake until the pastry is puffed, deep golden brown at the edges, and nicely golden brown between the plums, 40 to 45 minutes. Cool briefly, then loosen or remove the rim of the tart pan.

If a tiny pool of syrupy juice collects in the center of the halved plums, use a small knife to spread the shiny syrup over the cut surface of the plums for a glistening glaze. Serve warm or at room temperature, lightly dusted with powdered sugar, if desired.

NOTE: Plums that are both sweet and tart—especially those that make you pucker slightly when you taste the flesh nearest the skin—are especially delicious and dramatic with the sweet almond dough. I have used Santa Rosa, Laroda, Friar, and Elephant Heart plums and Flavor King pluots with great results. The small French and Italian prune plums and "sugar" plums are not tangy enough here.

walnut sponge cake

Loaded with nuts yet light, this sponge cake is mildly moist and very flavorful, with a perfect accent of lemon zest. I eat slices out of hand, but more civilized nibblers may enjoy a cup of fragrant tea and conversation on the side. Lightly sweetened whipped cream and sweetened blackberries or other berries are also pleasing. For a festive occasion, dollop the cream on top of the cake and decorate with the berries. Nut fanciers can substitute different nuts—for example, toasted skinned hazelnuts or raw or toasted almonds.   serves 8 to 10

2½ cups (10 ounces) walnut or pecan halves or large pieces

5 large eggs, separated, at room temperature

Finely grated zest of 1 small lemon, preferably organic or unsprayed

1 teaspoon pure vanilla extract or 1 tablespoon brandy or rum

⅓ plus ¼ cup sugar

⅛ teaspoon salt

¼ teaspoon cream of tartar

Powdered sugar for dusting (optional)

1 cup lightly sweetened whipped cream, and about 1 pint berries, plain or sweetened, for serving (optional)

EQUIPMENT

An 8 by 3-inch round pan with a removable bottom or an 8-inch springform pan

POSITION A RACK in the lower third of the oven and preheat the oven to 325°F. Line the bottom of the pan with parchment paper.

By hand or in a food processor, coarsely chop ½ cup of the nuts. Pulse the remaining 2 cups nuts in a food processor (make sure the bowl is dry) until finely ground. Combine the nuts and set aside.

In the bowl of a stand mixer (or a small bowl if using a hand-held mixer), combine the egg yolks, lemon zest, vanilla, ⅓ cup of the sugar, and the salt. Beat at high speed with the whisk attachment until thick and pale yellow. Unless you have a second mixer bowl, scrape the yolks into another large bowl and set aside.

Wash the mixer bowl and whisk attachment (or beaters) and dry them. Put the egg whites and cream of tartar into the clean mixer bowl (or a large bowl if using a hand-held mixer) and beat at medium-high speed (high speed with the hand-held) until soft peaks form when the beater is lifted. Gradually beat in the remaining ¼ cup sugar, then continue to beat at high speed until stiff but not dry peaks form when the beater is lifted.

Scrape half of the egg whites over the yolks, pour half of the nuts on top, and use a large rubber spatula to fold them in until almost completely incorporated. Repeat with the remaining egg whites and nuts, folding just until incorporated. Scrape the batter into the pan and spread it evenly.

(CONTINUED)

Bake until the cake springs back when lightly pressed and a toothpick inserted in the center comes out clean, 50 to 55 minutes. Cool the cake for 5 to 10 minutes in the pan on a rack. Run a thin knife around the inside of the pan to loosen the cake, detach the sides of the pan, and let the cake cool completely on the rack. Peel the parchment paper from the bottom of the cake.

Sift a little powdered sugar over the cake before serving, if desired. Serve plain or with whipped cream and berries. Or, omit the powdered sugar and top the cake with the cream and berries. The cake (without the cream and berries) keeps at least 3 days, wrapped airtight, at room temperature.

salted peanut butter toffee cookies

Encrusted with toffee-coated peanuts and accented with flaky salt, these melt-in-your-mouth cookies are festive enough for the holiday cookie tray but easy enough for everyday. They are irresistible to peanut lovers of all ages.

makes about fifty-six 1½-inch cookies

1⅓ cups (6 ounces) all-purpose flour

½ teaspoon baking soda

¾ teaspoon regular salt or 1 teaspoon coarse sea salt, such as fleur de sel

8 tablespoons (1 stick) unsalted butter, melted

½ cup (3.5 ounces) firmly packed brown sugar (dark or light)

½ cup sugar

1 large egg

1 teaspoon pure vanilla extract

1 cup natural chunky peanut butter (not unsalted)—stir well to blend in the oil before measuring

1 cup (5 ounces) toffee peanuts or coconut toffee peanuts, very coarsely chopped

EQUIPMENT
Baking sheets

MIX THE FLOUR, baking soda, and salt together thoroughly in a medium bowl and set aside.

In a large bowl, mix the melted butter with both sugars. Whisk in the egg, vanilla, and peanut butter. Add the flour mixture and mix with a rubber spatula or wooden spoon just until evenly incorporated.

Cover the dough and refrigerate for an hour or two, or up to 2 days.

Position the racks in the upper and lower thirds of the oven and preheat the oven to 325°F. Line the baking sheets with parchment paper.

Pour the chopped nuts into a shallow bowl. Scoop about 2 level teaspoons of dough for each cookie, shape into a 1-inch ball (or fat little log), and coat heavily with the chopped nuts, pressing in any pieces that fall off, so that there are no bald spots. Place the balls 2 inches apart on the lined baking sheets.

Bake the cookies until they are lightly colored on top, 15 to 18 minutes, rotating the sheets from top to bottom and front to back halfway through baking. The cookies will seem very soft to the touch, but they will firm up as they cool. Set the baking sheets on a rack to cool completely.

The cookies can be stored in an airtight container for at least 2 weeks.

sesame brittle ice cream

Exotic butter brickle! I was astonished that sesame seeds could produce such a distinctly American style of ice cream. Don't hesitate to serve it; it's laced with sweet crunchy bits of homemade sesame brittle and it's irresistible.   makes 1 quart

½ cup unsalted tahini (pure ground toasted sesame seeds)

1 cup heavy cream

2 teaspoons Asian sesame oil (see Note, page 83)

2 cups whole milk

½ cup sugar

⅛ teaspoon salt

Caramelized Sesame Seed Brittle Garnish (page 81), chopped into pieces no longer than ½ inch

EQUIPMENT

Ice cream machine

An 8-inch stainless steel skillet

IN A MEDIUM BOWL, whisk together the tahini and cream until smooth. Whisk in the sesame oil. Add the milk, sugar, and salt and whisk until very smooth. Cover and chill until ready to freeze.

For an extra-cold start, put the ice cream mixture in the freezer for 20 minutes, stirring once or twice to prevent freezing. Freeze the cream mixture according to the instructions for your ice cream machine. Add the sesame brittle at the very last minute, just to mix it in.

Serve soft or transfer to an airtight container and freeze until hard enough to scoop, at least 3 to 4 hours. If the ice cream gets too hard, before serving let it stand for a few minutes, put it in the refrigerator for 15 minutes or longer, or microwave it on low (defrost) for a few seconds at a time until scoopable.

caramelized nut
brittle garnish

Top ice cream or a bowl of ricotta with this caramelized walnut or pine nut brittle,
or garnish Lebni Tart (page 39) or Chilled Oranges in Rum-Caramel Syrup (page 120).

makes 2 cups

1 cup sugar

¼ teaspoon salt

¾ to 1 cup (3 to 4 ounces) whole, broken,
or coarsely chopped nuts such as almonds,
toasted skinned hazelnuts (see page 25),
or walnuts, pecans, or pine nuts

EQUIPMENT

A large stainless steel skillet

NEAR THE STOVE, set a baking sheet lined with parchment paper or foil to be used for
the finished brittle, and a white saucer to aid in judging the color of the caramel.

Mix the sugar and salt and spread it in the dry skillet. Set the pan over medium-
high heat without stirring until the sugar begins to melt into clear syrup around the
edges. Turn the heat down to medium and continue melting the sugar without stirring—shake the pan to redistribute it—for as long as the syrup remains clear. When
the syrup begins to color, stir it with a silicone spatula or wooden spoon, mixing and
spreading until all the sugar is melted and evenly colored. If some of the syrup colors
too fast before the rest, turn the heat down—or take the pan off the heat for a few
moments—and continue to stir until the sugar is completely melted. Drop a bead
of syrup on the white plate to judge the color accurately. When the drop looks pale
amber on the saucer, add the nuts and stir gently to coat them with the syrup (brisk
stirring may cause the caramel to crystallize). Continue to stir until a drop of syrup is
reddish amber or the color of medium-dark honey. Immediately scrape the contents
of the pan onto the foil and spread it as thin as possible. *Do not touch the hot caramel.* While
the caramel is still quite warm—and to prevent it from becoming sticky—slide the
foil into a resealable plastic bag and seal it until needed. After cooling break or chop as
desired and return the pieces to the sealed bag until needed.

caramelized sesame seed brittle garnish

Use an 8-inch skillet. Decrease the sugar to ½ cup and the salt to ⅛ teaspoon. Substitute
¼ cup sesame seeds for the nuts.

sesame seed cake

I love the flavor and scent of the sesame and vanilla in this pretty little cake, which has an irresistible velvet texture. Black sesame seeds look exotic, but regular natural seeds are equally tasty. I toast my own—although toasting the black ones is an exercise in using the nose and palate only, as you can't tell doneness by their color. If you are new to sesame seeds, start with the natural ones so you can watch as well as smell and taste them as they toast. Or get thee to an Asian grocery for a package of toasted black seeds, which are quite acceptable. Serve the cake plain or with Heavenly Honey Ice Cream (page 177).

serves 8 to 10

1⅓ cups (6 ounces) all-purpose flour

½ teaspoon baking soda

¼ teaspoon baking powder

¼ teaspoon salt

2 large eggs, at room temperature

2½ teaspoons Asian or toasted sesame oil (see Note)

1 teaspoon pure vanilla extract

8 tablespoons (1 stick) unsalted butter, softened

1 cup sugar

½ cup buttermilk, at room temperature

¼ cup toasted black or natural sesame seeds

EQUIPMENT

An 8-inch round cake pan

POSITION A RACK in the lower third of the oven and preheat the oven to 350°F. Spray the sides of the cake pan with vegetable oil spray and line the bottom with parchment paper.

Mix together the flour, baking soda, baking powder, and salt thoroughly in a medium bowl and sift three times. Set aside.

In a small bowl, whisk the eggs together briefly with the sesame oil and vanilla. Set aside.

In the bowl of a stand mixer or another large bowl, beat the butter at medium speed for a few seconds until creamy. Add the sugar and beat at medium speed (high speed with a hand-held mixer) until light colored and fluffy, 2 to 3 minutes. Beat in a little of the egg mixture at a time, taking about 2 minutes to add it all. Stop the mixer, add one third of the flour mixture, and beat on low speed only until no flour is visible. Stop the mixer and add half of the buttermilk, then beat only until the liquid is absorbed. Repeat with half of the remaining flour, then all of the remaining buttermilk, and finally the remaining flour with the sesame seeds, scraping the bowl as necessary and beating only enough to incorporate the ingredients each time.

Scrape the batter into the prepared pan. Bake until a toothpick inserted in the center of the cake comes out clean, 35 to 40 minutes. Cool in the pan on a rack for 10 minutes, then slide a thin knife or spatula around the sides of the cake to detach it from the pan. Invert the cake onto a rack and remove the pan and parchment liner. Turn the cake right side up and let cool completely on the rack.

The cake keeps in an airtight container at room temperature for at least 4 days. Or freeze, well wrapped, for up to 3 months.

NOTE: Asian sesame oil, not to be confused with Asian chili oil or with light untoasted sesame oil, is available in the Asian section of large supermarkets. Asian sesame oils are toasted as a matter of course, even if the labels do not specify this. If you buy a non-Asian brand (such as any produced by natural foods companies), be sure the label says "toasted," as untoasted oil will not deliver adequate flavor here. If you cook Asian dishes only occasionally, the sesame oil in your cupboard could be rancid; and even 2½ teaspoons of it can add an unpleasant flavor. Buy a fresh bottle, and keep it refrigerated unless you will use it up in less than 3 months (measure and bring to room temperature before using).

Exciting new cookie recipes emerged from experimenting with flours, grains, seeds, nuts, teas, herbs, flours, and sugars, not to mention chocolate and cocoa. I was particularly rewarded to discover that whole-grain flours, even those with high protein, could produce elegantly tender cookies; that aromatic flavors from herbs, spices, teas, and flowers could be translated into perfect crisp wafers; that freshly ground or grated spices make a big difference; and that enticing flavors and textures result from adding coarsely ground ingredients—chocolate, cacao nibs, coffee beans, vanilla beans, sugar, and salt and pepper—either to the dough or the cookie tops.

The high protein and gluten content of many whole-grain flours makes for delicious hearty breads (which I adore) but usually heavy pastries. I found, though, that I could capture the great flavors of these grains without activating gluten if I used the right recipes. Liquid activates gluten development, which in turn makes cakes and cookies tough. Shortbread and butter cookie recipes contain almost no liquid: they are made without milk or eggs (which are about 20 percent water) or any other liquid other than the small amount of water in the butter. With no liquid to absorb, whole-grain flours behave surprisingly like finely ground nuts in shortbread and butter cookies—they make the cookies tender. In fact, one batch of whole wheat short-bread had to be cut into dainty squares rather than long fingers or wedges because the crumb was so tender that long pieces broke in half from their own weight when picked up. That experience let me imagine a whole wheat pound cake. I wondered if Rose Levy Beranbaums's method of beating the butter and flour together first could protect the flour enough from the eventual addition of liquid to produce a meltingly tender cake. I was rewarded with pound cakes and variations made with whole wheat, kamut, and corn flours.

Early attempts to flavor baked goods with herbs, flowers, teas, and even citrus zest left me unimpressed. I found it hard to get clear bright flavors commensurate with the heavenly aromas and true tastes of these ingredients. A simple, elegant tuile recipe changed my luck and became the basis for a number of spectacular little cookies. The basic tuile is a thin, crisp, light but buttery wafer made with egg whites and a small amount of flour. The flavors of jasmine tea, dried lavender, fresh thyme, crushed saffron, grated citrus peels, ground-up vanilla beans, and freshly grated cinnamon simply sing in this recipe. Surely it is the butter that carries the flavors, but I think that the clarity of the flavors is greatly enhanced by the absence of egg yolk, which can have a dulling effect. Regardless, I was rewarded with a breathtaking array of delicately aromatic wafers to enjoy unaccompanied or to adorn ices creams, sorbets, compotes, custards, and creams. (The same cookie is brilliantly successful with corn flour and chestnut flour—and no doubt other flours with no gluten.)

I am always intrigued by the differences in flavor and texture that result from using the same ingredient in different forms or in different ways. I once made a cookie dough and then discovered I had forgotten half of the sugar. I unwrapped the dough, pressed it out flat, and sprinkled on the missing sugar, then rolled up the dough and kneaded it gently to distribute the sugar. After a rest (for the dough, not me), I formed and baked the cookies. The late addition of sugar made them wonderfully tender and slightly crunchy. Now I use the technique with a mixture of crunchy Demerara sugar, coarse sea salt, and ground-up vanilla beans, and with both unsweetened chocolate and cacao nibs. Sometimes ingredients are better on top of cookies than in them: Corn Tuiles with Salt and Pepper (page 90) are good with the seasonings mixed in the batter, but they are spectacular if the salt and pepper are sprinkled on top of the cookies instead. Similarly I sometimes grate a bit of cinnamon stick over the tops of lace cookies (see page 189) rather than adding the spice to the batter.

A few final words: Perfect, irresistible homemade cookies are within the reach of any home cook. Cookie recipes are the simplest in the baker's repertoire. Ingredients lists are brief and familiar, and instructions few and uncomplicated. But the very simplicity of a recipe can mislead the cook into thinking that it can be executed casually, that its details are whimsical, or its measurements flexible. In realty, cookies are tiny pastries, subject to all the rules of baking and prone to toughness. The intuitive cook who prides herself on never following a recipe exactly may need a gentle reminder: it matters how you measure, how you mix, what baking sheets you use, and how they are prepared. The temperature of the oven matters, as does the position of the cookies in the oven. Before you begin, read about bleached versus unbleached all-purpose flour (page 21), review the method for measuring flour properly (page 3), and read the information on baking sheets (page 7). Then, if you follow the recipes and instructions carefully—and they are so simple—your cookies will be sublimely flavorful, tender, delicate, and perfectly baked.

olive oil and sherry pound cake

Don't be afraid of the olive oil: extra virgin olive oil with sherry and a hint of fresh orange zest produces a subtle and flavorful cake, not overly sweet, with a satisfying close-grained texture. This cake improves after a day or two, and toasted slices are nice for breakfast even as much as a week later.   serves 16

3 cups (13.5 ounces) all-purpose flour

2 teaspoons baking powder

¼ teaspoon salt

2 cups sugar

1 cup flavorful extra virgin olive oil

2 teaspoons grated orange zest (from 1 medium orange)

5 large cold eggs

1 cup medium (amontillado) sherry

EQUIPMENT

A 10- to 12-cup tube or Bundt pan or two 8 by 4-inch (4 cups) loaf pans

POSITION A RACK in the lower third of the oven and preheat the oven to 350°F. Grease and flour the pans. (Or, if you prefer, line the bottom and sides of the loaf pans with parchment.)

Mix the flour, baking powder, and salt thoroughly in a large bowl and sift together. Set aside.

In the bowl of a stand mixer (with the whisk attachment if you have one), beat the sugar, oil, and orange zest on high speed until well blended. Add the eggs one at a time, beating well after each addition; continue to beat until the mixture is thick and pale, 3 to 5 minutes. Stop the mixer and add one-third of the flour mixture. Beat on low speed just until blended. Stop the mixer and add half of the sherry. Beat just until blended. Repeat with another third of the flour, followed by the remaining sherry, and then the remaining flour.

Scrape the batter into the pan(s). Bake until the cake tester comes out clean, 50 to 60 minutes for either the tube pan or the loaves. Cool the cake in the pan(s) on a rack for about 15 minutes before unmolding.

If using a tube pan, slide a skewer around the tube. If the sides of the pan are straight, slide a thin knife or spatula around the sides to release the cake (unless lined with paper). If using a Bundt or other decorative pan, tap one side of the pan against the counter to release the cake, then tap the other side. Invert the cake onto a rack. Turn the preferred side up before cooling the cake completely. Wrapped airtight, the cake keeps well at room temperature for up to 3 days, or freeze for up to 3 months.

whole wheat sablés

There is nothing chewy, dense, or heavy here, just meltingly tender, buttery cookies with the nutty flavor of whole wheat. The flavor of wheat is perfection with almost any nuts or dried fruit combinations, but it is especially good with the cacao nibs and hemp seeds in the variations that follow. Spelt flour may be substituted for whole wheat.

makes about forty-eight 2-inch cookies

1 cup (4.5 ounces) all-purpose flour

Scant 1 cup (4 ounces) whole wheat flour

½ pound (2 sticks) unsalted butter, softened

½ cup sugar

¼ teaspoon salt

1 teaspoon pure vanilla extract

EQUIPMENT

Baking sheets

POSITION A RACK in the lower third of the oven and preheat the oven to 350°F. Whisk the all-purpose and whole wheat flours together. Set aside. In a medium bowl, with the back of a large spoon or with an electric mixer, beat the butter with the sugar, salt, and vanilla for about 1 minute, until smooth and creamy but not fluffy. Add the flour and mix just until incorporated. Scrape the dough into a mass and, if necessary, knead it with your hands a few times, just until smooth.

Form the dough into a 12 by 2-inch log. Wrap and refrigerate for at least 2 hours, or, preferably, overnight.

Position the racks in the upper and lower thirds of the oven and preheat the oven to 350°F. Use a sharp knife to cut the cold dough log into ¼-inch-thick slices. Place the cookies at least 1½ inches apart on the ungreased baking sheets.

Bake until the cookies are light golden brown at the edges, 12 to 14 minutes, rotating the baking sheets from top to bottom and front to back halfway through the baking. Let the cookies firm up on the pans for about 1 minute, then transfer them to a rack with a metal pancake turner and let cool completely.

The cookies are delicious fresh but are even better the next day. They can be stored in an airtight container for at least 1 month.

hempseed whole wheat sablés

These have a subtle nutty flavor reminiscent of sunflower seeds and are as tender as can be.

Add ½ to ⅔ cup hempseed to the creamed butter before adding the flour. You can vary the recipe further by adding ½ cup finely chopped pecans and 2 tablespoons toasted sesame seeds.

hazelnut whole wheat sablés

Add 1 cup chopped toasted and skinned (see page 25) hazelnuts to the creamed butter before adding the flour.

nibby whole wheat sablés
(with or without currants)

PHOTOGRAPH ON PAGE 96

Toasted bits of cocoa beans are delicious with all kinds of whole-grain flavors.

Line the baking sheets with parchment paper (to avoid scorching the nibs). Mix ¼ cup cacao nibs into the creamed butter before adding the flour.

Stir in ½ cup currants, if desired, after the flour is added. If you use currants, reduce nibs to ⅓ cup.

corn tuiles with salt and pepper

Unexpected tangy sea salt and a warming bite of black pepper offset the sweet buttery corn in this crisp, delicate tuile. These are exciting cookies on their own, but they should also be tried with a selection of cheeses. In lieu of salt and pepper, try a flavored sea salt, such as the spicy Espelette, or luxurious truffled salt from your local palace of specialty foods, or order it by mail (see Resources, page 249).

See opposite for information about the virtues of foil versus silicone pan liners.

makes about forty 2½-inch tuiles

¼ teaspoon fine sea salt

¼ teaspoon freshly ground black pepper

3 tablespoons unsalted butter, melted and still warm

⅔ cup sugar

3 large egg whites

3½ tablespoons (1 ounce) all-purpose flour

⅓ cup (1.2 ounces) corn flour (see Note)

EQUIPMENT

Baking sheets

Silicone baking mats or heavy-duty foil

Small cups or a rolling pin for shaping the cookies (optional)

Offset spatula (optional)

PLACE A RACK in the center of the oven and preheat the oven to 300°F. Line the baking sheets with foil, dull side facing up, and smooth the foil to remove any wrinkles (which would distort the cookies). Or line with silicone mats. Lightly butter the foil or the silicone mats. Plan to bake only one sheet at a time.

In a small bowl, combine ⅛ teaspoon of the salt and the pepper. Set aside.

In another bowl, whisk together the butter, sugar, egg whites, flours, and the remaining ⅛ teaspoon salt. The batter will have the consistency of thin, runny Cream of Wheat cereal.

If using silicone mats, drop level teaspoons of batter 2 inches apart onto a baking sheet. Using a small offset spatula, spread the batter into rounds, ovals, or elongated shapes about 1/16 inch thick. Sprinkle a pinch of the salt and pepper over each. Bake, watching carefully, until the wafers are golden brown half to three-quarters of the way to the centers, but still pale in the centers, 10 to 15 minutes. If the cookies are not baked long enough, they will not be completely crisp when cool. As soon as you can coax a thin metal spatula under a cookie without destroying it, transfer it to a rack to cool flat. Or shape it by draping it over a rolling pin, nestling it into a little cup, or twisting it with your fingers. Working fast, remove the remaining tuiles; reheat if necessary. Repeat until all of the wafers are baked.

If using foil, drop level teaspoons of batter 2 inches apart onto a baking sheet. Sprinkle a pinch of the salt and pepper mixture over each. Bake, watching carefully, until the batter spreads and the cookies are golden brown half to three-quarters of the way to the centers but still look pale in the center, 10 to 15 minutes. If the cookies are not baked enough, they will not be completely crisp when cool. If the cookies do not spread thin in baking, try using a little more butter on the foil and/or spread the batter with an offset spatula or the back of the spoon. For flat tuiles, slide the foil sheet of cookies onto a rack to cool. For curved tuiles, grasp the edges of the foil when the sheet comes from the oven (without touching the hot pan or the cookies) and roll it into a fat cylinder, gently curving the attached cookies like potato chips. Crimp or secure the foil with a paper clip. When cool, unroll the foil carefully and remove the tuiles. Alternatively, remove individual tuiles from the foil while they are hot and shape them as described above.

Flat or curved, tuiles are easiest to remove from the foil when completely cool. Repeat until all of the wafers are baked.

Store the cooled tuiles in an airtight container for at least 1 month.

NOTES: Not to be confused with cornstarch, corn flour (see page 22) is very finely ground cornmeal that resembles soft, fine, yellow flour. It is available in 16-ounce packages in the baking aisle of better supermarkets, from specialty stores, or by mail-order from Bob's Red Mill (see Resources, page 249).

Even a little too much flour may result in a thick and tough rather than thin and crisp tuile. Review how to measure flour (see page 3) or, if you have one, use a digital scale.

■ ABOUT FOIL VERSUS SILICONE MATS

In the oven, spoonfuls of tuile batter on buttered foil spread automatically into gorgeously thin wafers with even more delicate browned edges. But the foil must be smooth and the baking sheet must not be warped, or the batter may wander into lovely but slightly random shapes. You can control the size and thickness of the cookies to some extent by how much butter you smear on the foil: a little more butter on the foil produces bigger thinner tuiles with shapes that may meander a bit rather than remaining round. These can be beautiful so long as they don't merge with adjacent cookies.

A silicone mat is more versatile, *if* you are willing to fuss a little more. The batter will not spread by itself even on buttered silicone. For thin, delicate tuiles, you must spread the batter very thin with a small offset spatula into the desired final size of the cookie before baking. However, silicone does allow you to control the shape—you can make round, oval, or elongated cookies. It is also easier to remove hot tuiles from silicone (foil tends to tear) if you want to form them into whimsical undulating, ruffled, or twisty shapes.

chestnut tuiles

The delicate flavor of chestnut in an equally delicate wafer. Yummy with Sour Cream
Ice Cream (page 49) or coffee ice cream.

makes about forty to forty-eight 2½-inch tuiles

3 tablespoons unsalted butter, melted and still warm

⅔ cup sugar

3 large egg whites

¼ cup (1.125 ounces) chestnut flour

3½ tablespoons (1 ounce) all-purpose flour

⅛ teaspoon salt

EQUIPMENT

Baking sheets

Silicone baking mats or heavy-duty foil (see page 91 for a discussion of foil versus silicone mats)

Small cups or a rolling pin for shaping the cookies (optional)

Offset spatula (optional)

PLACE A RACK in the center of the oven and preheat the oven to 300°F. Line the baking sheets with foil, dull side facing up, and smooth the foil to remove any wrinkles (which would distort the cookies). Or line with silicone mats. Lightly butter the foil *or* the silicone mats. Plan to bake one sheet at a time.

In a small bowl, whisk together all of the ingredients until blended. The batter will have the color and consistency of thin, runny Cream of Wheat cereal.

If using silicone mats, drop level teaspoons of batter 2 inches apart onto a baking sheet. Using a small offset spatula, spread the batter into rounds, ovals, or elongated shapes less than ⅛ inch thick. Bake, watching carefully, until the wafers are golden brown half to three-quarters of the way to the centers but still pale in the center, 10 to 15 minutes. If the cookies are not baked long enough, they will not be completely crisp when cool. As soon as you can coax a thin metal spatula under a wafer without destroying it, transfer it to a rack to cool. Or shape it by draping it over a rolling pin, nestling it into a little cup, or twisting it with your fingers. Working fast, remove the remaining wafers; reheat if necessary. Repeat until all of the wafers are baked.

If using foil, drop level teaspoons of batter 2 inches apart onto a baking sheet. Bake, watching carefully, until the batter spreads and the cookies are golden brown half to three-quarters of the way to the centers, but still look pale in the center, 10 to 15 minutes. If the cookies are not baked long enough, they will not be completely crisp when cool. For flat wafers, slide the foil sheet of cookies onto a rack to cool. For curved wafers, roll the foil up into a fat cylinder with hot cookies attached, or remove individual cookies while hot and shape as described above. Flat or curved, wafers are easiest to remove from the foil when completely cool. Repeat until all of the wafers are baked.

Stored in an airtight container, the wafers will last for at least 1 month.

nibby buckwheat butter cookies

Bits of roasted cocoa beans are a perfect complement to the nutty flavor of buck-wheat. Since buckwheat flour is low in gluten, it works like cornstarch (but with flavor!) to give cookies a fine sandy texture that is crunchy yet very tender. Serve the cookies with blackberry sorbet. Or turn them into linzer cookies (see page 94).

makes forty-eight 2½-inch cookies

1¼ cups (5.6 ounces) all-purpose flour

¾ cup (3 ounces) buckwheat flour

½ pound (2 sticks) unsalted butter, softened

⅔ cup sugar

¼ teaspoon salt

⅓ cup cacao nibs

1½ teaspoons pure vanilla extract

EQUIPMENT
Baking sheets

WHISK THE ALL-PURPOSE and buckwheat flours together in a medium bowl. Set aside.

In a medium bowl, with the back of a large spoon or with an electric mixer, beat the butter with the sugar and salt for about 1 minute, until smooth and creamy but not fluffy. Mix in the nibs and vanilla. Add the flours and mix just until incorporated. Scrape the dough into a mass and, if necessary, knead it with your hands a few times, just until smooth.

Form the dough into a 12 by 2-inch log. Wrap and refrigerate for at least 2 hours, or, preferably, overnight.

Position the racks in the upper and lower thirds of the oven and preheat the oven to 350°F. Line the baking sheets with parchment paper.

Use a sharp knife to cut the cold dough log into ¼-inch-thick slices. Place the cookies at least 1½ inches apart on the baking sheets.

Bake until the cookies are just beginning to color at the edges, 12 to 14 minutes, rotating the baking sheets from top to bottom and front to back halfway through the baking. Cool the cookies in the pans on a rack, or slide the parchment liners carefully onto the rack to free up the pans. Let cool completely. The cookies are delicious fresh but even better the next day. They can be stored in an airtight container for at least 1 month.

nibby buckwheat
linzer hearts

Dark berry preserves are delicious with buckwheat and with cacao nibs. The combination makes a dressy cookie for a special occasion.

makes about twenty 3½-inch cookies

Dough for Nibby Buckwheat Butter
Cookies (page 93), with 1 cup (4 ounces)
finely chopped walnuts added along with
the nibs

½ cup good-quality blackberry or black
raspberry preserves

Powdered sugar for dusting

EQUIPMENT

Baking sheets

A 3½-inch heart-shaped cookie cutter and
a 1½- or 2-inch heart-shaped cookie cutter

DIVIDE THE DOUGH in half and form into 2 flat patties. Wrap and refrigerate for at least 2 hours, or preferably overnight. (The dough can be refrigerated for up to 3 days, or frozen, well wrapped, for up to 3 months.)

Position the racks in the upper and lower thirds of the oven and preheat the oven to 325°F. Line the baking sheets with parchment paper.

Remove one dough patty from the refrigerator and let it sit at room temperature until supple enough to roll but still quite firm—it will continue to soften as you work. Roll the dough between two pieces of wax paper or plastic sheets (from a heavy-duty plastic bag) to a thickness of ⅛ inch. Turn the dough over once or twice while you are rolling it out to check for deep wrinkles; if necessary, peel off and smooth the paper or plastic over the dough before continuing to roll it. When the dough is thin enough, peel off the top sheet of paper or plastic and place it in front of you. Invert the dough onto that sheet and peel off the second sheet. Cut as many large hearts as possible with the 3½-inch cutter; dip the edges of the cutter in flour as necessary to prevent sticking. Use the point of a paring knife to lift and remove scraps as you transfer the cookies to the baking sheets, placing the cookies at least 1½ inches apart. Cut a smaller heart from the center of half of the large hearts with the 1½- or 2-inch cutter. If the dough gets too soft at any time while rolling, cutting, removing scraps, or transferring to the baking sheets, slide a cookie sheet underneath the paper or plastic sheet and refrigerate the dough for a few minutes, until firm. Repeat with the second piece of dough, then press all of the dough scraps together gently (don't overwork them with too much kneading)—including the tiny hearts, unless you want to bake them separately—and reroll to make more cookies.

Bake until the cookies are just beginning to color at the edges, 8 to 10 minutes, rotating the baking sheets from top to bottom and front to back halfway through the baking. The tiny hearts you cut out may be baked on a separate sheet; they will be done in 6 to 8 minutes. Cool the cookies in the pans on a rack, or slide the parchment liners carefully onto the rack to free up the pans. Let cool completely. The cookies are delicious fresh, but are even better the next day. The plain cookies can be stored in an airtight container for at least 1 month.

To assemble, shortly before serving, spread each whole heart cookie with a thin layer of preserves. Sift powdered sugar over the cut-out hearts. Place a sugared cut-out heart on top of each preserve-covered heart. Leftover cookies can be stored in an airtight container, but the moisture from the preserves will soften them.

sesame coins

These tender cookies with a giant sesame flavor were inspired by the taste of halvah.
Tahini (pure ground toasted sesame seeds, with no additives or preservatives) turned out to
be the best and purest source of flavor. The cookies look even more exotic topped with black
sesame seeds. If doubling the recipe, use 1 whole egg instead of 2 yolks.

makes about forty-eight 1½-inch cookies

⅔ cup (3 ounces) all-purpose flour

¼ teaspoon baking soda

⅔ cup unsalted tahini (pure ground
roasted sesame seeds)

4 tablespoons unsalted butter, melted

½ cup sugar

1 large egg yolk

½ teaspoon pure vanilla extract

½ teaspoon salt

3 tablespoons natural or black sesame
seeds

EQUIPMENT
Baking sheets
A 1½-inch round cookie cutter

WHISK THE FLOUR and baking soda in a small bowl until thoroughly blended. Set aside.

In a medium bowl, mix the tahini, butter, sugar, egg yolk, vanilla, and salt until
smooth. Add the flour mixture and work with your hands until blended. The dough
will be slightly crumbly, and you will have to push or squeeze it together.

Divide the dough in half-form it into 2 patties, and wrap the patties in plastic
wrap. Chill for at least 2 hours, or, preferably, overnight.

Position the racks in the lower and upper thirds of the oven and preheat the oven
to 325°F. Line the baking sheets with parchment paper.

Remove one piece of dough from the refrigerator and allow it to soften slightly.
Roll it between two pieces of wax paper or plastic wrap to a thickness of ¼ inch. If the
dough is crumbly, just push it together. Sprinkle the dough with half of the sesame
seeds and roll over them gently to secure them to the dough. Cut as many rounds
as possible, trying to minimize dough scraps, and transfer to the lined pans, spacing
the cookies 1 inch apart. Repeat with the second dough patty. Press all of the scraps
together, without overworking the dough, roll out, and cut additional cookies.

Bake until the edges of the cookies are golden brown, 10 to 12 minutes, rotating
the sheets from back to front and top to bottom halfway through baking. Set the baking sheets on racks to cool completely.

The cookies will keep in an airtight container for at least 1 month.

FRONT ROW: *Sesame Coins (this page) and Coffee-Walnut Cookies (page 202).*
BACK GROUPING, CLOCKWISE FROM TOP: *Chocolate Mint Sandwiches (page 167),
Golden Kamut Shortbread (page 67), Tropical Lace Cookies (page 189), My Gingersnaps
(page 210), and Nibby Whole Wheat Sablés (with currants; page 87).*

the flavors of fruit

Fruit is the least predictable of the dessert maker's ingredients. We must always question and judge. How ripe, sweet, or flavorful are those plums, berries, or melons? How tart are the apples? Are the lemons sweet and floral like Meyers or puckery like Eurekas?

I normally enjoy the precision and the control associated with pastry and dessert making (as opposed to more freewheeling savory cooking). But working with fruit is different. Precision must be abandoned to judgment and tasting. Seasonality and good shopping are paramount. Nothing is better than a store or a farmers' market where it is assumed that you may need to taste before you buy. Even dried fruit should be tasted before purchase, since its quality varies from producer to producer and crop to crop. Change your menu if the fruit is not good. Know that lackluster or rotten fruit does not improve when put into desserts. Blemished or unsightly fruit for making pies or tarts is often sold for less, but it is only a bargain if it is delicious.

I allowed myself to be quirky in my choices of recipes in this chapter. I love citrus—the fruit itself, the tart and puckery zest, and whole, homemade candied peels. I look forward each year to the stunning sequence of apples that ripen from late summer into winter, and I am likely to leave the skins on them for added flavor too, just as my mother does, wherever I can get away with it. I love the early Astrakhan, the short-lived Jonathon (on the brink of extinction!), and the dramatic Pink Lady, each in its time, among so many others. Among plums I prefer those with a pronounced contrast of sweet flesh with tart, even sour skin. I used to think most strawberries were more beautiful than delicious—until I found a farmer at my farmers' market who harvests his Seascape variety strawberries when they are still small and with their dainty stems attached; they have a sweet perfume and concentrated flavor, highlighted by perfect acidity. Tasting them was like tasting strawberries again for the very first time. I simply fell in love. For me the best of all fruit are like those pretty strawberries, those plums, those apples—it is always the magical balance of sweetness and acidity that creates the explosion of flavor and sensation on my tongue.

Helen's summer pudding

When berries are ripe and abundant, there is nothing purer or simpler than summer pudding. The late and beloved Helen Gustafson—once-actress, writer, hostess, and mistress of tea at Chez Panisse—described the lush berry-soaked dessert in her memoir, *The Agony of the Leaves*. I tasted it at one of her memorable and quirky Berkeley tea parties. Later, with the zeal of a missionary, Helen recited to me in detail the particulars of this underappreciated dessert. Sweetened whipped cream or rose cream is the obvious accompaniment, but I also like the contrast of tangy quark or lebni cheese with the tart-sweet berries.

serves 5 to 6 people

3 to 4 slices white sandwich bread with a tight crumb (nothing fluffy or with an open grain or crusty; Helen preferred Northridge English Muffin Toasting Bread)

3½ to 4 cups ripe berries, such as raspberries, blackberries, or boysenberries, including a handful of red currants if possible

½ cup sugar, or to taste

Lightly sweetened whipped cream or Rose Cream (page 103) for serving

EQUIPMENT
A 1-quart bowl (5 to 6 inches across the top and 3 to 4 inches deep is good)

GREASE THE BOWL and line it with a piece of plastic wrap long enough to hang over on two sides, opposite, pressing it into the bowl as smoothly as possible.

Cut the crusts from the bread. Use scissors to cut the bread into wedges. Line the inside of the bowl with the wedges, placing the narrow ends at the bottom. Use wet fingers to fit the bread pieces very snugly together, with no spaces in between. Set the lined bowl and the remaining bread aside.

Combine the berries and sugar in a nonreactive saucepan large enough to hold the berries in about 1½ layers. Heat the berries, turning them gently, until they begin to throw off their juices. Do not boil—the aim is not to cook the berries but only to warm them and coax forth their juices. You may taste and adjust the sugar, but Helen advised me to "stay on the tart side."

Spoon the berries and juices into the lined bowl. Fit more bread on top to cover the berries. Cover with the overhanging plastic wrap. Place a saucer small enough to fit inside the bowl on top of the wrap and weight it with a can of beans or similarly heavy object.

Set the bowl on a larger plate, in case juices overflow. Refrigerate at least overnight—1 or 2 days is even better, as the pudding is best when the bread is fully soaked with berry juices.

To unmold, pull back the plastic wrap and invert the bowl onto a serving platter with a rim to catch any juices; lift off the bowl. Serve the pudding with whipped cream.

strawberries with rose cream

Rose-scented whipped cream makes a seductive variation on the classic strawberries and cream. Rose water is an easy ingredient to have on hand; it is available at better super-markets, specialty stores, and Middle Eastern food stores. Avoid the small bottles sold in the wine or liquor department—these are not very flavorful. The Lebanese brand called Cortas is very nice. Use it again for Rose Water and Mint Ice Cream (page 223), or to flavor a pitcher of lemonade that even kids will love.   serves 6 to 8

3 pints ripe strawberries

ROSE CREAM
1 cup heavy cream

1 to 2 teaspoons rose water

1 tablespoon plus 1 teaspoon sugar, or to taste

1 lemon, preferably organic or unsprayed

WASH, PAT DRY, and hull the berries. Leave them whole if they are small, otherwise, cut them into halves or quarters.

To make the cream, in a chilled bowl, whip the cream with 1 teaspoon of the rose water until it begins to thicken. Add the sugar and whip until the cream holds a soft shape. Taste a bit of the cream on a strawberry; add a bit more sugar and/or drops of rose water to your taste, then finish whipping the cream to the desired stiffness.

If the berries aren't very sweet sprinkle them with a little sugar. Divide the berries among serving dishes or stemmed glasses. Grate a little lemon zest directly over each serving, and top with a dollop of the cream.

really raspberry coconut tart

Nothing but loads of fresh raspberries, both raw and cooked, fill this easy tart with a toasted coconut crust. You can substitute blackberries, blueberries, small strawberries, or your seasonal favorite.

serves 8

FOR THE CRUST

⅔ cup (1.4 ounces) unsweetened shredded dried coconut

⅓ cup sugar

8 tablespoons (1 stick) unsalted butter, melted and still warm

¾ teaspoon pure vanilla extract

¼ teaspoon salt

1 cup (4.5 ounces) all-purpose flour

FOR THE FILLING

2 tablespoons sugar

1 tablespoon all-purpose flour

6 to 7 cups (five 6-ounce packages) raspberries, rinsed and spread on two layers of paper towels to drain

Powdered sugar for dusting

Whipped cream or crème fraîche for serving (optional)

EQUIPMENT

Baking sheet or pizza stone

A 9½-inch fluted tart pan with a removable bottom

To make the crust, position a rack in the lower third of the oven. Place your darkest, heaviest baking sheet (or a pizza stone) on the rack and preheat the oven to 425°F.

Set a medium bowl near the stove. Spread the coconut in a wide heavy skillet, set over medium heat, and stir constantly until the coconut begins to color slightly. Turn the heat down (once hot, coconut can burn quickly) and continue to stir until the coconut is mostly light golden brown flecked with some white. I often take the pan off of the heat early and continue to stir, letting the residual heat of the pan finish toasting the coconut slowly and evenly. The whole process takes less than 5 minutes. Immediately scrape the coconut into the bowl.

Stir the sugar, melted butter, vanilla, and salt into the coconut. Add the flour and mix just until well blended. Press the dough evenly over the bottom and up the sides of the tart pan. This may take a little patience, as there is just enough dough; to avoid ending up with extra-thick edges, press the dough squarely into the corners of the pan.

To make the filling, mix the sugar and flour together in a medium bowl. Add 2½ cups of the berries with a rubber spatula and gently fold or toss to coat them with the sugar mixture. Pour the berries (including any loose flour or sugar) into the crust and spread them evenly.

Set the pan on a square of foil, and fold the edges of the foil up and loosely over the edges of the crust to protect them temporarily. Set on the hot baking sheet and bake for 15 minutes. Turn the oven down to 350°F, unfold the foil to expose the crust edge, and bake until the crust is deep golden brown and the berry juices are bubbly, 25 to 30 minutes more. About halfway through, use a fork to gently break up the berries.

Remove the tart from the oven and arrange the remaining berries attractively, as close together as possible, over the hot berries. Cool completely on a rack.

Remove the sides of the tart pan and dust the tart with powdered sugar before serving plain or with whipped cream, crème fraîche, or ice cream. The tart is best served within a few hours of baking, but the rare leftovers are hard to resist even the morning after.

chunky blackberry sauce

With both the bright flavor of fresh fruit and the deeper jammy notes from cooked berries, this is the sauce that you will spoon over a slice of Lebni Tart (page 39) or any cheesecake, atop a Quark Soufflé (page 52), beside a quivery panna cotta, or around a scoop of ice cream. It's less a recipe than a concept, with endless possibilities that include other berries, the substitution of wine for water, the addition of cinnamon or other spices, and/or the insinuation of a few fresh lemon thyme leaves (especially good with the soufflé) into the simmering sauce. Just taste as you go. Or, when you don't need a sauce, dish it into a bowl, top it with crème fraîche or a dollop of fresh cheese, and call it dessert.

makes 2 cups

3 cups fresh blackberries

2 tablespoons sugar

2 tablespoons water or dry red wine

Drops of fresh lemon juice to taste

1 to 2 teaspoons kirsch, or to taste (optional)

PUT ONE-THIRD to a half of the berries in a medium saucepan, add the sugar and water or wine, and cook, covered, over medium heat until the berries release their juices, 2 to 3 minutes. Stir, cover, and cook until the berries have collapsed and the juices are sweet, rich, and syrupy. Fold in the remaining berries and just warm them through. Taste and adjust the flavor with sugar, drops of lemon juice, and kirsch, if desired. Serve warm or chilled.

rustic plum tart

The soul of simplicity, this tart is a late-summer treasure. Teach the recipe to a child, or take it on vacation. The unabashedly sweet pastry is golden brown and crunchy at the edges, chewy within. It is a dramatic foil for tart-sweet plums or sour cherries. The dough is simply pressed into the bottom of a tart pan (or cake pan, or pie plate) and the fruit arranged on top, not too close together, skin side up or down, depending on the size. In the oven, the dough puffs up around the plums to form a crusty surface and raised edges, while the plum juices turn to a sparkling glaze without your lifting a finger. Serve it with whipped cream, ice cream, or nothing at all. Nibble leftovers for breakfast.   serves 8

1 cup (4.5 ounces) all-purpose flour

¾ cup sugar

½ teaspoon baking powder

⅛ teaspoon salt

1 large egg, lightly whisked

3 tablespoons firm but not hard unsalted butter

4 to 6 juicy, flavorful plums, such as Santa Rosas, Elephant Hearts, Friars, or Larodas or pluots (see Note)

EQUIPMENT

A 9½-inch fluted tart pan with a removable bottom (or 9- to 10-inch cake pan or glass pie plate)

POSITION A RACK in the lower third of the oven and preheat the oven to 375°F (350°F if using a glass pie plate). Generously butter the tart pan (or cake pan or pie plate).

To make the dough by hand, mix the flour, sugar, baking powder, and salt together in a medium bowl. Add the egg and butter and use a pastry blender, a large fork, or a couple of knives to cut the mixture together, as though you were making pie dough. The dough is ready when it resembles a rough mass of damp yellow sand with no dry flour showing.

To make the dough in a food processor, combine the flour, sugar, baking powder, and salt in the bowl of the food processor and pulse to mix. Add the egg and butter, cut into a few chunks, and pulse just until the mixture resembles damp yellow sand and is beginning to clump around the blade.

Press the dough evenly over the bottom but not up the sides of the pan.

If the plums are no bigger than 2 inches in diameter, cut them in half and remove the pits. Cut larger plums into quarters or sixths, removing the pits. Leaving a margin of ½ inch around the edge of the pan, arrange halved plums cut side up over the dough, with a little space between each one. Arrange wedges skin side up (they look beautiful that way after baking), pressing them slightly into the dough so that they will not turn onto their sides while baking.

Bake until the pastry is puffed, deep golden brown at the edges, and nicely golden brown in the center between the plums, 50 to 55 minutes (perhaps 10 minutes less if you are using a glass pie plate—in which case, you can lift the pan and check underneath to be sure the pastry is well browned on the bottom as well). Set the tart on a rack to cool for 10 minutes, and then loosen the rim of the tart pan, if you used one, before cooling further. If you find a tiny pool of syrupy juice in the center of halved plums, use a small table knife to spread the shiny syrup over the cut surface of the plum for a glistening glaze. Serve warm or at room temperature.

sour cream–topped plum tart

Here is a richer, more decadent treatment for the plum tart.

While the tart is in the oven, mix ¾ cup sour cream with ¼ teaspoon pure vanilla extract and 1 tablespoon sugar. When the tart is done, spread the sour cream over it, leaving a border of bare crust around the edges. Return the tart to the oven for 5 minutes to set the topping.

NOTE: Plums that are both sweet and tart—especially those that make you pucker slightly when you taste the flesh nearest the skin—are especially delicious and dramatic here because the dough is quite sweet. I have used Santa Rosa, Friar, Laroda, and Elephant Heart plums and Flavor King pluots with great results. The small French and Italian prune plums and "sugar" plums are not tangy enough for this dessert. I shop in the farmers' market at the height of the season so I can taste each variety of plum before choosing.

dried fruit and nut cake

My friend Christine Blaine gave me this recipe many years ago when she was the retail director of my dessert company. Chock-full of crunchy nuts and moist dried fruit, it was especially appealing for having no artificially colored (and universally reviled) bits of candied fruit. This is an even more treasured recipe now that there are so many more dried fruits with which to create variations. (For the cake in the photograph, I used dates, dried Angelino plums, and dried pears.) And now, why not add some homemade (and really *delicious*) Candied Citrus Peel (page 131)? Please be inventive with this fantastic recipe. Add slices to the cheese tray, or serve with after-dinner liqueurs. Or keep some in your desk for an emergency burst of energy.   makes 1 large loaf cake or 2 small ones

¾ cup (3.4 ounces) all-purpose flour

¼ teaspoon baking soda

¼ teaspoon baking powder

½ teaspoon salt

¾ cup (5.25 ounces) firmly packed light or dark brown sugar or raw sugar, such as light muscovado or grated piloncillo

1 cup dried apricots, plums, pluots, pears, or peaches, or a mixture (to measure, leave apricots or similar-size fruit whole and cut larger fruit in halves or thirds)

2 cups quartered moist dates or any other favorite dried fruits

3 cups (12 ounces) walnut halves

3 large eggs

1 teaspoon pure vanilla extract

EQUIPMENT

A 9 by 5-inch 8 cup loaf pan or two 8 by 4-inch (4 cups) loaf pans

POSITION A RACK in the lower third of the oven and preheat the oven to 300°F. Spray the loaf pans with vegetable oil spray or line the bottom and sides with parchment paper.

In a large bowl, whisk the flour with the baking soda, baking powder, and salt to combine. Add the brown sugar, all the dried fruit, and the nuts and mix thoroughly with your fingers. Set aside.

In a small bowl, beat the eggs with the vanilla until light. Pour the egg mixture over the dry ingredients and mix well with a wooden spoon or your hands until all the fruits and nuts are coated with batter. Scrape into the prepared pan(s).

Bake until the top is deep golden brown and the batter clinging to the fruit seems set, about 1 hour for smaller loaves, 10 to 15 minutes longer for a large loaf. Tent loosely with foil if the cake appears to be browning too much. Cool completely in the pan(s) on a rack.

When completely cool, remove the cake from the pan(s). The cake keeps, wrapped airtight in foil or plastic wrap, for several weeks at room temperature or at least 3 months in the refrigerator. It can also be frozen for at least 6 months.

To serve, cut into thin slices with a sharp heavy knife.

cardamom-roasted figs

The recipe for these sweet, spicy, and syrupy figs was described to me at a dinner party one evening, leaving me to work out the details. Serve the figs warm or cold with vanilla ice cream or a dollop of crème fraîche. Or halve the figs and serve them with (or even arranged atop) the Lebni Tart (page 39).   serves 6

18 to 20 cardamom pods

1 pound ripe Mission figs (18 to 20 figs)

2½ tablespoons sugar, or to taste

2½ tablespoons balsamic vinegar,
or to taste

2 tablespoons water

EQUIPMENT

A 1½- to 2-quart baking dish

POSITION A RACK in the lower third of the oven and preheat the oven to 375°F.

Use a heavy object such as a mallet or skillet to lightly smash each of the cardamom pods so that you can remove the papery outer covering. Remove the seeds from each pod. Use a small paring knife to push the seeds into 18 or 20 tiny heaps (depending on how many figs you have). Rinse the figs and trim off the tough stems. Cut a small gash in the side of each fig. Use the moist figgy knifepoint to scoop up and place one heap of seeds inside each fig. Put the stuffed figs in the baking dish and sprinkle with the sugar. Drizzle the vinegar and water over the figs.

Cover the dish tightly with foil and bake until the figs are very tender and the juices are thickened and syrupy, 1 hour to 1 hour and 15 minutes. If the juices are still thin and copious toward the end of baking, uncover the dish for the last 10 to 15 minutes, checking frequently until the juices are reduced and syrupy (they will thicken even further on cooling). If the syrup gets too thick, add a little water. Toward the end, taste the syrup and adjust the sugar and/or vinegar if needed.

Serve the figs warm or hot. They can be kept in a covered container in the refrigerator for at least a week. Reheat them in the microwave, if desired.

Bea's apple crisp

By the 1970s, my mother's magnificent double-crusted Thanksgiving apple pie—perfected during my little girlhood—had given way to a series of lighter, simpler, more creative experiments. Around the turn of the twenty-first century, The Pie became The Crisp. The apples are never peeled, and dried apricots dwell therein. My brothers and I love it, and our children don't even remember the pie with a top and bottom crust and no apricots. So I had to write it down now, before it became something else.

You might assume that the crisp is best served warm or at room temperature. But I think it's extra flavorful cold, even after two or three or four days in the fridge. That makes it extra versatile. Whipped cream is always nice, but not essential.

Apple skins add flavor and body to the juices. If some or all of the apples are red (but crisp and at least a little on the tart side), the filling will have a beautiful rosy hue. Chunks rather than wedges are the preferred cut because small squares of apple skin are pleasant to eat, while long thin pieces suggest that the cook was lazy rather than smart like a fox.

serves 6 to 8

FOR THE TOPPING

½ cup (2.25 ounces) all-purpose flour

½ cup rolled oats

Scant 1 cup (3.5 ounces) coarsely chopped walnut pieces

½ cup sugar

5 tablespoons unsalted butter

⅛ teaspoon salt

FOR THE FILLING

Grated zest and juice of 1 bright-skinned orange, preferably organic or unsprayed

½ cup (2½ ounces) dried apricots, coarsely chopped

¼ to ½ cup sugar, depending on the tartness of the apples

1 teaspoon ground cinnamon

6 medium crisp flavorful apples with a decent balance of sweetness and acidity (I have used Pippins, Granny Smiths, Sierra Beauties, and new-crop Jonathans, or a mixture)

EQUIPMENT

A 2-quart baking dish

POSITION A RACK in the lower third of the oven. Preheat the oven to 350°F. Liberally butter the baking dish.

To make the topping, combine all of the ingredients and mix well. Set aside.

To make the filling, in a medium saucepan, combine the orange zest, juice, and chopped apricots, bring to a simmer, and cook until the apricots are soft. Set aside.

In a large bowl mix the sugar and cinnamon. Halve and core the apples. Cut each half twice in each direction to make 9 chunks. Add the chunks to the bowl and toss the apples with the sugar and cinnamon. Stir in the apricots and juice from the saucepan.

Scrape the mixture into the buttered baking dish and spread evenly. Distribute the crumbly topping evenly over the apples. Bake until the crisp is browned on top and the juices are bubbling and thickened, 1¼ to 1½ hours. Serve warm or cold.

summer apple carpaccio

There is no raw or cured beef or tuna involved in this version of carpaccio, just a fan of almost translucent apple slices to accompany a scoop of ice cream, be it sophisticated Rose Water and Mint (page 223) or crowd-pleasing Vanilla Bean (page 55) with a drizzle of caramel sauce (see page 227). Apple slices can also be arranged to form roses: children love them served with or atop Tropical Cinnamon Toasts (179).

Since the apples are prepared without the expected cinnamon and cloves, they burst with refreshing apple-y flavor. Begin serving this dessert in mid summer when the earliest new-crop apples show up in farmers' markets and good supermarkets. Continue through the fall, enjoying each new apple at its best. The apples are quickest to prepare, and have the best firm texture, baked one by one in a microwave oven: by the time you've peeled and sliced the last apple, the others are already cooked and cooling!   serves 8

4 flavorful apples, washed and peeled

3 to 4 tablespoons of sugar

1½ to 2 pints ice cream, such as Rose Water and Mint or Vanilla Bean, homemade or purchased

Caramel Sauce or Tropical Cinnamon Toasts (Optional)

EQUIPMENT

8 microwave-safe saucers

Offset spatula (optional)

CUT ONE APPLE in half lengthwise from the stem to the blossom end. Remove and discard the core. Place one apple half cut side down on a cutting board and slice it crosswise into ⅛-inch slices, leaving the slices in place.

Transfer to a saucer, keeping the slices together in the shape of the apple half. Sprinkle with 1 to 1½ teaspoons sugar (depending on the tartness of your apples). Cover with a piece of wax paper loosely tucked under the saucer.

Microwave on high for 1 minute in an 800 watt oven, or for 45 seconds in a 1000 watt oven. Cool the covered apple on the saucer, undisturbed, to reabsorb its juices and firm up. Repeat with each of the remaining apple halves, cutting and sprinkling each while the previous one is cooking, until all are done. Cool the apples completely, or chill them, before shaping fans or roses. You may cover and refrigerate the baked apples up to 4 days before serving them.

To serve, fan out the slices attractively on eight dessert plates. Or shape the slices into roses as follows: starting with one sliced apple half on its saucer, twist the middle slice, without removing it, into a cone or spiral to form the bud at the center of the rose. Wrap one or two adjacent slices partially around the bud to resemble the inner petals of the rose. Continue to arrange the adjacent slices, working from the center outward, until the apple looks like an open garden rose. Use a offset spatula to transfer the rose to a serving plate. Serve apple fans or roses with a scoop of ice cream (with sauce or cinnamon toasts, if desired).

NOTE: Absent a microwave, bake the apples in a conventional oven preheated to 350°F with a rack in the lower third. Slice all of the apple halves as described and transfer them to a 9 by 13-inch baking dish, keeping the sliced halves together in their original shape. Sprinkle each half with sugar, cover with foil, and bake for 20 minutes. Uncover and baste the apples with their juice. Cook, uncovered, for an additional 10 to 20 minutes or until fork tender. Cool completely before serving.

lemon tart

An elegant classic, made simple with a no-fail crust and myriad do-ahead options. This one belongs in everyone's repertoire. Since I like my lemon desserts tart and tangy, not creamy and mild, this tart tart is my cup of tea, just as it is. But, you may dish it up with dollops of lightly sweetened whipped cream and a side of berries.   serves 8 to 10

FOR THE CRUST

8 tablespoons (1 stick) unsalted butter, melted

¼ cup sugar

¾ teaspoon pure vanilla extract

⅛ teaspoon salt

1 cup (4.5 ounces) all-purpose flour

FOR THE FILLING

Grated zest of ½ lemon, preferably organic or unsprayed

¼ cup fresh lemon juice, strained, preferably from an organic or unsprayed fruit

¼ cup sugar

3 tablespoons unsalted butter, cut into pieces

1 large egg

1 large egg yolk

EQUIPMENT

9½-inch fluted tart pan with a removable bottom

Baking sheet

POSITION A RACK in the lower third of the oven and preheat the oven to 350°F.

To make the crust, in a medium bowl, combine the butter with the sugar, vanilla, and salt. Add the flour and mix just until well blended. If the dough seems too soft and gooey, let it stand for a few minutes to firm up.

Press the dough evenly over the bottom and up the sides of the tart pan to make a very thin, even layer. This takes a little patience, as there is just enough dough; to avoid ending up with extra-thick edges, press the dough squarely into the corners of the pan.

Place the pan on a baking sheet and bake until the crust is a deep golden brown, 20 to 25 minutes. Check after 15 minutes to see if the dough has puffed up from the bottom of the pan; if it has, lift and gently slam down the baking sheet to settle the dough, or press the dough down with the back of a fork and prick it a few times.

Meanwhile, to make the filling, set a medium strainer over a medium bowl and place near the stove. In a small nonreactive saucepan, combine the lemon zest, juice, sugar, and butter and bring to a simmer over medium heat.

In a small heatproof bowl, whisk the egg and yolk lightly to combine. Gradually pour the hot liquid over the eggs, whisking constantly. Scrape the mixture back into the saucepan and whisk over medium heat until thickened and just beginning to simmer around the edges.

Pour the mixture into the strainer and rap the strainer against the bowl to coax the mixture into the bowl. Press only very gently on the solids, to avoid pushing any bits of cooked egg through the strainer. Scrape any filling clinging to the underside of the strainer into the bowl.

When the crust is ready, remove it from the oven, leaving the oven on. Pour the filling into the hot crust and spread it evenly over the crust. Return the tart to the oven for 5 minutes to set the surface slightly. Cool the tart completely on a rack.

Serve the tart at room temperature or chilled. The filling sets a little more firmly when chilled. Store the tart in the refrigerator if you are not serving it within a few hours. It *is* best served on the day it is made, although the crust stands up beautifully through the next day.

■ THE VERSATILE LEMON TART

While my lemon tart recipe is simple as can be, there may be times when you want to serve a fresh lemon tart but you don't want to make the crust and the filling on the same day as you are eating it. You have many options.

I used to be curious why some, but not all, chefs bake their lemon tart for a few minutes after adding the filling, even though the crust is already fully baked and the filling fully cooked. So I tested my tart both ways. As it turns out, the final baking gives the shiny filling a slightly matte surface and a firmer set when it cools, which is nice for slicing if you are serving the tart unchilled. However, if you chill the tart before serving, the filling will firm up anyway, so you can skip the final bake if you like.

Do-ahead options? Both the crust and filling can be made ahead. Once cooled, the crust can be wrapped and stored at room temperature for 2 to 3 days; the filling can be kept in an airtight container in the refrigerator for 1 week. If you spread the cold filling into the cooled crust, you can serve the tart as is or return to a preheated 350°F oven until the filling is hot, 15 to 20 minutes. You can also fill a cooled crust with freshly made hot filling, or spread chilled filling into a freshly made hot crust. In both cases, the choice of whether or not to finish the tart in the oven is up to you.

very tangy lime or lemon bars

I love lemon and lime desserts but often find them overly sweetened or their puckery-ness "tamed" with too much baking soda. (Baking soda reduces the acidity of the citrus juice.) An esteemed New England cooking magazine once pronounced my lemon bars too sour, though my cooking students and guests continue to declare them the best ever. Perhaps it's a New England versus California thing. I mention this so you will know what you are getting into here: very special (and very tangy) citrus bars with a tender, crunchy crust.

makes 16 large bars or 25 smaller bars

FOR THE CRUST

8 tablespoons (1 stick) unsalted butter, melted

¼ cup sugar

¾ teaspoon pure vanilla extract

¼ teaspoon salt

1 cup (4.5 ounces) all-purpose flour

FOR THE TOPPING

1 cup plus 2 tablespoons sugar

3 tablespoons all-purpose flour

3 large eggs

1½ teaspoons finely grated lime or lemon zest, preferably from an organic or unsprayed fruit

½ cup strained fresh lime or lemon juice, preferably from an organic or unsprayed fruit (see Note)

Powdered sugar for dusting (optional)

EQUIPMENT

An 8-inch square baking pan

POSITION A RACK in the lower third of the oven and preheat the oven to 350°F. Line the bottom and up the sides of the baking pan with foil.

To make the crust, in a medium bowl, combine the melted butter with the sugar, vanilla, and salt. Add the flour and mix just until incorporated. Press the dough evenly over the bottom of the pan.

Bake for 25 to 30 minutes, or until the crust is fully baked, well browned at the edges, and golden brown in the center.

While the crust is baking, make the topping. Stir together the sugar and flour in a large bowl until well mixed. Whisk in the eggs. Stir in the lemon or lime zest and juice.

When the crust is ready, turn the oven down to 300°F. Slide the rack with the pan out, and pour the filling onto the hot crust. Bake for 20 to 25 minutes longer, or until the topping no longer jiggles in the center when the pan is tapped. Set on a rack to cool completely in the pan.

Lift up the foil liner and transfer the bars to a cutting board. If the surface is covered with a thin layer of moist foam (not unusual), you can blot it gently to reveal the zest. Lay a square of paper towel on the surface and sweep your fingers over it gently to absorb excess moisture. Remove the paper and repeat with a fresh piece if necessary. Use a long sharp knife to cut into sixteen 2-inch or 25 daintier bars. Sift powdered sugar over the bars just before serving, if desired. The bars can be stored airtight in the refrigerator for several days or more. After 3 days, the crust softens but the bars still taste quite good for up to a week.

NOTE: Meyer lemons are less tart and more floral than most other lemons. If you want to use them, reduce the sugar in the topping to ½ cup plus 2 tablespoons.

lemon tuiles

If you can find them, Meyer lemons give these perfect simple tuiles an exceptional floral fragrance and flavor. You could also substitute mandarin orange or tangerine zest, or regular orange zest.   makes about forty 2½-inch tuiles

3 tablespoons unsalted butter, melted and still warm

1 tablespoon finely grated lemon zest, preferably from an organic or unsprayed fruit

⅔ cup sugar

3 large egg whites

¼ cup plus 3 tablespoons (2 ounces) all-purpose flour (see Note)

⅛ teaspoon salt

EQUIPMENT

Baking sheets (see page 91 for a discussion of foil versus silicone mats)

Small cups or a rolling pin for shaping the cookies (optional)

Offset spatula (optional)

PLACE A RACK in the center of the oven and preheat the oven to 300°F. Line the baking sheets with silicone mats or foil, dull side facing up, and smooth the foil to remove any wrinkles (which would distort the cookies). Lightly butter the foil or the silicone mats.

In a small bowl, whisk together all of the ingredients until blended. The batter will have the consistency of thin, runny Cream of Wheat cereal.

If using silicone mats, drop level teaspoons of batter 2 inches apart onto a baking sheet (bake only one sheet at a time). Using a small offset spatula, spread the batter into rounds, ovals, or elongated shapes about ¹⁄₁₆ inch thick. Bake, watching carefully, until the tuiles are golden brown, half to three-quarters of the way to the centers but still pale in the center, 10 to 15 minutes. If the cookies are not baked long enough, they will not be completely crisp when cool. As soon as you can coax a thin metal spatula under a tuile without destroying it, transfer it to a rack to cool flat. Or shape it by draping it over a rolling pin, nestling it into a little cup, or twisting it with your fingers. Working fast, remove the remaining tuiles; reheat if necessary. Repeat until all of the tuiles are baked.

If using foil, drop level teaspoons of batter 2 inches apart onto a baking sheet (bake only one sheet at a time). Bake, watching carefully, until the batter spreads and the cookies are golden brown half to three-quarters of the way to the centers but still pale in the center, 10 to 15 minutes. If the cookies are not baked long enough, they will not be completely crisp when cool. If the cookies do not spread thin in baking, try using a little more butter on the foil and/or spread the batter with the offset spatula or the back of a spoon. For flat tuiles, slide the foil sheet of cookies onto a rack to cool. For curved tuiles, grasp the edges of the foil when the sheet comes from the oven (without touching the hot pan or the cookies), and roll it into a fat cylinder, gently curving the attached cookies like potato chips. Crimp or secure the foil with a paper clip and set aside. When cool, unroll the foil carefully and remove the tuiles. Alternatively, as described above, remove individual tuiles from the foil while they are hot and shape them in small cups or with your fingers. You can control the size and thickness of the cookies to some extent by how much butter you smear on the foil: a little more butter on the foil produces bigger thinner tuiles with shapes that may meander a bit rather than remaining round. These can be beautiful so long as they don't merge with adjacent cookies. Flat or curved, tuiles are easier to remove from the foil when completely cool. Repeat until all of the tuiles are baked.

Store the cooled tuiles in an airtight container, where they will keep for at least a week.

NOTE: Even a little too much flour may result in a thick and tough rather than thin and crisp tuile. Review how to measure flour (see page 3) or, if you have a digital scale, use it here.

chilled oranges in rum-caramel syrup

This easy, stylish recipe is an old favorite, adapted from a recipe in a French fashion magazine circa 1972. You can serve it as you would fruit compote for brunch, or as a refreshing, light dessert after a spicy meal. Or spoon a moat of it around a scoop of vanilla or honey ice cream (see page 177) or a trembling panna cotta. Or try the variations with balsamic vinegar, orange flour water, or rose water below. Any and all versions are extra dressy and enticing sprinkled with crunchy Caramelized Nut Brittle Garnish (page 81) just before serving. A very versatile dish indeed.   serves 8

8 good eating oranges, preferably organic
or unsprayed

¼ to ⅓ cup dark rum

1 cup sugar

EQUIPMENT

A 12-inch stainless steel skillet

ZEST 2 OF THE ORANGES, using a zester or Microplane to make fine shreds. Or use a vegetable peeler to peel wide strips of zest from the oranges and then cut the zest into very fine slivers with a chef's knife. Set aside.

Use a sharp knife to remove the skin and all of the white membrane from all of the oranges. Cut the oranges crosswise into ¼-inch slices, or "supreme" them by cutting the sections from the membranes (use the technique described on page 123). Remove any seeds. Arrange in a shallow serving dish, drizzle the rum over the oranges, and sprinkle with the zests. Set aside.

To make the caramel, set a white saucer by the side of the stove to use to judge the color of the caramel. Spread the sugar in the dry skillet. Set the pan over medium-high heat and heat, without stirring, until the sugar begins to melt into clear syrup around the edges. Turn the heat down to medium and continue melting the sugar without stirring—shake the pan to redistribute it—for as long as the syrup remains clear. When the syrup begins to color, stir it with a silicone spatula or wooden spoon, mixing and spreading the syrup and sugar together, until all the sugar is melted and beginning to color evenly. If some of the syrup starts to color too quickly before the rest, turn the heat down, or take the pan off the heat for a few moments, and continue to stir. Drop a bead of syrup onto the white plate to judge the color. When the syrup looks pale amber on the saucer, turn the heat down even lower, or remove the pan, and stir until a drop of syrup is reddish amber, or the color of medium-dark honey.

Immediately pour the hot caramel over the orange slices. The oranges may be prepared to this point and kept, covered, in the refrigerator, for up to 2 days. If you serve the oranges after a brief chilling, some of the caramel will have hardened into a thin brittle layer on top of the oranges, providing a pleasing crunch. Lengthier chilling will melt the caramel completely, bathing the oranges in sweet rummy caramel syrup without a crunchy layer. The choice is yours.

chilled oranges in caramel-balsamic syrup

Substitute 1 tablespoon balsamic vinegar for the rum. Before serving, taste the syrup and add more vinegar to taste if necessary. If you like, grind a little fresh black pepper over the oranges, or pass the pepper grinder at the table.

chilled caramel oranges
with orange flower or rose water

I've turned a memorable Moroccan salad into dessert—with hats off to Paula Wolfert for her inspiring recipes.

Substitute 2 teaspoons orange flower or rose water for the rum. Before serving, taste the syrup and add a few drops of orange or rose water if necessary.

chilled oranges with caramelized-walnuts

Just before serving, sprinkle any version of oranges with syrup with chopped Caramelized Nut Brittle Garnish (page 81) made with walnuts. (It's just as good with other kinds of caramelized nuts.)

melon sorbet

Icy cool and refreshing. Choose a very ripe, flavorful melon to begin with; musk-melon, cantaloupe, Crenshaw, Persian, or any other melon (except watermelon) may be used. The key to great sorbet is in the tasting and adjusting of sugar and salt, and sometimes lemon or lime juice. The goal is to lift and express the basic flavor of the fruit, not to flavor it. The last-minute adjustments are also the fun of making sorbet, for no decision is really a disaster, and the more you taste and adjust, the more accomplished you become.

makes 2½ cups

2 cups pureed melon

¼ cup water

3 tablespoons sugar

1 to 2 teaspoons vodka or grappa (optional)

Salt

A few drops of fresh lemon juice, preferably from an organic or unsprayed fruit

EQUIPMENT
Ice cream machine

IN A MEDIUM BOWL, mix the melon puree with the water and sugar, stirring to dissolve the sugar. Chill the mixture.

Before freezing, taste the mixure and add the vodka or grappa, if you like. Adjust the flavor with additional sugar as necessary, tiny pinches of salt, and drops of lemon juice until the puree tastes lively and slightly sweeter than you think it should be. For an extra-cold start, put the mixture in the freezer for 20 minutes, stirring once or twice to prevent freezing. Then, freeze according to the instructions for your ice cream machine.

Serve the sorbet soft or transfer it to an airtight container and freeze until hard enough to scoop, at least 3 to 4 hours. If the sorbet gets too hard, before serving let it stand for a few minutes or microwave it on low (defrost) for a few seconds at a time until scoopable.

pink grapefruit granita

In hot weather, this is a sparkler on your tongue. Don't let the fact that it is fat-free deter you. I noticed Romans eating granita with dollops of whipped cream. It is also a lovely topping for ice cream and berries.

makes about 3 cups

1½ cups grapefruit segments (see Box) and juice (without seeds or membranes)

¼ cup sugar

A few drops of fresh lime or lemon juice (optional)

COMBINE THE GRAPEFRUIT SEGMENTS, juice, and sugar in the bowl of a food processor and pulse to puree. Let stand for a few minutes, and then pulse again to make sure the sugar is dissolved. Taste and adjust the flavor with drops of lime or lemon juice if necessary.

Pour the mixture into a shallow baking dish. Freeze for about 1 hour, or until the mixture is starting to harden. Stir and freeze again until frozen hard.

Use a fork to scrape and break the mixture into shards and crystals. Return to the freezer to freeze completely. Scrape and toss the granita one more time. Keep frozen until serving. Serve in stemmed glasses, dolloped with whipped cream, if desired.

■ **TO REMOVE SEGMENTS OR "SUPREME" A GRAPEFRUIT**

Wash the grapefruit rind. Cut a generous slice from each end of the fruit to expose a round of bare fruit about 2 inches in diameter. Set the fruit on one cut end on a cutting board. With a sharp knife, starting at the top edge of the rind, follow the contour of the fruit using a downward sawing motion to cut a wide strip of rind, pith, and membrane from the fruit. Continue around the fruit, removing as much membrane as possible without wasting too much fruit. Trim any remaining membrane left on the surface of the fruit.

To segment, turn the fruit on the cutting board with one side facing up. Cut into the fruit next to a membrane and rotate the knife blade to peel the segment away from the opposite membrane, or simply cut both sides of the segment away from the membrane, whichever is easier for you. Remove all of the segments. Don't worry if the segments are not perfect. On the cutting board, reserve juice squeezed from the membrane and any segments with any juice.

mango sorbet

The naturally fibrous nature of mangoes produces sorbet with a creamy texture despite the absence of cream, fat, or excessive sugar. And what vibrant flavor! If your large mango yields more than 1 cup of puree, increase the other ingredients accordingly, or treat yourself to the extra fruit on the spot. For a sorbet reminiscent of a tropical bar drink, add 1 tablespoon rum to the ingredients. With or without the rum, consider serving the sorbet with Tropical Lace Cookies (page 189). makes 2 cups

1 large, very ripe sweet mango

¼ cup plus 2 tablespoons sugar

⅔ cup water

1 tablespoon plus 1 teaspoon fresh lemon juice

EQUIPMENT

Ice cream machine or food processor

PEEL THE MANGO and remove the flesh from around the pit. Puree the fruit in a food processor and measure it. Transfer 1 cup of the puree to a bowl and add the sugar, water, and lemon juice, stirring until the sugar dissolves. Chill.

For an extra-cold start, put the mixture in the freezer for 20 minutes, stirring once or twice to prevent freezing. Freeze the mixture according to the instructions for your ice cream machine.

Or, if you don't have an ice cream machine, pour the mixture into a cake or pie pan, cover, and freeze until hard, 3 to 4 hours, or until needed. Remove from the freezer and break the mixture into chunks with a fork and transfer to the clean bowl of the food processor. Process, scraping the bowl as necessary, until the mixture is smooth and the color lightens.

Serve the sorbet soft or transfer it to an airtight container and freeze until hard enough to scoop, at least 3 to 4 hours. If the sorbet gets too hard, before serving let it stand for a few minutes or microwave it on low (defrost) for a few seconds at a time until scoopable.

FROM TOP: *Sensational Strawberry Sorbet (page 128),*
Blackberry-Buttermilk Sherbet (page 129),
Mango Sorbet (this page).

banana ice cream

Bananas and cream are a natural. When ripening bananas threaten the fruit bowl, you can always make banana bread, but this simple ice cream is faster and easier (no cooking required), and it tastes a lot more like bananas! It's excellent all by itself, or try it with Salted Peanut Butter Toffee Cookies (page 79) or Tropical Lace Cookies (page 189).

makes about 3½ cups

2 cups pureed very ripe bananas (4 to 5 medium bananas)

1 cup heavy cream

3 tablespoons sugar

¾ teaspoon pure vanilla extract

⅛ teaspoon salt

EQUIPMENT

Ice cream machine

IN A MEDIUM BOWL, stir the banana puree with the cream, sugar, vanilla, and salt. Let stand briefly, then stir again to make sure that the sugar is dissolved. Chill. For an extra-cold start, put the mixture in the freezer for 20 minutes, stirring once or twice to prevent freezing. Freeze the mixture according to the instructions for your ice cream machine.

Serve soft, or transfer to an airtight container and freeze, until the ice cream is hard enough to scoop, at least 3 to 4 hours. If the ice cream gets too hard, before serving let it stand for a few minutes, put it in the refrigerator for 15 minutes or longer, or microwave it on low (defrost) for a few seconds until scoopable.

lime (or lemon) sherbet

This tangy and refreshing sherbet is easy but special enough for a dinner party, garnished perhaps with strips of candied citrus peel. Between your fruit bowl and your fridge, you may already have all of the ingredients on hand. And you can even make it without an ice cream machine. I find that 1 percent low-fat milk makes for a brighter flavor than whole milk does. Serve sherbet with lightly sugared strawberries or with Honey Snaps (page 174). Or serve in a martini glass with a shot of citron vodka over it.

makes 3⅓ cups

2⅔ cups 1% low-fat or whole milk

1 cup sugar

1½ teaspoons grated lime (regular or key lime) or lemon zest

½ cup fresh lime or lemon juice (from 3 to 4 regular limes, 5 to 6 key limes, or 2 to 3 medium lemons)

EQUIPMENT

Ice cream machine or food processor

COMBINE ALL OF the ingredients in a medium bowl and stir to blend. The mixture will thicken slightly as the lime juice reacts with the milk, and it will look slightly curdled—this is okay. Let stand for 2 to 3 minutes, then stir again to be sure that the sugar is completely dissolved. Chill.

For an extra-cold start, put the mixture in the freezer for 20 minutes, stirring once or twice to prevent freezing. Freeze the mixture according to the instructions for your ice cream machine. When the sherbet is almost frozen, remove the dasher and check to see if the zest has accumulated on it. If necessary, scrape the zest off the dasher and stir it back into the sherbet with a fork, then continue to freeze the sherbet.

Or, if you do not have an ice cream machine, pour the mixture into a cake or pie pan, cover, and freeze until hard, 3 to 4 hours, or until needed. Remove from the freezer and break the mixture into chunks with a fork and transfer to the clean bowl of a food processor. Process, scraping the bowl as necessary, until the mixture is smooth and the color lightens.

Serve the sherbet soft or transfer to an airtight container and freeze until hard enough to scoop, at least 3 to 4 hours. If the sherbet gets too hard, before serving let it stand for a few minutes or microwave it on low (defrost) for a few seconds at a time until scoopable.

sensational strawberry sorbet

PHOTOGRAPH ON PAGE 125

Of course, the key to great strawberry sorbet is to start with fresh, flavorful berries with a good balance of sweetness and tangy acidity. But the secret to a superior strawberry sorbet is cooking a small percentage of the berries, ever so briefly, to concentrate their flavor and soften them. The cooked berries add a layer of complexity to the flavor and a subtle creaminess to the texture, without compromising the essential bright, tangy flavor of fresh fruit. Tasted side by side with an all-raw or all-cooked sorbet, there's no contest. Try it.

makes 2¾ cups

1 pound (4 cups) ripe, flavorful strawberries, rinsed and hulled

⅓ cup plus 2 tablespoons water

⅓ cup sugar, plus more to taste

A few drops of fresh lemon juice, preferably from an organic or unsprayed fruit (only if necessary)

2 to 3 teaspoons vodka, kirsch, or framboise (optional)

EQUIPMENT
Ice cream machine

PUT 1 CUP of the berries in a small saucepan (6 inches or less in diameter) with a good lid, add the 2 tablespoons water, and bring to a simmer over high heat. Reduce the heat to medium, cover, and simmer the berries gently for 2 to 3 minutes only, just until most of the berries are barely fork-tender; if in any doubt about whether the berries are "done," stop the cooking—less is better than more. The berries will throw off juices, which will begin to concentrate into a small amount of fragrant syrup (which you should not allow to burn).

Scrape the berries and their juices into the bowl of a food processor or a blender. Add the remaining berries and the sugar, and puree until smooth. You should have about 2½ cups of puree. Stir in the remaining ⅓ cup water, transfer the puree to a bowl, and chill. Taste the puree and adjust the sugar if necessary; the puree should taste a little bit sweeter than you think it should. If the berries were excellent to start with, you won't need to adjust the flavor with drops of lemon juice, but if you must, do so with a light hand. Stir the puree well to be sure that any added sugar is dissolved. Add the optional spirits if you like. For an extra-cold start, put the mixture in the freezer for 20 minutes, stirring once or twice to prevent freezing. Freeze the puree according to the instructions for your ice cream machine.

Serve the sorbet soft or transfer it to an airtight container and freeze until hard enough to scoop, at least 3 to 4 hours. If the sorbet gets too hard, before serving let it stand for a few minutes or microwave it on low (defrost) for a few seconds at a time until scoopable.

basil- or mint-scented strawberry sorbet

A nuance of fresh basil or mint adds a lovely dimension to strawberries.

Stir a generous ⅓ cup (lightly packed) coarsely chopped fresh basil or mint into the puree before chilling it. Chill for at least 1 hour. Strain out and discard the herbs before freezing the sorbet.

blackberry-buttermilk sherbet

PHOTOGRAPH ON PAGE 125

Don't miss this robust bowl of big berry flavor. It's just the right balance of sweet with tart, and it's both icy and creamy. It's gutsy. It's delicious. Buttermilk in a glass may scare you, but it is a magical ingredient in many desserts and a star in this one. Make the sherbet with any fresh or frozen bush berries, such as raspberries, loganberries, marionberries, olallieberries, or boysenberries. *makes about 1 quart*

3 cups fresh blackberries, rinsed and drained, or individually quick-frozen berries (unsweetened), thawed, with their juice

1 cup plus 2 tablespoons sugar

3 cups buttermilk

EQUIPMENT

Ice cream machine

IN A MEDIUM BOWL, mash the berries with the sugar. Add the buttermilk and stir until the sugar dissolves. Chill. For an extra-cold start, put the mixture in the freezer for 20 minutes, stirring once or twice to prevent freezing. Freeze the mixture according to the instructions for your ice cream machine.

Serve soft or transfer to an airtight container and freeze until hard enough to scoop, at least 3 to 4 hours. If the sherbet gets too hard, before serving let it stand for a few minutes, put it in the refrigerator for 15 minutes or longer, or microwave it on low (defrost) for a few seconds at a time until scoopable. This ice cream does not keep for long; eat it within a few days.

lemon-basil sherbet

Lightly infused with the flavor of fresh basil, this is a wonderful, fresh way with lemon sherbet.

makes 3⅓ cups

1 cup sugar

½ cup fresh lemon juice (from 2 to 3 medium lemons, preferably organic or unsprayed)

A very large handful of fresh basil leaves

2⅔ cups 1% low-fat or whole milk

1½ teaspoons grated lemon zest, preferably from an organic or unsprayed fruit

EQUIPMENT

Ice cream machine or food processor

IN A MEDIUM BOWL, stir the sugar, lemon juice, and basil leaves together. Let stand for 1 hour.

Stir the milk into the lemon juice mixture, then strain the mixture, pressing lightly on the basil leaves; discard the basil. Add the lemon zest. Chill.

For an extra-cold start, put the mixture in the freezer for 20 minutes, stirring once or twice to prevent freezing. Freeze the mixture according to the instructions for your ice cream machine. When the sherbet is almost frozen, remove the dasher and check to see if the zest has accumulated on it. If necessary, scrape the zest off the dasher and stir it back into the sherbet with a fork before continuing to freeze the sherbet.

Or, if you do not have an ice cream machine, pour the mixture into a cake or pie pan, cover, and freeze until hard, 3 to 4 hours, or until you are ready to finish the sherbet. Break the mixture into chunks with a fork and transfer to the bowl of a food processor. Process, scraping the bowl as necessary, until the mixture is smooth and the color lightens.

Serve the sherbet soft or transfer to an airtight container and freeze until hard enough to scoop, at least 3 to 4 hours. If the sherbet gets too hard, before serving let it stand for a few minutes or microwave on low (defrost) for a few seconds at a time until scoopable.

candied citrus peel

PHOTOGRAPH ON PAGE 132

If you have ever tasted hand-made candied citrus peel, you know it is an entirely different animal from mass-produced commercial peel. To me, the good stuff is addictively delicious (whether or not it is dipped in chocolate). And it is fantastic in recipes. With abundant organic citrus in the market, and still so few artisan-made candied peels available for purchase, there is every reason to make your own. If you are smart and planful, you will get to work in the winter and early spring when citrus is truly in season and has the most flavor in both fruit and peel. I am not always so organized, but I do care that the peel is organic. Years ago I was horrified by the smell of chemicals that emanated from the blanching pot during my first candying experience.

This recipe presumes that you have not saved up citrus peel from other dishes or from fruit that you have eaten or served or juiced, which, of course, you can do; some cooks accumulate citrus peels in the freezer until they have enough to candy. You want about 4 cups of it for this recipe. It is also worth noting that purists candy only one type of peel in the same pot, but for every purist there are happy rule breakers.

Candied peel that is moist and chewy as well as tart and intensely flavorful includes some of the white pith under the colored zest layer of the skin. If you want a quicker zest-only garnish for desserts, skip to the Quick Citrus Zest Garnish, which follows.

makes 3 to 4 cups

4 bright-skinned preferably organic or
unsprayed oranges, 2 grapefruit, or
6 to 8 lemons, limes, or tangerines

1½ cups water

1½ cups sugar, plus more for dredging

EQUIPMENT
Instant-read or candy thermometer

USE A SHARP paring knife to score the peel of each fruit into quarters (or sixths if using grapefruit), cutting just through the skin from the top to bottom all around. Use your fingers to strip the peel from the fruit. It's okay if some fruit is left on the peel for now. You should have 3 to 4 cups peel. Save the fruit for another dish.

Place the peel in a 3- to 4-quart saucepan and fill the pan with cold water, leaving just enough space for it to boil. Bring the water to a full rolling boil. Drain the peel and dump it into a large bowl of cold water to cool for a minute. Drain and return the peel to the saucepan. Repeat the entire blanching and cooling sequence twice for thin-skinned Meyer lemons or tangerines, three times for oranges, regular lemons, or tangelos, or four times for grapefruit. (Blanching rids the fruit of excess harshness and astringency and tenderizes it. The number of blanchings is not cast in stone. With experience, you may increase or decrease the number to get the tenderness and flavor that you like. Even fruit of the same variety varies in texture, skin thickness, and bitterness, so use my guidelines as you will.)

(CONTINUED)

After the final blanching and draining, use a small sharp knife to scrape only the mushiest part of the white pith (and any fruit left on the peel) gently from the peel, leaving thicker lemon, orange, and grapefruit peels about ¼ inch thick and thinner tangerine or Meyer lemon peels about ⅛ inch thick (thinner skins, in fact, may need little or no scraping). Cut the peel into strips or triangles or whatever shape you like.

Place the peel in a smaller (2-quart) saucepan with 1½ cups water and the sugar. Bring to a simmer, stirring to dissolve the sugar. Wash the syrup and sugar off the sides of the pan with a wet pastry brush or a wad of wet paper towel. Adjust the heat and simmer the peel uncovered, with little or no stirring, very gently until the syrup registers between 220° and 222°F and the peel has been translucent for a few minutes; this will take a little more or less than an hour.

Remove from the heat and use a slotted spoon to transfer the peel to a rack set over a rimmed baking sheet, to catch the syrup drips. Spread the peel out in one layer and let cool and dry overnight.

Dredge the peel in sugar to coat. Stored in an airtight container in the refrigerator, the peel will keep for several months.

quick citrus zest garnish

This is an easy, attractive garnish for fruit salads, compotes, tarts (such as Bittersweet Citrus Tart with Jasmine Cream, page 163), or what have you. Use any organic (or at least unsprayed) citrus. Keep the zest in the fridge ready to drain, and use with or without a sprinkling of sugar. I've done this with regular and blood oranges, grapefruit, lemons, limes, etc.

makes about ⅔ cup

3 bright-skinned (preferably organic or unsprayed) oranges, 5 lemons, 6 limes, or 1 grapefruit

1 cup sugar, plus more for sprinkling if desired

⅔ cup water

USE A VEGETABLE PEELER, pressing firmly, to remove the orange zest in wide strips about 1½ to 2 inches long. Cut into very thin strips, about ⅛ inch wide.

Put the citrus zest in a small saucepan and fill with water. Bring to a boil and boil 5 minutes; drain. Repeat. Return the zest to the saucepan with the sugar and ⅔ cup water and bring to a simmer, stirring until the sugar dissolves. Cover and simmer for about 5 minutes, or until the zest is translucent and tender.

Transfer the zest and syrup to a small bowl. Cover and refrigerate overnight. (The zest can be refrigerated for several weeks.)

Using a slotted spoon, transfer the citrus zest to paper towels to drain before using. Sprinkle with additional sugar, if desired.

the flavors of chocolate

Americans are more knowledge-

able about chocolate and have more choices for eating and cooking with it than ever before. Chocolate, even so-called baking chocolate, is no longer a generic flavor and hardly a rote purchase. Some of us are as fussy about choosing chocolate as we are about selecting cheese, wine, olive oil, or coffee beans. And what fun this is!

Chocolate now comes in myriad strengths (varying percentages of cacao), blends, and styles; scores of cocoas are available. We can buy the European-style hazelnut chocolate called gianduja as well as unsweetened chocolate that is smooth and palatable. Home cooks can even purchase bits of pure roasted cacao beans called nibs. Such richness of choice naturally invites us to create new recipes. But the explosion of new forms and the better quality of chocolate ingredients also beg us to revisit and reinvent all of our old favorites, from cozy chocolate pudding and killer brownies to soufflés and sorbets. Better chocolate *does* make better desserts.

Better chocolate—like all exquisite ingredients—also encourages the cook to taste and refine her or his palate, and to work with simple recipes that honor the ingredient. More than ever, I myself want chocolate desserts with simple clear flavors. When I take a bite of dessert, I want to savor the earthy or roasted nutty flavors, the fruity and floral characteristics, smoky notes, or any nuance that can be tasted in the chocolate itself, whether it's French, Belgian, or American—without distraction or excessive sweetness. The recipes in this chapter, as well as Bittersweet Citrus Tart with Jasmine Cream (163) and Iced Citron Vodka Chocolates with Fresh Mint (243) elsewhere in the book, call for a variety of types of chocolate, used in a variety of ways. As a bonus, most are amazingly simple to make. For more technical information about chocolate, see page 16, and for more personal chocolate chat, see page 156.

new bittersweet brownies

These new brownies have a texture between very moist cake and rich chocolate mousse. One secret is whipping the eggs with the salt; another is using lots of 70% bittersweet chocolate. If you bake in a round rather than a square pan and serve wedges topped with whipped cream (on plates with forks), people will think you made something very fancy indeed.

makes sixteen 2-inch brownies

8 ounces 70% bittersweet chocolate, coarsely chopped

6 tablespoons unsalted butter, cut into several pieces

3 large eggs

1 cup sugar

Scant ¼ teaspoon salt

1 teaspoon pure vanilla extract

⅓ cup plus 1 tablespoon (1.2 ounces) all-purpose flour

EQUIPMENT
An 8-inch square baking pan

POSITION A RACK in the lower third of the oven and preheat the oven to 350°F. Line the bottom and sides of the baking pan with foil.

Place the chocolate and butter in a heatproof bowl and set in a wide skillet of almost-simmering water. Stir frequently until the mixture is melted and smooth and quite warm. Remove from the pan and set aside.

In a medium bowl, beat the eggs, sugar, salt, and vanilla with a hand-held mixer on high speed until the eggs are thick and light colored, about 2 minutes. Whisk in the warm chocolate. Fold in the flour.

Scrape the batter into the lined pan and spread evenly. Bake until a toothpick inserted in the center comes out clean, 25 to 30 minutes. Cool in the pan on a rack.

Invert the brownies on a rack and peel off the foil. Turn right side up on a cutting board and cut into sixteen 2-inch squares.

nibby bittersweet brownies

Stir 2 tablespoons cacao nibs into the batter. Sprinkle 2 more tablespoons cacao nibs over the batter in the pan before baking.

After grating nutmeg for another recipe, I stopped to taste a brownie, still warm from the oven. The aroma of nutmeg from my fingers came on just seconds before the taste of intense bittersweet chocolate. The effect was memorable. The nutmeg enhanced the chocolate flavor without destroying its clarity, as it might have done were the nutmeg actually mixed into the batter. Could one ask guests to handle nutmeg before eating brownies? But simply dusting the brownies with the spice right out of the oven, I found, gave the same effect. You may do the same with freshly grated stick cinnamon, or ground cardamom, or any type of pure ground chile powder. If you live with a brownie purist who doesn't want his or her brownies messed with, set some aside before dusting the rest. For a dinner party, bake in a round pan, and never refer to the dessert as brownies. Serve wedges slightly warm and sprinkle with the spice at the table. Dollop with whipped cream, or (even more exciting) whipped crème fraîche. And you have a sophisticated and seriously sensuous dessert without having defiled any brownies.

my chocolate pudding

This has been my chocolate pudding for close to a decade, with the recent addition of ten seconds in the food processor at the finish. The pudding is a little richer, more bittersweet, and a little less starch-bound than the pudding I grew up with, but it is definitely more pudding than pot de crème or custard. The set is soft and the texture both dense and light. Even when chilled, it "spoons" beautifully, so to speak. The processor step, with my thanks to Dorie Greenspan for a sensational idea, adds a silken dimension and lightness to the texture. You can vary the intensity of the chocolate flavor by choosing a more or less bittersweet chocolate, ranging from 50% cacao on up to 70% or so. You can also increase or decrease the sugar to your taste. Whipped cream on top is very nice.   serves 6 to 8

2 large eggs

⅓ cup sugar

⅓ cup (1.1 ounces) unsweetened cocoa powder (I prefer natural)

2 tablespoons cornstarch

2 pinches of salt

2 cups whole milk

1 teaspoon pure vanilla extract

3 ounces bittersweet or semisweet chocolate (I like to use a 70% bittersweet), chopped medium-fine

EQUIPMENT

Six 4-ounce custard cups or ramekins or 8 smaller cups

SET THE FOOD PROCESSOR near the stove. Have a whisk, a heatproof (silicone) spatula, and a ladle on hand.

In a medium bowl (preferably glass or crockery, because it is heavy and will stay put when you whisk in the hot pudding), whisk the eggs thoroughly. Set the whisk and bowl near the stove.

In a medium heavy saucepan, mix the sugar, cocoa, cornstarch, and salt. Pour about ⅓ cup of the milk into the pan and whisk to make a smooth paste. Whisk in the remaining milk. Heat the milk mixture over medium heat, stirring with the heatproof spatula, until it begins to bubble around the edges. Adjust the heat to maintain a steady low boil and stir constantly for 2 minutes, sweeping the bottom and sides of the pan constantly to avoid scorching. Remove from the heat.

Ladle about 1 cup of the hot mixture gradually over the eggs, whisking constantly to prevent scrambling. Scrape the egg mixture back into the pan and whisk vigorously to blend. Set the pan over low-medium heat and whisk for just 30 seconds, without simmering or boiling, to be sure the eggs are hot enough. Off the heat, add the vanilla and chocolate and whisk until the chocolate is melted.

Scrape the pudding into the processor and process for 10 seconds. Divide the pudding among the cups or ramekins. Let cool and serve, or chill before serving.

cocoa-pecan roll

This rustic-looking roulade is a thin sheet of moist, chocolaty soufflé cake with a hint of toasted pecans rolled up around lightly sweetened whipped cream. The recipe is simple, but be sure to use the best and most aromatic (preferably natural) cocoa powder.

Of course, you can substitute walnuts or almonds or hazelnuts for the pecans, or crème fraîche for the heavy cream. And the cream may be flavored with a splash of rum, brandy, or Scotch. This cake needs no embellishment, but no one ever turned down a handful of fresh berries, or an ice cream roll made by spreading a pint of softened ice cream over the cake, then rolling and freezing it. Serve it with Cocoa Fudge Sauce (page 161) or caramel sauce (see page 227).

serves 10

FOR THE CAKE

⅓ cup (1.5 ounces) pecan halves

1 tablespoon all-purpose flour

½ cup plus ⅓ cup sugar

½ cup (1.63 ounces) unsweetened cocoa powder

⅛ teaspoon salt

4 tablespoons unsalted butter, melted and still hot

2 tablespoons water

½ teaspoon pure vanilla extract

3 large eggs, separated

2 large egg whites

⅛ teaspoon cream of tartar

About 1 tablespoon unsweetened cocoa powder for dusting

FOR THE FILLING

1 cup cold heavy cream

½ teaspoon pure vanilla extract

1½ tablespoons sugar, or to taste

Powdered sugar for dusting (optional)

EQUIPMENT

Rimmed baking sheet or 12 by 16-inch or 11 by 17-inch jelly-roll pan

TO MAKE THE CAKE, position a rack in the lower third of the oven and preheat the oven to 350°F. Spread the nuts on the baking sheet and toast for 5 to 8 minutes, or until fragrant and lightly colored. Transfer the nuts to a plate to cool completely. Line the baking sheet with parchment paper or foil.

Combine the pecans and flour in the bowl of a food processor or a mini processor and pulse until the nuts are finely ground. Set aside.

In a large bowl, combine the ½ cup sugar with the cocoa and salt. Whisk in the hot melted butter, water, and vanilla. Whisk in the egg yolks. Set aside.

In a clean dry mixer bowl, or other large bowl, beat the 5 egg whites and cream of tartar with an electric mixer at medium speed until soft peaks form. Gradually sprinkle in the remaining ⅓ cup sugar, beating at high speed until the whites are stiff but not dry. Fold about one-quarter of the egg whites into the cocoa mixture. Scrape the remaining egg whites on top of the batter, pour the nut mixture over them, and fold just until the egg whites and nuts are incorporated.

Scrape the batter into the lined pan and spread it evenly. Bake until the cake is slightly puffed all over and a toothpick inserted in two or three places emerges clean, about 10 minutes. Cool completely in the pan on a rack.

Use a very fine strainer (I use a tea strainer) to dust the top of the cake evenly with 1 tablespoon of cocoa. Run a knife around the edges of the pan to detach the cake. Cover the cake with a sheet of foil long enough to extend over the ends of the pan. Holding the foil against the edges of the pan, invert the cake, and peel off the pan liner.

To make the filling, in a chilled medium bowl, whip the cream with the vanilla until it begins to thicken. Sprinkle in the sugar and beat until the cream holds a shape but is not completely stiff; it will stiffen further when you spread it.

Spread the cream evenly over the cake. Starting at one short end, use the foil under the cake to help you roll the cake. At first the cake will crack as you roll it— do not worry, the cracking will get less severe as the roulade gets fatter, and a little cracking on the finished roulade ends up looking quite appetizing anyway. Wrap the roulade in the foil and refrigerate until serving time.

To serve, unwrap the roulade and transfer it to a platter. Sift a little more cocoa over it, or sift in a little powdered sugar for contrast. Slice and serve.

gianduja roulade

A thin layer of bittersweet chocolate and toasted hazelnut soufflé cake rolled up around chocolate hazelnut cream. Dreamy, rich, and impressive. serves 10

FOR THE FILLING

6 ounces milk-chocolate-based gianduja, coarsely chopped, or 5 ounces dark-chocolate gianduja

1 cup heavy cream

FOR THE CAKE

⅓ cup (1.5 ounces) hazelnuts (plus a few extra for testing doneness)

2 tablespoons all-purpose flour

6 ounces 70% bittersweet chocolate, coarsely chopped

8 tablespoons (1 stick) unsalted butter, cut into chunks

4 large eggs, separated

⅔ cup sugar

⅛ teaspoon salt

⅛ teaspoon cream of tartar

Cocoa powder for dusting

Powdered sugar for dusting (optional)

EQUIPMENT

Rimmed baking sheet or a 12 by 16-inch or 11 by 17-inch jelly-roll pan

TO MAKE THE FILLING, place the gianduja in a medium bowl. Bring the cream to a simmer and pour it over the gianduja. Stir until the gianduja is completely melted. Cover and chill the mixture until very cold, 4 hours or more.

To make the cake, position a rack in the center of the oven and preheat the oven to 350°F.

Spread the nuts in a baking pan or pie pan and toast until flavorful and golden brown in the center, 10 to 15 minutes. Cool completely, then rub off the loose skins. Line the baking sheet or jelly-roll pan with parchment paper.

Combine the nuts with the flour in a clean food processor (or mini processor) bowl, and pulse until the nuts are finely ground. Set aside.

Combine the chocolate and butter in a large heatproof bowl, set it in a wide skillet of barely simmering water, and stir occasionally until the mixture is melted and smooth. Off the heat, stir in the egg yolks, ⅓ cup of the sugar, and the salt.

In a clean dry mixer or other large bowl, beat the egg whites and cream of tartar with a stand mixer on medium speed until soft peaks form. Gradually sprinkle in the remaining ⅓ cup sugar, and continue beating at high speed until the whites are stiff but not dry.

Use a rubber spatula to fold about one-quarter of the egg whites into the chocolate mixture. Scrape the remaining egg whites into the bowl, pour the nut mixture over them, and fold until no streaks remain.

Spread the batter evenly in the prepared pan. Bake until a toothpick inserted into the center of the cake comes out just clean, 8 to 10 minutes. Cool completely in the pan on a rack.

Sift a light dusting of cocoa over the top of the cake. Run a knife around the edges of the pan to detach the cake. Cover the cake with a sheet of foil long enough to extend over the ends of the pan. Holding the foil against the edges of the pan, invert the cake, and peel off the pan liner.

Whip the gianduja cream until it thickens and holds its shape. Spread the cream evenly over the cake (if it is so stiff it tears the cake, spread it with a warmed spatula). Starting at one short side, roll the cake, using the foil to help you. At first the cake will crack as you roll it—do not worry, the cracking will get less severe as the roulade gets fatter, and a little cracking on the finished roulade looks quite appetizing anyway. Wrap the roulade in the foil and refrigerate for at least 2 hours, or until firm.

To serve, unwrap the roulade and slide it onto a platter. Sift a little more cocoa over it, and, if desired, a little powdered sugar for contrast. Slice and serve.

nutty chocolate sponge cake

If you normally consider sponge cakes dry and flavorless, this one will turn your head. It's exceedingly moist and light, with plenty of rich flavor from nuts and ground bitter-sweet chocolate. It may sound similar to the Italian Chocolate-Almond Torte (page 148), but the texture is much lighter (both are exquisite). Use walnuts, pecans, almonds, or toasted hazelnuts with the skins rubbed off. Although this was originally a Passover recipe, I've always considered it too good to be limited to a holiday that not everyone celebrates. Why shouldn't a spectacular chocolate nut torte be as popular as bagels? I tried to "secularize" the recipe by substituting flour for the matzo meal and the starch, but the result lacked finesse—it was a tad heavy and damp rather than moist and light. So it's matzo meal or plain crackers pulverized in your food processor (which is essentially what matzo meal is) with one of several starch choices. Matzo meal is available in large supermarkets. You can use the rest of the box to bread a pork chop or a piece of fish—or to make the torte several more times.

serves 10 to 12

1 cup whole almonds blanched or unblanched (5 ounces) or walnuts (4 ounces)

2 tablespoons cracker meal, such as matzo meal or pulverized unsalted saltines, water biscuits, cream crackers, or plain matzo

2 tablespoons potato starch, rice flour, or cornstarch

5 to 6 ounces bittersweet or semisweet chocolate, coarsely chopped

Grated zest of 1 medium orange, preferably organic or unsprayed

9 large eggs, separated, at room temperature

1 cup sugar

⅛ teaspoon salt

Rounded ¼ teaspoon cream of tartar

Powdered sugar for dusting

EQUIPMENT

A 9- or 10-inch plain tube pan, preferably with a removable bottom

POSITION A RACK in the lower third of the oven and preheat the oven to 350°F. If the pan does not have a removable bottom, line the bottom with parchment paper, or grease the bottom only and dust with flour.

Combine the nuts, cracker meal, starch, chopped chocolate, and orange zest in a food processor and pulse until most of the nuts are finely ground (some can be coarser). Set aside.

In the bowl of a stand mixer or use a hand mixer and a small bowl, beat the egg yolks with ½ cup of the sugar and the salt until very thick and pale yellow. Scrape the yolks into another large bowl. Wash the beaters and mixer bowl and dry them.

In the clean bowl, beat the egg whites and cream of tartar until soft peaks form when the beaters are lifted. Gradually, add the remaining ½ cup sugar and beat until the peaks are stiff but not dry when the beaters are lifted. Scrape half of the egg whites on top of the yolks, pour half of the nut mixture on top, and use a large rubber spatula to fold in until almost completely incorporated. Repeat with the remaining egg whites and nuts, folding just until incorporated.

Scrape the batter into the tube pan and spread it evenly. Bake until the cake springs back when lightly pressed and a wooden skewer inserted into the center comes out clean, 40 to 45 minutes. Cool the cake in the pan (right side up) on a wire rack for 10 minutes.

Slide a slim knife or small metal spatula around the sides of the cake to detach it from the pan, pressing against the pan sides to avoid tearing the cake. Then detach the cake from the tube with a knife or a metal skewer. Let the cake cool completely in the pan on the rack.

If the pan sides are not removable, invert the cake onto a wire rack or a serving platter and remove the parchment liner if you used one. Otherwise, pull up on the tube to lift the cake from the pan sides, and slide the knife under the cake and around the tube to detach it. Transfer the cake to a serving platter. Serve the cake right side up or upside down—whichever looks best to you—sprinkled with powdered sugar.

NOTE: If you *are* making this torte for Passover, use matzo meal or matzo cake meal and potato starch. If dusting the bottom of the pan, use matzo meal. Omit the cream of tartar if you are strict about ingredients that can be considered leaveners, although in this recipe the cream of tartar is not used as leavening per se. To stabilize the egg whites without cream of tartar, begin adding the sugar to the egg whites a little earlier than usual—when the egg whites are white and foamy but have not started to stiffen. Continue beating as described.

Italian chocolate-almond torte

torta cioccolata

The soul of simplicity, this jewel of a chocolate dessert was inspired by Claudia Roden's *torta di mandorle e cioccolata* in her magnificent *Book of Jewish Food.* The torte is rich and quite sophisticated, yet simple to make. Lots of ground, rather than melted, unsweetened chocolate and plenty of almonds folded into egg whites (no yolks) produce a uniquely moist, rich torte with a nutty texture but without the dense heaviness you might expect.

serves 10

1 cup (5 ounces) unblanched or blanched whole almonds

7 ounces good-quality unsweetened chocolate, roughly chopped

1 cup sugar

⅛ teaspoon salt

7 large egg whites (1 cup)

¼ teaspoon cream of tartar

Powdered sugar or unsweetened cocoa powder for dusting

Sweetened whipped cream for serving (optional)

EQUIPMENT

A 9-inch springform pan or a 9 by 3-inch round pan with a removable bottom

POSITION A RACK in the lower third of the oven and preheat the oven to 350°F. Grease the sides of the springform pan and line the bottom with parchment paper.

Combine the almonds, chocolate, ½ cup of the sugar, and the salt in a food processor and pulse until the almonds and chocolate are very finely chopped but not completely pulverized. Set aside.

In the clean dry bowl of a stand mixer or using a hand-held mixer and a large bowl, beat the egg whites with cream of tarter until soft, moist peaks are formed when the beaters are lifted. Gradually add the remaining ½ cup sugar and continue to beat until the egg whites are stiff but not dry. Add one-third of the nut mixture to the egg whites and fold in with a large rubber spatula until nearly incorporated. Fold in half of the remaining nuts, then fold in the rest of the nuts.

Scrape the batter into the prepared pan and spread it evenly. Bake until the torte has risen and is golden brown on top and a toothpick inserted in the center of the cake comes out clean, or with a little melted chocolate, 25 to 30 minutes. Set the pan on a rack to cool for 10 minutes. Remove the sides of the pan and invert the cake onto the rack. Remove the bottom of the pan and then the parchment liner. Turn the cake right side up and cool completely. Cover or wrap tightly, and store for up to 3 days at room temperature.

To serve, transfer the cake to a serving plate. Dust with powdered sugar or cocoa, and serve slices with a dollop of whipped cream, if desired.

nibby ice cream

An infusion of cacao nibs in cream produces a unique ice cream with the subtle evocative flavors of unrefined cacao. Lightly sweetened and balanced with milk, the result is slightly icy, not too rich, and very refreshing. This recipe remains one of my favorite simple recipes from my book *BitterSweet: Recipes and Tales from a Life in Chocolate.*

makes about 3½ cups

1½ cups heavy cream
1½ cups whole milk
⅓ cup cacao nibs
½ cup sugar

⅛ teaspoon salt

EQUIPMENT
Ice cream machine

BRING THE CREAM, milk, nibs, sugar, and salt to a simmer in a medium saucepan over medium heat. Remove from the heat, cover, and let steep for 20 minutes.

Pour the cream mixture through a fine strainer, pressing on the nibs to extract their liquid; discard the nibs. Refrigerate at least 4 but preferably 12 hours.

For an extra-cold start, put the mixture in the freezer for 20 minutes, stirring once or twice to prevent freezing. Freeze the mixture according to the instructions on your ice cream maker.

Serve soft or transfer to an airtight container and freeze until the ice cream is hard enough to scoop, at least 3 to 4 hours. If the ice cream gets too hard, before serving let it stand for a few minutes, put it in the refrigerator for 15 minutes or longer, or micro-wave it on low (defrost) for a few seconds at a time until scoopable.

chocolate sorbet

Use the best cocoa you can find for this exquisite sorbet. It is packed with intense bittersweet chocolate flavor. I also make it with raspberry vodka instead of rum, or with no liquor at all. For a more "gently" flavored chocolate-sherbet effect, make the base with only 1 cup of water and add 1 cup milk along with the vanilla.

Prolonged heat can damage the flavor of good cocoa—cook the cocoa mixture only until it begins to simmer at the edges, no more.

makes 1 quart

1 cup (3.25 ounces) unsweetened cocoa powder

Scant 1 cup sugar

2 tiny pinches of salt

2 cups boiling water

¼ teaspoon pure vanilla extract

1½ tablespoons rum (optional)

EQUIPMENT

Ice cream machine

COMBINE THE COCOA, sugar, and salt in a heavy 3-quart saucepan, and whisk in about ½ cup of the boiling water to form a thick paste. Whisk in the remaining water. Stir the mixture over medium heat until tiny bubbles start to appear around the edges of the pan. Remove from the heat and stir in the vanilla. Transfer to a bowl, cover, and refrigerate until cold, at least 4 hours. Just before freezing the sorbet, stir in the rum, if using. For an extra-cold start, put the mixture in the freezer for 20 minutes, stirring once or twice to prevent freezing. Freeze according to the instructions for your ice cream machine.

Serve soft or transfer to an airtight container and freeze until hard enough to scoop, at least 3 to 4 hours. If the sorbet gets too hard, before serving let it stand for a few minutes, put it in the refrigerator for 15 minutes or longer, or microwave it on low (defrost) for a few seconds at a time until scoopable.

milk chocolate sorbet

Is it sorbet or is it ice cream? It's made with water, but the chocolate itself is rich and loaded with milk, so the results are creamy, yet icily cold like sorbet. You decide. The essential flavor comes from the milk chocolate, so choose one that you really love. This very simple recipe invites creative variations. Substitute strong coffee for the water, or add cinnamon or other spices. Or concoct a sundae with caramel sauce (see page 227) flavored with nutmeg or cardamom or Raw Sugar Toffee Sauce (page 185), and top with pecans or salted peanuts and whipped cream.

makes 4 cups

1 pound milk chocolate, coarsely chopped

1½ ounces good-quality unsweetened chocolate, coarsely chopped

2¼ cups boiling water

EQUIPMENT

Inversion (stick) blender or regular blender or food processor

Ice cream machine

COMBINE THE CHOCOLATES in a medium bowl. Pour the boiling water over the chocolate and wait for 30 seconds, then stir until the chocolate is melted and smooth. Blend with the inversion blender for 1 minute, or use a regular blender or food processor (see Note). Cool to room temperature (do not chill).

Freeze the sorbet according to the instructions for your ice cream machine.

Serve soft or transfer to an airtight container and freeze until hard enough to scoop, at least 3 to 4 hours. If the sorbet gets too hard, before serving let it stand for a few minutes, put it in the refrigerator for 15 minutes or longer, or microwave it on low (defrost) for a few seconds at a time until scoopable.

gianduja sorbet

Substitute milk-chocolate-based gianduja for the milk chocolate in the recipe.

NOTE: The blending step homogenizes the ingredients and produces a noticeably smoother sorbet with a fuller and more resonant flavor.

gianduja soufflés

Gianduja lovers will delight in these sophisticated soufflés with a rich hazelnut-chocolate flavor. You can prepare the soufflés ahead and chill them, then simply bake before serving.

serves 6

10 ounces milk-chocolate-based gianduja

4 large eggs, separated,
at room temperature

¼ cup (1.5 ounces) all-purpose flour

⅛ teaspoon salt

1 cup whole milk

½ teaspoon pure vanilla extract

¼ teaspoon cream of tartar

2 tablespoons plus 2 teaspoons sugar

EQUIPMENT

Six 6-ounce ramekins or custard cups

Baking sheet

BUTTER AND SUGAR the ramekins.

Using the coarse holes of a box grater, grate and set aside 2 ounces of the gianduja. Coarsely chop the remaining gianduja and set it aside (it is used first).

Put the egg yolks in a medium bowl near the stove, and have a rubber spatula at hand.

In a small heavy saucepan, combine the flour and salt. Whisk in just enough of the milk to make a smooth paste, then whisk in the remaining milk. Cook over medium heat, whisking constantly, until the mixture has the consistency of a medium-thick cream sauce, 2 to 3 minutes. Gradually whisk about ¼ cup of the hot sauce into the egg yolks to warm them up, so they won't scramble. Scrape the yolks back into the saucepan and cook for a minute or two, whisking constantly, to make a thick pastry cream. With a rubber spatula, scrape the pastry cream into the egg bowl. Add the chopped gianduja and stir until it is completely melted and incorporated into the pastry cream. Stir in the vanilla. Set aside.

In a clean dry mixer bowl or other large bowl, combine the egg whites with the cream of tartar. Beat at medium speed in a stand mixer (at high speed if using a hand-held mixer) until soft peaks form when the beaters are lifted. Gradually sprinkle in the sugar and beat until the whites are stiff but not dry. Fold one-quarter of the egg whites into the pastry cream. Fold in the remaining egg whites with the grated gianduja, just until incorporated.

Divide the mixture among the ramekins. If you are not baking right away, chill until ready to bake, up to several hours.

Position a rack in the lower third of the oven and preheat the oven to 375°F.

Put the ramekins on a baking sheet and bake for 16 to 18 minutes, until the soufflés are puffed and cracked on the top and a toothpick inserted in the center emerges coated with thick moist batter. Serve immediately.

nutella bread pudding

This was something of an accident. I didn't intend to fuel the current frenzy for Nutella, but I ran out of chocolate filling for the bread pudding I was trying to make and I needed a stand-in for the visual effect. I substituted the you-know-what just because it was the right color. It was the best move of the day. You will love it.　　serves 6 to 8

Enough ¼-inch slices of home-style or bakery white bread or baguette, with or without the crusts, to cover the bottom of an 8-inch square baking dish, not too tightly, with 2 layers of bread

¼ to ⅓ cup Nutella

5 large eggs

½ cup sugar

Scant ⅛ teaspoon salt

1¼ cups milk

1¼ cups heavy cream

EQUIPMENT

An 8-inch square baking dish

POSITION A RACK in the lower third of the oven. Preheat the oven to 325°F. Put the bread in the bottom of the baking dish to make sure you have sliced enough to make two layers.

Remove the bread from the dish. If the bread is fresh, lay slices on a baking sheet and bake for 5 minutes on each side, or until very lightly toasted. Let the slices cool.

Spread one side of each slice of bread with Nutella. Cut or break large whole slices (not baguette slices) into 4 pieces each. Arrange the bread, Nutella side facing up, in the baking dish in one layer of overlapping pieces, with rounded crusts or trimmed angles showing attractively.

In a medium bowl, whisk the eggs, sugar, and salt together. Gradually whisk in the milk and cream. Pour the egg mixture through a strainer into the baking dish. Cover the pudding with plastic wrap and press any floating bread pieces back into the egg mixture. Let stand for at least 15 minutes to allow the bread to absorb the liquid.

Preheat the oven to 325°F. Put a kettle of water on to boil.

Uncover the pudding and place it in a baking pan large enough to hold it with a little space on all sides, and then into the oven. Pull the oven rack out and carefully pour enough boiling water into the large pan to come halfway up the sides of the baking dish. Bake until a knife inserted into the pudding comes out free of custard (or with a little Nutella clinging to it), 50 to 55 minutes. Cool for at least 1 hour.

Serve the pudding warm or at room temperature. Cold leftover pudding is divine, but you could also reheat it in the microwave on medium power for a few seconds.

I'm a constant nibbler of chocolate. I often eat a little piece of a chocolate bar instead of dessert just to savor the intense and subtle flavors without distraction from other ingredients, and to enjoy the remarkable choice of chocolates that we didn't have even ten years ago. As for whether the best chocolate is blended from a variety of beans or made from a single source of beans, let us hope the ongoing debate is never resolved. Let producers continue to give us even better chocolates to justify their arguments!

Some forms of chocolate—like cacao nibs, chocolate with varying percentages of cacao, the newest unsweetened chocolates, and gianduja—are still relatively unfamiliar to American chocolate lovers and cooks.

Nibs, bits of roasted hulled cacao beans, were barely on the radar screen of professional chefs only a few years ago. While experimenting for a 1998 article in *Pastry Arts & Design*, I invented a salad with cacao nibs for a luncheon meeting of the American Institute of Food and Wine. That may have been the first salad with cacao nibs ever served—regardless, the salad inspired me to create more savory and sweet recipes using nibs. It was fun, but futile at the time since home cooks could not buy nibs. So I suggested that the owners of Scharffen Berger Chocolate Maker package cacao nibs for sale, and they did. I then had a close call in 2003, just before the publication of my book *BitterSweet: Recipes and Tales from a Life in Chocolate,* with an entire chapter of nibby recipes: John Scharffenberger casually mentioned that he was discontinuing the sale of nibs because sales were slow. To my immense relief, John got busy with other projects and forgot about the nibs. Lucky! Today sweet and savory dishes with cacao nibs—salads included—are found on restaurant menus and recipes using them appear in food magazines. The crunchy little nuggets of roasted cacao beans with a wallop of chocolate flavor have become a cult ingredient. See Nibby Cocoa Wafers (page 166), Nibby Bittersweet Brownies (page 138), and the Nibby Whole Wheat Sablés (page 89), where their earthy flavor perfectly complements the nutty flavor of stone-ground whole wheat with hazelnuts and currants. And don't forget to sprinkle some nibs on your salad.

The *newest* unsweetened chocolate bars (sometimes labeled 99% or 100% cacao) are also exciting and are a far cry from the harsh, gritty squares that made us gag and grimace as children when we sneaked a taste of baking chocolate. The new unsweetened chocolate is processed like fine eating chocolate: it is conched until smooth and palatable enough to nibble pleasurably. Like espresso, this is an acquired taste but also an opportunity to rethink the use of unsweetened chocolate. Now we can flaunt the flavor and quality of good unsweetened chocolate by folding bits or even great chunks of it into cakes, soufflés, and cookies rather than always disguising it with oceans of sugar and melting and blending it into batters.

In fact, incorporating ground or chopped rather than melted chocolate in a recipe is an underused tool in the cook's arsenal. With it, we can add layers of flavor and create more textures as well. Of course, adding pieces of chocolate to a dough or batter is nothing new—that's what chocolate chips are made for. But the technique deserves to be used in more ways, with more types of chocolate. I often avoid packaged chips and chop my own from a variety of different chocolates, because I love all the choices these offer. Like chips and chunks, pulverized bits of chocolate remain intact after baking and cooling, making it possible to pack a huge amount of chocolate flavor into a cake, or cookie, or soufflé without adding significant density to the final product. For the Italian Chocolate-Almond Torte, (page 148), I grind a full 7 ounces of unsweetened chocolate to the size of coarse bread crumbs and fold it into an airy batter, where it adds intense flavor while leaving the torte light and moist, rather than heavy and dense. Ground chocolate also enhances crunchy Extra-Bittersweet Cocoa Wafers (page 166), Nutty Chocolate Sponge Cake (page 146), and Gianduja Soufflés (page 153).

Gianduja? Europeans have been savoring this unctuous marriage of chocolate and toasted hazelnuts for generations. Thirty years ago, when I opened my dessert shop Cocolat, hazelnut desserts appealed only to our European clientele and the most sophisticated American customers. But, sparked perhaps by the recent Nutella rage, America now loves hazelnuts with chocolate. Unlike Nutella, gianduja resembles a bar of chocolate. It is softer to the tooth than a plain chocolate bar (because of the oil from the hazelnuts), and it melts smooth and rich on the tongue. Its intense hazelnut and chocolate flavor is deeper, more lingering, and less sweet than that of Nutella. Bite into a warm baguette split and stuffed with chunks of gianduja, and you will be a convert. Keep a bar of gianduja in your desk drawer for nibbling, and another in your cupboard for desserts. Try Gianduja Sorbet (page 152), Gianduja Soufflés (page 153), and Gianduja Roulade (page 144)—and don't miss the divine, but accidental (really), Nutella Bread Pudding (page 154).

I continue to find that the taste of chocolate is not just one, but many tastes. And I remain convinced that the best chocolate recipes are those that are simple enough to let the chocolate shine forth with all of its flavor and nuance. Happily, what's best for the chocolate also makes life simpler for the cook.

white chocolate soufflé cakes with fresh berries

Not so tall as a classic soufflé, but far more flavorful, these little white chocolate soufflé cakes could be savored with no embellishment at all, but they are transformed with a handful of sugared raspberries (or blackberries) in the bottom of each cup. Magically, you get the enticing counterpoint of hot berries with their tart, sweet juices beneath warm white chocolate. Do try the spectacular molten variations with their hidden sauces of warm bittersweet chocolate infused with orange or raspberry.

All of these soufflés can be prepared several hours in advance and baked at the last minute.

serves 6

36 raspberries or small blackberries

3 tablespoons sugar, plus extra to coat the ramekins

3 large eggs, separated, at room temperature

3 tablespoons all-purpose flour

3 pinches of salt

¾ cup whole milk

6 ounces white chocolate, finely chopped

Scant ½ teaspoon pure vanilla extract

Scant ¼ teaspoon cream of tartar

EQUIPMENT

Six 6-ounce ramekins or custard cups

Baking sheet

BUTTER AND SUGAR the ramekins. Put 6 berries in the bottom of each one and sprinkle with ½ teaspoon of the sugar. Set aside.

Put the egg yolks in a medium bowl near the stove. Have a wire whisk and a heat-proof silicone or rubber spatula at hand.

In a small heavy saucepan, combine the flour and salt. Whisk in just enough of the milk to make a smooth paste, then whisk in the remaining milk. Cook over medium heat, whisking constantly, until the mixture has the consistency of a medium-thick cream sauce, 2 to 3 minutes. Gradually whisk about ¼ cup of the hot sauce into the egg yolks to warm them up, so they won't scramble. With the spatula, scrape the yolk mixture back into the saucepan and cook for a minute or two, whisking constantly, to make a thick pastry cream. Scrape the pastry cream into the yolk bowl. Add the white chocolate and stir until it is completely melted and incorporated into the pastry cream. Stir in the vanilla.

In a clean dry mixer bowl or other large bowl, combine the egg whites and cream of tartar. Beat at medium speed in a stand mixer (at high speed if using a hand-held mixer) until soft peaks form when the beaters are lifted. Gradually sprinkle in the remaining 2 tablespoons sugar and beat until the whites are stiff but not dry. Fold one-quarter of the egg whites into the pastry cream. Fold in the remaining egg whites just until incorporated.

Divide the mixture among the ramekins. If you are not baking right away, chill until ready to bake, up to several hours.

Position a rack in the lower third of the oven and preheat the oven to 375°F. Put the soufflés on a baking sheet and bake for 18 minutes, or until they are puffed and golden brown on top—they should still quiver when tapped and seem soft in the center. Serve immediately, or allow to cool and settle for a few minutes and then serve.

white chocolate soufflé cakes with chocolate-orange sauce

Lots of extra drama for just a few extra steps—here are the same sweet vanilla-scented soufflés with an unexpected molten heart of orange and bittersweet chocolate.

To make the sauce, place a dinner plate or Pyrex pie pan in the freezer to chill. Combine 3 ounces bittersweet or semisweet chocolate (no more than 62% cacao), chopped; 2 tablespoons unsalted butter; 2 tablespoons fresh, preferably organic orange juice; and 1 teaspoon sugar in a medium heatproof bowl, set it in a skillet of barely simmering water, and melt the chocolate and butter, stirring frequently until smooth. Remove from the heat and stir in 1 teaspoon Grand Marnier and ¼ teaspoon gently packed, finely grated orange zest, preferably from an organic or unsprayed fruit. Taste the mixture to adjust the sweetness with pinches of extra sugar if you think it necessary, stirring well to make sure that the sugar is dissolved. Scrape the mixture into a puddle on the chilled plate and freeze for 10 minutes or so, until firm. When the chocolate mixture is firm, use a teaspoon or a tiny scoop to scrape it into 6 large "truffles" (they need not be perfectly round). Refrigerate until needed. Omit the raspberries and sugar in the bottom of each ramekin, and make the soufflé mixture as directed. Divide the mixture among the ramekins and chill until ready to bake.

When ready to bake, spoon up a heaping teaspoon of batter from the center of the top of one soufflé; place a truffle in the depression, and cover it with the spoonful of batter. Repeat with the remaining soufflés. Bake and serve as directed.

white chocolate soufflé cakes with chocolate-raspberry sauce

Follow the instructions for White Chocolate Soufflé Cakes with Chocolate-Orange Sauce, substituting 2 tablespoons strained raspberry puree (made from fresh or thawed frozen unsweetened berries) and 1 teaspoon raspberry eau-de-vie (eau-de-vie framboise), raspberry vodka, or kirsch for the orange juice and Grand Marnier. Increase the sugar to 2 teaspoons, or more to taste, and omit the orange zest.

raspberry–chocolate chunk muffins

I fed hundreds of these rather elegant muffins to my daughter's rowing team carpool during her freshman year of high school. Fourteen-year-old "women" rowers come off the lake hungry. Ironically, in spite of the whole wheat flour, these sensational muffins are more delicate than they are he-man hearty. The girls each simply had to devour two or three of them while driving from the lake to first-period classes. The key to greatness? The raspberries go into the batter frozen (even if you start with fresh berries) to prevent them from overcooking while the muffins bake. And chocolate chips are fine, but a bar of great chocolate cut into chunks easily raises the standard. Don't pass up the muffins for lack of fourteen-year-olds—they (the muffins) are divine for a fancy brunch.   makes 12 muffins

1½ cups (6.75 ounces) all-purpose flour

½ cup (2.25 ounces) whole wheat flour

1 tablespoon baking powder

½ teaspoon salt

¼ teaspoon freshly grated nutmeg

2 large eggs

Scant ⅔ cup sugar

1 cup whole or 1% low-fat milk

5 tablespoons unsalted butter, melted and still warm

5 to 6 ounces frozen fresh raspberries or individually quick frozen raspberries (see Note)

4 ounces semisweet or bittersweet chocolate, chopped into little chunks, or ⅔ cup chocolate chips

EQUIPMENT

Muffin pan with 12 cups

Pleated paper muffin liners

POSITION A RACK in the lower third of the oven and preheat the oven to 400°F. Line the muffin tin with pleated paper liners.

In a medium bowl, thoroughly mix the flours, baking powder, salt, and nutmeg. Set aside.

In another bowl, whisk the eggs and sugar together. Whisk in the milk and butter. Pour the wet mixture over the flour mixture and fold gently until all of the dry ingredients are moistened but the batter is still very lumpy and uneven. Dump the frozen berries and the chocolate into the bowl and fold just until they are distributed throughout the batter. Do not try to create a smooth, homogeneous-looking batter, or your muffins will be tough.

Divide the batter among muffin cups. Bake until a toothpick inserted into the cakey part of a muffin emerges free of batter (other than a little melted chocolate or raspberries), 15 to 18 minutes. Cool on a rack.

Enjoy the muffins warm or at room temperature.

NOTE: If using fresh berries, spread the picked-over berries on a tray and place in the freezer until frozen. (If not using them right away, transfer to a freezer bag and freeze until needed.) Or buy unsweetened "individually quick frozen" raspberries from the grocery store. Keep the raspberries in the freezer until the moment they are needed.

cocoa fudge sauce

My favorite chocolate sauce is actually made with superb cocoa, which gives it extra big chocolate flavor. It's divine over ice cream, but it can also be cooled and used to frost a cake or cookies.

makes 1½ cups

½ cup (1.625 ounces) unsweetened cocoa powder (I prefer natural)

½ cup sugar

A pinch of salt

½ cup heavy cream

3 tablespoons unsalted butter, cut into bits

½ teaspoon pure vanilla extract (optional)

PLACE THE COCOA, sugar, and salt in a medium saucepan. Stir in just enough of the cream to make a smooth thick paste, then stir in the rest of the cream and add the butter pieces. Stir over low heat until the butter is melted and the sauce is smooth and hot but not simmering. Taste and add the vanilla, if desired. Spoon the warm sauce over ice cream. Or, for frosting, cool until spreadable.

The sauce keeps in a covered container in the refrigerator for a week, or it can be frozen for up to 3 months and thawed in the microwave or at room temperature. To reheat, put the sauce in a heatproof bowl set in a wide skillet of barely simmering water, and stir occasionally until the sauce is the desired consistency. Or microwave on medium power, using short bursts and stirring frequently. Do not allow the sauce to simmer or boil.

NOTE: Cocoas vary. Taste and adjust with sugar if the sauce tastes too harsh or bitter, or tone down the intensity with a little extra butter or cream.

bittersweet citrus tart
with jasmine cream

The subtle citrus notes in this dark chocolate tart come from pink grapefruit and blood orange zest. The flavor and scent of jasmine-infused cream adds an exotic sensuality to an easy but elegant dinner party dessert.   serves 10 to 12

FOR THE TOPPING

1 cup heavy cream

1 tablespoon good-quality jasmine tea
(I use Yin Hao or Jasmine Downy Pearls)

2 teaspoons sugar, or more to taste

FOR THE CRUST

8 tablespoons (1 stick) unsalted butter, melted

¼ cup sugar

¾ teaspoon pure vanilla extract

⅛ teaspoon salt

1 cup (4.5 ounces) all-purpose flour

FOR THE FILLING

8 ounces bittersweet or semisweet chocolate (see Note), finely chopped

5 tablespoons unsalted butter, cut into small pieces

½ teaspoon very lightly packed grated blood (or regular) orange zest, preferably from an organic or unsprayed fruit

½ teaspoon very lightly packed pink grapefruit zest, preferably from an organic or unsprayed fruit

1 large egg yolk, at room temperature

¼ cup boiling water

Quick Citrus Zest Garnish
(page 133) or Candied Citrus Peel
(page 131) for garnish (optional)

EQUIPMENT

A 9½-inch round or a 4 by 14-inch rectangular fluted tart pan with a removable bottom

Instant-read thermometer

Pastry bag and tip (optional)

MAKE THE COLD TEA INFUSION for the topping early in the day or a day ahead. Stir the cream and tea leaves together in a bowl. Cover and chill for 8 to 12 hours. Even if you are not using the cream right away, strain the tea out and discard it after 12 hours. Refrigerate the cream until needed.

To make the crust, position a rack in the lower third of the oven and preheat the oven to 350°F.

In a medium bowl, combine the melted butter with the sugar, vanilla, and salt. Add the flour and mix just until well blended. If the dough seems too soft, let it stand for 5 minutes to firm up.

Press the dough evenly across the bottom and up the sides of the tart pan; to avoid ending up with extra-thick edges, press the dough squarely into the corners of the pan. Place the pan on a cookie sheet and bake until the crust is a deep golden brown, 20 to 25 minutes; press it down with the back of a spoon or prick it with a fork if it bubbles up. Let cool completely on a rack before making the filling.

(CONTINUED)

To make the filling, place the chocolate, butter, and citrus zest in a small heatproof bowl (stainless steel is best), set it in a wide skillet of not-quite-simmering water, and stir frequently until the chocolate and butter are completely melted and smooth. Remove the bowl, set a fine strainer over it, and set aside. Leave the skillet over low heat.

Place the egg yolk in a small bowl and gradually whisk in the boiling water. Place the egg bowl in the skillet and stir constantly with a silicone spatula, sweeping the bottom of the bowl to prevent the egg from cooking, until the mixture registers 160°F on the instant-read thermometer. Remove the bowl from the skillet and immediately scrape the yolk mixture into the strainer set over the bowl of chocolate. Stir gently, without whisking or beating, just until the egg is incorporated completely into the chocolate and the mixture is smooth (except for the bits of zest).

Pour the filling into the cooled tart shell and spread it evenly. Place in a covered container (or cover with an inverted bowl if you don't have an appropriate container), and refrigerate at least until the filling is set (3 to 4 hours), or up to 2 days.

About 30 minutes before serving, remove the tart from the refrigerator, to soften the filling and bring back its sheen. Remove the pan sides, and place the tart on a platter.

Whip the jasmine-infused cream until thickened. Add the sugar (you want the cream only gently sweetened so that the sweetness doesn't overpower the subtle flavor of the jasmine and the tea) and whip until it holds a soft shape, or a little stiffer if you plan to pipe the cream.

Using a pastry bag, decorate the tart with the jasmine cream or serve plain wedges with dollops of cream. If desired, add the citrus zest garnish or candied peel.

NOTE: If you use chocolate that exceeds 62% cacao, the recipe must be adjusted as follows: Use only 6 ounces chocolate marked 64% to 66%; use only 5½ ounces chocolate marked 66% to 72% and dissolve 1 to 2 teaspoons sugar in the boiling water before adding it to the egg yolk.

cocoa wafers

Ages ago I developed a simple, crisp, "plain" chocolate wafer made with cocoa, perfect with a dish of ice cream or a cup of coffee. I've packed them into lunch boxes, made icebox cakes with them, and smashed them up for cheesecake crusts. But new ideas and changes in the quality of ingredients periodically send me back to the drawing board to reinvent even my favorite recipes. The cookies are now better than ever: superbly crisp yet tender, with exceptional cocoa flavor. They are not too sweet and not too rich. Clarity of flavor came with editing out the eggs in the original and extra tender crispness came with the inclusion of a little milk. Please use a superior type of cocoa powder.

makes fifty to sixty 1¾-inch wafers

1½ cups (6.75 ounces)
all-purpose flour (see Note)

¾ cup (2.4 ounces) unsweetened
cocoa powder (I prefer natural)

1 cup plus 2 tablespoons sugar

¼ teaspoon salt

¼ teaspoon baking soda

14 tablespoons (1¾ sticks)
unsalted butter, slightly softened

3 tablespoons whole milk

1 teaspoon pure vanilla extract

EQUIPMENT

Baking sheets

COMBINE THE FLOUR, cocoa, sugar, salt, and baking soda in the bowl of food processor and pulse several times to mix thoroughly. Cut the butter into about 12 chunks and add them to the bowl. Pulse several times. Combine the milk and vanilla in a small cup. With the processor running, add the milk mixture and continue to process until the mixture clumps around the blade or the sides of the bowl. Transfer the dough to a large bowl or a cutting board and knead a few times to make sure it is evenly blended.

Form the dough into a log about 14 inches long and 1¾ inches in diameter. Wrap the log in wax paper or foil and refrigerate until firm, at least 1 hour, or until needed.

Position the racks in the upper and lower thirds of the oven and preheat the oven to 350°F. Line the baking sheets with parchment paper. Cut the log of dough into slices a scant ¼ inch thick and place them 1 inch apart on the lined sheets. Bake, rotating the baking sheet from top to bottom and back to front about halfway through baking, for 12 to 15 minutes. The cookies will puff up and deflate; they are done about 1½ minutes after they deflate. Cool the cookies on the baking sheets on racks, or slide the parchment onto racks to cool completely (see Note). The cookies may be stored airtight for up to 2 weeks or frozen up to 2 months.

NOTE: These cookies should crisp up as they cool. If they don't, you are not baking them long enough—in which case, return them to the oven to reheat and bake a little longer, then cool again.

nibby cocoa wafers

Bits of roasted cacao beans add extra chocolate intensity and a nutty texture.

Add ⅓ cup cacao nibs after pulsing in the butter.

extra-bittersweet cocoa wafers

Finely ground unsweetened chocolate makes extra-flavorful wafers. I like them completely crisp, which takes a little more time after cooling, because the bits of ground chocolate have to harden again. Otherwise the cookies are a little chewy, and also delicious.

In the bowl of a food processor, combine 1½ ounces of good-quality unsweetened chocolate with half of the sugar called for in the recipe. Pulse until the chocolate bits are the size of sesame seeds. Add the remaining sugar, the flour, cocoa, salt, and baking soda, and pulse to mix. Proceed as directed.

chocolate chunk cookies with cherries and pecans

makes about forty-eight 2-inch cookies

The crisp wafers are transformed into chunky, crusty-edged cookies with moist, cakey interiors loaded with chewy tart cherries, rich nuggets of chocolate, and plenty of toasty pecans.

Make the dough as directed, but instead of kneading it, use a rubber spatula to mix in 6 ounces bittersweet or semisweet chocolate, cut into small chunks, or 1 cup bittersweet or semisweet chocolate chips or chunks; 1⅓ cups (5.2 ounces) chopped toasted pecans; and 1 cup (6 ounces) dried sour cherries. Drop level tablespoons of dough 2 inches apart on the lined baking sheets. Bake until the surfaces of the cookies look dry and the cookies are soft but not too squishy when pressed lightly with your finger, 10 to 12 minutes. Rotate the sheets from top to bottom and from back to front about halfway through baking. Cool the cookies as directed.

chocolate mint sandwiches

PHOTOGRAPH ON PAGE 96

makes forty-eight 2-inch sandwich cookies

For mint and chocolate lovers, these dainty crisp sandwich cookies, made with extra-thin cocoa wafers, have cut-out tops to reveal the cool mint-laced white chocolate filling within.

Make the dough as directed, but form it into a log about 16 inches long and 1½ inches in diameter. Wrap and refrigerate until firm, at least 1 hour.

When ready to bake, with a thin sharp knife, score the log at 1-inch intervals. Cut 6 very thin slices per inch, placing them 1 inch apart on the lined baking sheets. Using a small cookie cutter (or improvise with a bottle cap), cut out and remove a ⅞-inch round from the center of half of the slices. Bake, rotating the baking sheets from top to bottom and back to front about halfway through baking, for 10 to 12 minutes: the cookies will puff up and deflate; they are done about 1 minute after they deflate. Cool completely before filling.

To make the filling, place 6 ounces white chocolate, finely chopped, in a clean dry microwave-safe bowl. Microwave on medium power for 3 minutes. Use a clean dry rubber spatula to stir the chocolate, and then microwave it at 5- to 10-second intervals, stirring after each one, until most of the chocolate is melted. Stir until completely melted. Mix in 3 drops mint oil (not extract). Taste and add up to 3 more drops if necessary. Spread ½ teaspoon of filling almost to the edges of the bottom of a cookie without a hole, and set a cookie with a hole on top. Repeat until all of the cookies are filled.

When the filling is set, the cookies may be stored airtight at room temperature for up to 2 weeks or frozen for up to 2 months.

Mexican chocolate soup
with cinnamon toasts

Spicy-sweet Mexican chocolate makes a playful and very satisfying dessert, complete with hot, cold, creamy, crunchy, and spicy elements. Make this after you've returned from Mexico with tablets of hand-crafted chocolate from a small artisan producer (if you have a choice, ask for the *semi-amargo,* which is a little less sweet than the usual). Or poke around your local Mexican grocery, or just go to the supermarket.

Make the cinnamon toasts just before serving. serves 5 to 6

10 to 12 ounces (three and a half to four 3-ounce tablets) Mexican chocolate, such as Ibarra or Abuelita brands, or five to six 2-ounce tablets (if you have smaller tablets from Mexico), coarsely chopped

4 cups water

6 small scoops Vanilla Bean Ice Cream (page 55) or store-bought vanilla, dulce de leche, or coffee ice cream

A double recipe of Tropical Cinnamon Toasts (page 179), just made

IN A MEDIUM SAUCEPAN, melt the chocolate with 1 cup of the water over medium heat, whisking until it is dissolved. Stir in the remaining water, and whisk to a boil. Cover and set aside until ready to serve, or up to several hours.

When ready to serve, reheat the soup and whisk until frothy. Place a scoop of ice cream in the center of each of six shallow soup bowls. Ladle the hot soup around the ice cream. Garnish with the cinnamon toasts, and serve immediately.

the flavors of honey
and sugar

Unrefined sugars from cane or palm trees are a staple of indigenous diets in tropical locations where these plants abound. Dishes flavored and sweetened with honey predate biblical times. My focus is on the flavors of these ingredients—nuances of earthiness, ripe fruit, or smoke in the sugars or the floral, grassy, treacly character of the honeys—rather than their sweetness. With them I made suave flans and rustic ice creams, chewy caramels, and crisp shattering cookies. I laced a rich brioche and a gooey bread pudding, filled nutty cookies, and topped ice cream with fragrant raw sugars. (For more about raw sugars, see page 28 and 194.) I acted without prejudice against white sugar—and with no concern for any health advantage that honey or raw sugars may have. My goal was to highlight and enjoy the taste, rather than to test the ability of honey or tropical sugar to replace white sugar. Seeking clarity and a fresh perspective, I rarely added spices or other distracting flavors except in variations. I passed up the traditional (and ancient) repertoire of dense honey cakes, medieval gingerbreads, and spiced holiday fare, to choose instead recipes that romance and reveal the flavors in the honey or sugar itself. These recipes are so minimal and so uncomplicated that a mere change from one type of honey to another—from local to Alabama wildflower honey, or from acacia to sage honey—or one sugar to another, makes a dessert that tastes different, according to the source of the honey or sugar. For honey collectors, the curious cook, or anyone excited to sample sugars, these recipes offer infinite possibilities for tasting and experimenting.

honey snaps

I almost went mad trying to find a crisp, crunchy honey cookie that didn't go limp, chewy, or sticky (honey tends to do all this to cookies). Finally I turned to a recipe for brandy snaps given to me by my friend Elizabeth Thomas, a Berkeley cooking teacher. Hallelujah. These are great if you love honey, or you can use golden syrup as Elizabeth does. If you don't want to curl the snaps into little cylinders, just skip that step and call 'em wafers. The plain snaps can be served as cookies—they are delicious with tea. Or use a pastry bag fitted with a medium star tip to fill the snaps with lightly sweetened whipped cream. Fill them immediately before serving so that they will not soften before they are eaten.

makes thirty-six 4-inch cylinders or wafers

4 tablespoons unsalted butter

3 tablespoons honey

¼ cup sugar

¼ teaspoon ground ginger

½ cup (2 ounces) sifted before measuring all-purpose flour (see Note)

2 pinches of salt

EQUIPMENT
Baking sheets

POSITION A RACK in the center of the oven and preheat the oven to 400°F. Butter the baking sheet.

In a small saucepan, heat the butter, honey, sugar, and ginger over low heat, until the butter is melted. Remove the pan from the heat and stir in the flour and salt. Mix well.

Drop 6 teaspoons of batter onto each of the baking sheets, allowing plenty of room for spreading. Place one sheet at a time in the oven and bake until the cookies are golden, 3 to 5 minutes. While they are baking, butter the handle of a wooden spoon.

Exchange the sheet of unbaked cookies for the baked ones. Allow the cookies to cool for a few seconds, then lift one with a metal spatula onto the wooden spoon handle (or a cooling rack, if you don't want to curl them). Curl the hot cookie around the handle with your fingers and slide it to the end of the spoon. Form the second cookie near the bowl of the spoon, and remove the first one to a cooling rack. Repeat, forming and removing cookies as fast as you can. If they harden before you can roll them, return the baking sheet to the oven for a few seconds to soften, and then roll them. If the first set of cookies does not spread or curl properly, add a tiny bit of extra butter and/or honey to the batter before continuing. Do not bake more than 6 cookies at a time, or you will not be able to keep up! Cool the cookies completely before storing in an airtight container, where they will keep for several days.

NOTE: Even a little too much flour may result in a thick and tough, rather than thin and crisp, snap. Review how to measure flour (page 3), or if you have a digital scale, use it here.

cinnamon snaps

The cinnamon flavor starts subtly before it really kicks in and begins to warm the palate. Finally, the buttery, spicy sweetness is reminiscent of the taste of cinnamon toast.

Substitute golden syrup for the honey. Add 1 rounded teaspoon freshly grated stick cinnamon (if possible) or ½ teaspoon regular ground cinnamon to the melted butter mixture.

heavenly honey ice cream

This very simple but seductive dessert celebrates the unique flavors and aromas of honey, from the most delicate to the robust. Serve the ice cream plain or with Fresh Thyme Tuiles (page 218), Lavender Tuiles (page 216), Lemon Tuiles (page 118), or Honey Snaps (page 174); or garnish with pistachios, walnuts, toasted almonds, strawberries, or fine strips of candied orange or Meyer lemon peel (see page 131). Or make a heavenly *affogato* (an Italian dessert/drink) by pouring a double shot of espresso around a scoop of it.   makes about 4 cups

½ cup milk

½ cup honey

Slightly rounded ⅛ teaspoon salt

2¼ cups heavy cream

EQUIPMENT

Ice cream machine

HEAT THE MILK in a small saucepan until it begins to simmer around the edges. Pour the milk into a medium bowl and allow it to cool completely (to avoid curdling when the honey is added). Add the honey and salt, stirring to dissolve the honey. Stir in the cream. Chill the mixture for at least 4 hours, but preferably 12.

For an extra-cold start, put the mixture in the freezer for 20 minutes, stirring once or twice to prevent freezing. Freeze according to the instructions for your ice cream maker.

Serve soft or transfer to an airtight container and freeze until hard enough to scoop, at least 3 to 4 hours. If the ice cream gets too hard, before serving let it stand for a few minutes, put it in the refrigerator for 15 minutes or longer, or microwave it on low (defrost) for a few seconds at a time until scoopable.

heavenly honey-orange flower ice cream

Serve with ripe cantaloupe or Charentais melon or slices of persimmon.

Use a vegetable peeler to remove a strip of orange zest about ¾ inch wide and 6 inches long from a large orange, preferably organic or unsprayed. Heat the zest with the milk. Remove the zest before adding the cream, and add ¼ teaspoon orange flower water. Taste and adjust the flavor with drops of orange flower water if necessary before freezing. (Depending on the brand and your sensitivity to this flavor, you may have to increase the amount significantly.)

honey panna cotta

Honey fanciers will find panna cotta a subtle showcase for all kinds of delicate or robust honey flavors. The only honey that has disappointed me so far was a big commercial brand—good reason to buy from small producers at farmers' markets, or wherever you find them, and it's more fun besides. You can garnish the panna cotta with a drizzle of the same honey you used to make it and serve with Lemon Tuiles (page 118). For best results, measure gelatin like a miser, or you risk turning an exquisite dish into Jell-O. If you want to pursue the perfect panna cotta, sheet gelatin is a more accurate way to go.   serves 6

1¼ cups whole milk

2½ teaspoons unflavored gelatin (see Note)

3 cups heavy cream

⅓ cup honey, plus extra for drizzling

⅛ teaspoon salt

EQUIPMENT

Instant-read thermometer

6 wide margarita glasses or six 6-ounce ramekins

POUR THE MILK into a small bowl and sprinkle the gelatin over it. Set aside (without stirring) to let the gelatin soften, 5 to 10 minutes.

Meanwhile, in a small saucepan, heat the cream, honey, and salt until steaming hot, stirring from time to time to dissolve the sugar. Off the heat, add the milk and gelatin and stir well to dissolve the gelatin. Set the bowl in a larger bowl of water and ice cubes and stir frequently until the mixture thickens and registers 50°F on the instant-read thermometer.

Divide the mixture evenly among the glasses or ramekins. Cover with plastic wrap and chill for at least several hours, or overnight.

Serve the panna cotta in the glasses or ramekins. Or wrap each ramekin briefly in a wrung-out hot wet towel and unmold the panna cotta onto dessert plates.

NOTE: You can substitute 3 leaves of sheet gelatin for the granulated gelatin. Soak the leaves in the cold milk to soften them, then fish the softened sheets from the milk and stir them into the hot cream until dissolved. Stir in the milk, and proceed as directed.

tropical cinnamon toasts

SEE PHOTOGRAPH FOR MEXICAN CHOCOLATE SOUP PAGE 168

Have you forgotten how good cinnamon toast is? These toasts are even better. Use them to garnish a dish of ice cream or Mexican Chocolate Soup (page 167). Or just nibble on them. The lighter raw sugars—light muscovado, palm sugar, piloncillo—are great with vanilla ice cream or fresh pineapple. Toasts made with dark muscovado are especially delicious with coffee ice cream. This is a versatile recipe. You can use fresh or slightly stale bread. Or, if your bread is fresh and you want a little extra crispness, toast the slices briefly before covering with the cinnamon mixture.   makes 4 to 6 toasts

4 to 6 fresh or slightly stale baguette slices (sliced on the diagonal up to 1 inch thick and 6 inches long for maximum drama—or any size slices that you have on hand) or 2 to 3 slices regular bread, cut in half on the diagonal to make 4 or 6 pieces

2 tablespoons firmly packed raw sugar, such as grated piloncillo or palm sugar or light or dark muscovado sugar (see Note)

½ teaspoon ground cinnamon (Mexican or regular) or 1 rounded teaspoon freshly grated cinnamon stick

1 tablespoon unsalted butter, softened

Pinch of salt

PLACE THE BREAD on a baking sheet and preheat the broiler with the rack 4 to 5 inches from the heating element, or use a toaster oven. Mix the sugar, cinnamon, butter, and salt together. Spread the mixture on the bread.

Broil until the edges of the bread are dark brown and the sugar is bubbly. Serve at once.

NOTE: Yes, you could substitute regular brown sugar for the raw sugars, but then you would be missing something special.

honey caramels

Honey collectors will enjoy trying regional or varietal honeys in this recipe, with or without the walnuts. The year my brother's family moved to Alabama, they brought a taste of their new home, Alabama wildflower honey, back to Berkeley for Thanksgiving. I made caramels with it and carried them back to Birmingham for Christmas a few weeks later. For the more delicate honeys, increase the honey to ⅓ cup and reduce the corn syrup to ⅔ cup.

makes eighty 1-inch caramels

2 cups (8 ounces) broken or coarsely chopped walnut pieces (optional, but shown in photo)

¾ cup light corn syrup

¼ cup honey

2 cups sugar

⅜ teaspoon fine sea salt

2 cups heavy cream

3 tablespoons unsalted butter, cut into chunks and softened

1 tablespoon plus 1 teaspoon pure vanilla extract

EQUIPMENT

A 9-inch square baking pan

Candy thermometer

LINE THE BOTTOM and sides of the baking pan with aluminum foil and grease the foil. If using the walnuts, spread them in the prepared pan. Set aside.

Combine the corn syrup, honey, sugar, and salt in a heavy 3-quart saucepan. Cook over medium heat, stirring with a silicone spatula or wooden spoon, until the mixture simmers around the edges. Wash the sugar and syrup from the sides of the pan with a wet pastry brush. Cover and cook for 3 minutes. (Meanwhile, rinse the spatula or spoon for use again later.) Uncover the pan and wash down the sides once more. Attach the candy thermometer to the saucepan, without letting it touch the bottom of the pan, and cook, uncovered, without stirring until the mixture reaches 305°F.

Meanwhile, heat the cream in a small saucepan until tiny bubbles form around the edges of the pan. Turn off the heat and cover the pan to keep the cream hot.

When the sugar mixture is at 305°F, turn off the heat and stir in the butter chunks. Gradually stir in the hot cream; it will bubble up and steam dramatically. Turn the burner back on and adjust it so that the mixture boils energetically but not violently. Stir until smooth. Continue to cook, stirring occasionally, to about 245°F. Then cook, stirring constantly, to 248°F for soft chewy caramels or 250°F for firmer chewy caramels.

Remove the pan from the heat and stir in the vanilla. Pour the caramel into the lined pan. Let set for 4 to 5 hours, or overnight, until firm.

Lift the pan liner from the pan and invert the sheet of caramel onto a sheet of parchment paper. Peel off the liner and turn the caramel right side up. Cut the caramels with an oiled knife into 1-inch squares, skinny bars (as shown in the photograph), or any desired shape. Wrap each caramel individually in wax paper or cellophane.

muscovado bread pudding

The flavor of raw sugar is accentuated in these individual bread puddings, which resemble flowers with golden brown petals. If you don't want to fuss with individual puddings, see the Note.

serves 8

10 slices fresh or stale homemade
or bakery-style white bread (such as
Pepperidge Farm or Orowheat buttermilk
or potato bread)

6 tablespoons unsalted butter, melted

1 cup (7 ounces) firmly packed light or dark
muscovado sugar or grated piloncillo sugar

¼ teaspoon salt

6 large eggs

3 tablespoons sugar

1 teaspoon pure vanilla extract

3 cups milk (or use a combination of milk
and half-and-half)

EQUIPMENT

Eight 6-ounce ramekins or custard cups

POSITION A RACK in the lower third of the oven and preheat the oven to 325°F. Butter the ramekins or custard cups.

If the bread is fresh, lay the slices on a baking sheet and bake for 5 minutes on each side, or until very lightly toasted. Let cool on a rack.

Meanwhile, combine 4 tablespoons of the melted butter with the muscovado sugar and half of the salt in a small bowl. Set the remaining melted butter aside in a warm spot.

Cut off the bread crusts (don't worry about leaving a little crust on the corners). Spread each slice with a slightly rounded tablespoon of the muscovado butter. Cut each slice into quarters. Set aside.

In a medium bowl, whisk the eggs, sugar, the remaining salt, and vanilla together. Gradually whisk in the milk. Pour enough of the mixture through a strainer into a shallow baking pan to come to a depth of about ¼ inch; reserve the rest. Lay 5 bread pieces, sugar side up, in the egg mixture. Let the bread soak just long enough to become flexible (some bread will soak more quickly than other) but not too soggy to handle (once you know your bread, you may be able to soak more than 5 pieces at one time). Arrange 4 overlapping pieces of bread around the inside of a buttered ramekin, tucking the end of the fourth piece under the first one. Bend the fifth piece into a shape that will fit into the bottom of the ramekin and insert it, using a dinner knife if necessary to press it in place. Repeat to assemble the remaining pudding, straining more of the egg mixture into the baking pan as needed. When the ramekins are filled, divide any leftover egg mixture among them, reserving any that doesn't fit. Let stand for 15 minutes to absorb the liquid. Preheat the oven to 325°F. Put a kettle of water on to boil. After 15 minutes drizzle any remaining egg mixture into the pudding if it will fit.

Brush the unsugared edges of the bread with the reserved melted butter. Wipe any smudges off the ramekins and set them in a baking pan large enough to hold them with space between them. Set the pan in the oven. Pull out the rack and carefully pour enough boiling water into the pan to come halfway up the sides of the ramekins. Bake until the pudding is puffy, the edges of the bread are golden, and a knife inserted into the pudding comes out wet but mostly clear rather than milky, 35 to 45 minutes.

Serve warm or at room temperature, in the ramekins or unmolded.

NOTE: To make one large bread pudding, arrange the sugar-coated bread quarters in an overlapping pattern in a 9 by 13-inch or other 3-quart baking dish. Strain the egg mixture over the bread. Cover the pudding with plastic wrap and press any floating bread pieces back into the egg mixture. Let stand for at least 15 minutes to allow the bread to absorb the liquid. Put the baking dish in a large pan, add enough boiling water to come halfway up the sides of the baking dish, and bake until a knife inserted into the pudding comes out clear, 45 to 55 minutes. Cool for 1 hour before serving.

pecan penuche shortbread
with rum

This sweet, slightly addictive shortbread has the flavor of brown sugar fudge, with a whisper of rum.

makes twenty-five 1½-inch squares

12 tablespoons (1½ sticks) unsalted butter, melted and still warm

½ cup (3.5 ounces) firmly packed grated piloncillo sugar or light muscovado sugar

1 tablespoon dark rum

1 teaspoon pure vanilla extract

⅜ teaspoon salt

1½ cups (6.75 ounces) all-purpose flour

⅔ cup (2.6 ounces) pecans, coarsely chopped

Turbinado, Demerara, or granulated sugar for sprinkling

EQUIPMENT
An 8-inch square baking pan

LINE THE BOTTOM and four sides of the baking pan with foil. In a medium bowl, combine the melted butter with the sugar, rum, vanilla, and salt. Add the flour and half of the pecans and mix just until incorporated. Pat and spread the dough evenly in the pan. Let stand for at least 2 hours, or overnight (no need to refrigerate).

Position a rack in the lower third of the oven and preheat the oven to 300°F.

Sprinkle the remaining pecans over the top of the shortbread and press them gently into the dough. Bake for 45 minutes. Remove the pan from the oven, leaving the oven on. Sprinkle the surface of the shortbread with pinches of the turbinado sugar. Let the shortbread cool for 10 minutes.

Using the foil, remove the shortbread from the pan, being careful to avoid breaking it. Use a thin sharp knife to cut it into squares. Place the pieces slightly apart on a baking sheet lined with parchment and return to the oven for 15 minutes to toast it lightly. Cool on a rack.

Shortbread keeps for several weeks in an airtight container.

raw sugar toffee sauce

Easy to make, this sensational sauce tops coffee or vanilla ice cream, fresh pine-
apple, toasted pecans, or bananas . . . just to begin my list! makes 1½ cups

¾ cup (5.25 ounces) firmly packed raw
sugar (see Note)

1 cup heavy cream

⅛ teaspoon salt

IN A MEDIUM SAUCEPAN, whisk together the sugar, cream, and salt. Bring to a simmer
over low heat and cook 5 minutes, stirring frequently. Remove from the heat. Serve
warm or at room temperature. The sauce keeps for several weeks in the refrigerator.

NOTE: Use light muscovado, dark muscovado, piloncillo, or palm sugar. For the muscovado
or piloncillo sugar, add ½ teaspoon dark rum, if desired. For the palm sugar, I like to add
½ teaspoon pure vanilla extract (optional).

flans with raw sugar sauce

These are almost too easy! Forget about caramelizing sugar for the molds. Just press some flavorful raw sugar into the bottom of each dish, and pour the flan mixture on top. The sugar dissolves into a sauce when the flans are chilled.   serves 8

⅔ cup (4.7 ounces) firmly packed light or dark muscovado sugar or grated piloncillo

⅜ teaspoon salt

5 large eggs

¾ cup sugar

3 cups half-and-half

EQUIPMENT

Eight 6-ounce custard cups or ramekins

POSITION A RACK in the lower third of the oven and preheat the oven to 350°F. Put a kettle of water on to boil.

Combine the muscovado sugar thoroughly with ¼ teaspoon of the salt, pinching or mashing the sugar to eliminate lumps. Divide the mixture among the custard cups or ramekins and press the sugar lightly with another small cup to even it out and compact it. Set the cups in a baking pan (or pans) large enough to hold them with space between them.

In a large bowl, whisk the eggs, sugar, and the remaining ⅛ teaspoon salt until well combined. Heat the half-and-half in a saucepan over medium heat until steaming (140° to 145°F); it will be just too hot for you to insert a finger for more than a moment at this temperature. Gradually whisk the half-and-half into the eggs. Strain the mixture into another bowl to eliminate any bits of egg.

Ladle the flan mixture very gently onto the sugar in the custard cups or ramekins, disturbing the sugar as little as possible. Some of the sugar may float up, but it will eventually settle back down in the bottom. Place the baking pan in the oven, pull out the rack, and carefully pour enough boiling water into the pan to come halfway up the sides of the custard cups or ramekins. Slide the rack back into the oven and bake until the custard is just a little wobbly in the center, 20 to 25 minutes. Remove the pan from the oven and remove the cups with tongs. Let cool for 15 minutes, then refrigerate at least 4 hours, but preferably 12 for maximum sauce.

To serve, run a thin knife around the edge of each cup and invert onto a rimmed plate or into a shallow bowl.

tropical sugar ice cream

This is icy, refreshing, and rather like a rustic ice cream than a perfectly smooth commercial product. And it offers instant gratification—you just mix the ingredients and freeze. So easy and fresh. The muscovado has nuances of maple and coffee, while the piloncillo flavor is ripe and fruity. Pour a shot of espresso around either ice cream. Or make a banana split with toasted pecans, whipped cream, and Raw Sugar Toffee Sauce (page 185) made with the same sugar as the ice cream.   makes about 3½ cups

1½ cups whole milk

1½ cups heavy cream

½ cup (3.5 ounces) firmly packed light muscovado sugar or grated piloncillo sugar

⅛ teaspoon salt

EQUIPMENT

Ice cream machine

COMBINE ALL of the ingredients in a bowl, stirring well to dissolve the sugar.

For an extra-cold start, put the mixture in the freezer for 20 minutes, stirring once or twice to prevent freezing. Freeze according to the instructions for your ice cream machine.

Serve soft or transfer to an airtight container and freeze until hard enough to scoop, at least 3 to 4 hours. If the ice cream gets too hard, before serving let it stand for a few minutes, put it in the refrigerator for 15 minutes or longer, or microwave it on low (defrost) for a few seconds at a time until scoopable.

NOTE: You can make this ice cream a bit smoother and denser, and slightly chewier, if you heat the milk with the sugar until the mixture begins to simmer around the edges (175°F), stirring to dissolve the sugar. Cool the milk, stir in the cream, and chill it at least 4 hours but preferably 12 hours.

It's an interesting experiment. In addition to texture changes, the flavor of the raw sugar becomes more intense. However, the overall flavor of the ice cream is not as balanced and pleasing because the fresh milk flavor is lost! (My thanks to food scientist and cook Shirley Corriher for her endless wisdom and her book *Cookwise,* which belongs in every cook's kitchen, regardless of whether we follow the rules! The reason I don't always follow the milk-heating rule is that I like the fresh taste of uncooked milk—yet another trade-off between flavor and texture.)

tropical lace cookies

PHOTOGRAPH ON PAGE 96

These are pretty and delicious accompanying all kinds of creamy desserts, including ice creams, sorbets, panna cotta, and ricotta cheese. Anyone who loves strawberries dipped in sour cream and brown sugar will like these with strawberries and Sour Cream Ice Cream (page 49). I grate plenty of cinnamon over the cookies that I plan to serve with ricotta cheese.

makes sixteen to twenty 4-inch cookies

3 tablespoons unsalted butter

¾ cup (5.25 ounces) firmly packed grated piloncillo, palm sugar, or light muscovado sugar

1 tablespoon dark rum

1 large egg

⅛ teaspoon salt

2 tablespoons all purpose flour

½ cup finely chopped pecans, walnuts, or almonds (or sliced almonds), or unsweetened shredded dried coconut

A nutmeg or cinnamon stick for seasoning (optional)

EQUIPMENT

Baking sheets

Small cups or a rolling pin for shaping the cookies (optional)

POSITION A RACK in the center of the oven and preheat the oven to 350°F. Line the baking sheets with parchment paper, heavy-duty aluminum foil, or silicone baking mats. If shapes are desired, set out small cups or a rolling pin.

In a medium saucepan melt the butter. Stir in the sugar, and remove from the heat. Add the rum, egg, and salt and beat until smooth. Stir in the flour and nuts. Let the batter rest for 5 minutes.

Drop tablespoons of batter about 3 inches apart on one of the prepared baking sheets (bake only one sheet at a time). If using a silicone mat, spread the batter very thin (about ¹⁄₁₆ inch) into rounds, ovals, or long tongue shapes. If using foil or parchment paper, the batter should spread by itself when in the oven—if it does not, spread it as described. Bake until the cookies are browned all over, 8 to 10 minutes. Remove the pan from the oven. If desired, grate nutmeg or cinnamon over the tops of the hot cookies.

For flat cookies, slide the foil or parchment off the pan onto a rack to cool; let cookies baked on silicone cool for 30 seconds before transferring them to a rack to cool. If the cookies are to be shaped, let rest 30 seconds, then slide an offset spatula under each and shape as desired by draping the cookies over a rolling pin, nestling them into a cup, rolling them into cornets, or pinching or twisting them into any desired shape before they cool. Cool completely before storing in an airtight container.

The cookies keep for at least a week.

coconut palm cream cake

Coconut sugar (see page 29) is made from the nectar of the coconut palm. It has subtle hints of coconut flavor with nuances of maple and coffee. In Southeast Asia, it is used in both savory and sweet cooking. Here I've used it in a Western-style layer cake, splashed with rum and lime juice and filled with whipped cream and coconut. Instead of the rum and lime juice, you could brush the cake with ¼ cup rum mixed with ¼ cup strong coffee, or just use about ¼ cup straight rum.

If you want to be extra festive and fancy, use a propane torch to caramelize the top.

serves 12

FOR THE CAKE

⅔ cup (1.4 ounces) unsweetened shredded dried coconut

2¼ cups (8 ounces) sifted (before measuring) cake flour

1½ teaspoons baking powder

¼ teaspoon baking soda

⅜ teaspoon salt

3 large eggs, at room temperature

12 tablespoons (1½ sticks) butter, slightly softened

⅔ cup (7 ounces) coconut sugar (see Note)

⅓ cup plus 1 tablespoon sugar

1 teaspoon pure vanilla extract

¾ cup whole milk, at room temperature

2 tablespoons fresh lime juice

¼ cup dark rum

2 tablespoons water

FOR THE FILLING

1 cup heavy cream

2 teaspoons sugar

⅔ cup (1.4 ounces) unsweetened shredded dried coconut

Powdered sugar for dusting or ⅓ cup grated palm sugar or ¼ cup coconut sugar to caramelize the top of the cake

EQUIPMENT

Two 9-inch round cake pans

A propane torch (optional)

TO MAKE THE CAKE, position a rack in the lower third of the oven and preheat the oven to 350°F. Grease the sides of the cake pans and line the bottoms with parchment paper.

To toast the coconut, set a plate near the stove. Spread the coconut in a wide heavy skillet and stir constantly over medium heat until it begins to color slightly. Turn the heat down (once coconut is hot, it burns easily) and continue to stir until most of the coconut is light golden brown flecked with some white. (I often take the pan off the heat a little early and continue to stir, letting the residual heat from the pan toast the coconut more slowly and evenly.) Immediately scrape the coconut onto the plate to stop it from browning, and cool completely before using.

Mix the flour, baking powder, soda, and salt, then sift it three times. Set aside.

In a small bowl, whisk the eggs together briefly to combine the whites and yolks. Set aside.

(CONTINUED)

In the bowl of a stand mixer or another large bowl, combine the butter, coconut sugar, ⅓ cup sugar, and vanilla. Beat on medium speed (or high speed if using a hand-held mixer) until light and fluffy, 3 to 4 minutes. Beat in the eggs a little at a time, taking about 2 minutes to add all of them.

Add one-quarter of the flour mixture and beat on low speed just until no flour is visible. Stop the mixer and add one-third of the milk. Beat just until it is absorbed. Repeat twice, adding another quarter of the flour and then another third of the milk each time. Finally add the last of the flour and the toasted coconuts. Scrape the bowl as necessary, and beat only enough to incorporate the ingredients after each addition.

Divide the batter evenly between the two pans and spread it level. Bake until a toothpick inserted into the center comes out clean, 20 to 25 minutes. Cool the layers in the pans on a rack for about 5 minutes, then unmold and cool completely (right side up) on the rack.

Combine the lime juice, rum, water, and 1 tablespoon of sugar in a small bowl, stirring to dissolve the sugar.

To assemble the cake, place one cake layer on a plate. Brush it with about one-third of the rum syrup.

To make the filling, whip the cream with the sugar until it just holds a very soft shape—it should seem slightly underwhipped. Fold in the (untoasted) coconut. Spread all of the coconut cream over the moistened cake layer. Brush the least-good-looking side of the second cake layer with half of the remaining rum syrup. Set the cake moist side down on the coconut filling. Brush the top of the cake with the remaining rum syrup.

Wrap the cake carefully, to keep its shape. Refrigerate for at least several hours, or overnight, to allow the coconut to absorb moisture from the cream.

To serve, you can simply sift powdered sugar over the cake just before serving, or you can top the cake with caramelized palm or coconut sugar up to 3 hours before serving: If using grated palm sugar, sprinkle it over the top of the cake as evenly as you can. If using gooier coconut sugar (impossible to sprinkle and too thick to spread), heat it very gently in a small saucepan until it flows like honey, then pour it over onto the top of the cake and spread it with a heated icing spatula.

To caramelize the top, sweep the propane torch all over the sugared surface, always moving it and keeping enough distance to avoid scorching, until the sugar melts, bubbles, and finally turns reddish amber and clear. If you don't get to reddish amber, the sugar will not harden when it cools. Before serving, refrigerate the cake for at least 15 minutes to harden the top; or refrigerate for up to several hours, and remove from the refrigerator 30 to 60 minutes before serving.

NOTE: To use molded lumps of hard palm sugar instead of the gooier coconut sugar, grate the hard sugar and use 1 firmly packed cup (7 ounces, the same weight as ⅔ cup coconut sugar).

pecan polvorones with muscovado filling

These melt-in-your-mouth pecan tea cakes are filled with a gorgeous mahogany- hued toffee sauce made simply by simmering dark muscovado sugar in heavy cream.

makes forty-eight 2-inch cookies

FOR THE COOKIES

1½ cups (6 ounces) pecan or walnut halves or pieces

⅓ cup sugar

¼ teaspoon salt

½ pound (2 sticks) unsalted butter, slightly softened and cut into chunks

2 teaspoons pure vanilla extract

2 cups (9 ounces) all-purpose flour

FOR THE FILLING

⅔ cup (4.6 ounces) firmly packed dark muscovado sugar

⅓ cup heavy cream

Scant ⅛ teaspoon salt

EQUIPMENT

Baking sheets

To make the cookies, pulse the nuts in the bowl of a food processor until most are finely ground and the largest pieces are about ¼ inch. Transfer to a bowl and set aside.

Wipe the processor bowl with a paper towel to remove excess oil from the nuts. Add the sugar and salt and process until fine and powdery. Add the butter and the vanilla and pulse until the mixture is smooth. Add the flour and pulse until the dough starts to clump together. Add the nuts and pulse just until combined. Transfer the dough to a bowl and knead it by hand briefly to make sure it is evenly mixed.

Line the baking sheets with parchment paper. Shape the dough into 1-inch balls (½ ounce each), and place them slightly apart on one of the prepared sheets. Press the handle of a wooden spoon dipped in flour (or your finger) into each ball to form a depression. Cover and chill the cookies for at least 2 hours, or preferably, overnight.

Position the racks in the upper and lower thirds of the oven and preheat the oven to 325°F.

Remove the cookies from the refrigerator and place them 1 inch apart on the lined baking sheets. Bake for 10 minutes. Rotate the sheets from top to bottom and front to back. Continue baking until the cookies are lightly colored on top and light golden brown on the bottom, 10 to 12 more minutes. Transfer pans to racks to cool.

Meanwhile, to make the filling, combine the muscovado sugar with the cream and salt in a small saucepan. Bring to a boil over low heat, stirring, until the sugar is dissolved. Boil gently for about 2 minutes without stirring. Cool the sauce briefly.

Spoon a little filling into the depression in each cookie. Allow the filling to cool completely. The cookies can be stored in an airtight container for at least a week.

Refined white sugar is a staple of the dessert kitchen. As a cook, a pastry chef, and a serious chocolate lover, I could never turn my back on it. The virtue of granulated white sugar—ultrarefined, pristinely clean, bleached, and stripped of all character and nutrients—is its very absence of flavor and its straight-ahead sweetening power. It sweetens without interfering. It yields the stage to more important ingredients and, when used with finesse, it actually highlights other flavors. The finest chocolates are sweetened with white sugar, so we taste the pure flavors of the cacao. Chocolates sweetened with less refined sugar taste of the chocolate *and* the molasses in the sugar; the clarity and complexity of the cacao flavor is compromised. White sugar is a supremely versatile ingredient, as essential as salt. I can't imagine a kitchen without it.

In fact, for years I never paid attention to raw sugars. If I needed brown sugar for oatmeal cookies, I opted for a national brand, chose light or dark, and enjoyed the resulting chewiness and mild caramel flavor. Period. Things changed when I brought home a dozen different raw and other specialty sugars one day and lined them up for tasting alongside the usual browns. I compared colors, stuck my nose deep into the bags, and finally tasted.

Originally all browns sugars were semirefined—sugar with some of the natural molasses left in them. But commercial brown sugar is made by adding some molasses to refined white sugar. The result has a pleasing caramel or butterscotch flavor but no hint of its origins, nothing that suggests *terroir*. However, although the process is considerably more sanitary than it once was, raw sugars are still semirefined sugars, with varying amounts of natural molasses left in them. By contrast with commercial brown sugars, they burst with complex, earthy fruit flavors and aromas: literally the taste and scent of the earth, the plants, and the musky humid climates they come from.

My samples varied in color and consistency from coarse crunchy grains with a light caramel hue and flavor to match to amber and russet sugars with the moist consistency of familiar supermarket brown sugar. Most compelling were the softer, darker sugars. At the top of the color and flavor spectrum, dark muscovado is deep mahogany brown, almost black, with dark flavors of molasses, ripe tropical fruits, and smoke. A whiff took me back to a night drive through a sugarcane field in Martinique more than twenty years ago. In color and relative sweetness and intensity, piloncillo is similar to ordinary dark brown sugar, but the flavor is brighter and more interesting, with caramel and molasses notes and a slight flavor and aroma of smoke—familiar to anyone who has wandered through the markets of Mexico. Palm sugar has notes of maple and coffee and nuances of coconut. These sugars embody a world of flavor.

Yet, for all of my rhapsodizing, it was immediately clear that raw sugar would never replace white sugar in my repertoire. (But it might threaten ordinary brown sugar, suddenly so boring and characterless by comparison.) After very little experimentation, I realized that raw sugars are flavoring ingredients as much as they are sweeteners. To treat them as mere sugar is to miss their essence; indeed, if they are used when only a sweetener is needed, their rich and compelling flavors can actually get in the way. Peaches are sweet, but we don't throw a peach into a recipe just for its sweetness, and no more would I use a flavorful tropical sugar without considering its flavor.

Repeatedly, I found that the most exciting recipes treat raw sugar as a star flavor—often in contrast with other elements. Raw sugars taste strong when substituted for refined sugar, but when treated as flavors on their own, they are surprisingly delicate. The tropical sugars seem to need salt—and sometimes even a little white sugar—to reveal the full glory of their flavors. When I replaced white sugar with piloncillo in a custard for bread pudding (see page 182) the result was nice. But when I spread the piloncillo *on* the bread instead, with a little salt and butter, and sweetened the custard with only white sugar, the improvement was dramatic: the pudding was spectacular, with the bright, fruity, ripe flavors of the piloncillo. Encouraged, I laced a buttery babka with veins of muscovado sugar and used raw sugars (with a pinch of salt) in place of caramelized sugar to line flan molds. I made stunning simple sauces for fruit or ice cream by cooking raw sugar with a little cream (and salt).

White sugar remains in my kitchen. But piloncillo, light and dark muscovado, and palm sugar are also now fully esconced there. When I stop thinking about new recipes, I might get around to revisiting traditional spice cakes, gingersnaps, blondies, oatmeal and chocolate chip cookies. . . . Who knows, recipes that traditionally call for brown sugar might get a big lift from an infusion of *terroir*.

tropical swirl babka

Exquisitely rich buttery brioche dough makes the best babka in the world. Filled with piloncillo or muscovado sugar mixed with butter and salt, this version is sumptuous, gorgeous to behold, and far too good to reserve for breakfast. Don't miss the spiced versions either. Babka is good plain or toasted.   serves 10 to 12

¾ cup (5.25 ounces) firmly packed dark muscovado, light muscovado, or grated piloncillo sugar

⅛ teaspoon salt

4 tablespoons unsalted butter, softened

Desiré's Brioche dough (page 42), chilled as directed

EQUIPMENT

An 8- to 10-cup plain tube pan

Baking sheet

Instant-read thermometer (optional)

MIX THE SUGAR, salt, and butter. Scrape the cold dough out onto a floured surface. Use a rolling pin to roll it into a rectangle about 18 by 12 inches and ½ inch thick. Spread the sugar mixture evenly over the dough, leaving a 1-inch margin on one long side. Moisten the margin with a little water. Beginning at the long side opposite the margin, roll up the dough as you would a jelly roll. Press firmly to seal the seam.

Turn the roll seam side down and cut it into 18 slices, about 1 inch wide. Toss the slices gently into the tube pan, without particularly arranging them. (If you lay them flat in the pan, they will not stick together properly.) If necessary, rearrange the slices so they come to about the same level all around the pan. Cover the pan loosely with plastic wrap and let the dough rise in a warm place until doubled, about 2 hours.

Position a rack in the lower third of the oven and preheat the oven to 350°F.

Place the tube pan on a baking sheet. Bake until the top of the babka is deeply browned and the bottom of the pan sounds hollow when tapped, or until an instant-read thermometer registers 200°F when inserted in the center of the bread, 50 to 60 minutes. Cool in the pan on a rack.

To unmold, slide a skewer around the tube and a slim knife or spatula around the sides of the pan to release the cake. Invert on a rack. Turn right side up to serve. Wrapped tightly, babka keeps at least 3 days.

cinnamon swirl babka

Use light muscovado or grated piloncillo sugar for the filling and add 1 tablespoon ground cinnamon or *canela* (Mexican cinnamon) to it.

espresso-muscovado swirl babka

A little espresso accentuates the dark roasted flavors of the sugar.

Use dark muscovado sugar in the filling and add 1 tablespoon instant espresso powder to it.

orange-muscovado swirl babka

Use dark muscovado sugar in the filling and add 2 teaspoons grated orange zest, preferably from an organic or unsprayed fruit, to it.

the flavors of
herbs and spices,
flowers
and leaves

Flavors considered too weird, exotic, or "ethnic" for the mainstream kitchen only a few years ago now take pride of place. Consider aniseed and fennel, saffron, cardamom, lavender, and all kinds of chilies, to name a few. Today, the idea of thyme (or tarragon or oregano . . .), truffled salt, or black pepper in a sweet buttery cookie, or of chilies in a brownie, is more appetizing than shocking. Flavors from other cuisines kindle a spark of reinvention too—we borrow them easily, as the distinction between sweet and savory flavors grows intriguingly illusive.

With a world of flavors available, we are free to play. And so I did. In some recipes I used spices that we normally taste in concert with others as a solo voice instead. Familiar flavors like vanilla taste fresh and haunting when allowed to star—in crisp tuiles, for example—rather than playing the usual background role or silent partner with chocolate. Likewise, nutmeg is dramatic and cinnamon spectacular in the spotlight. I love to put a single exotic flavor—like cardamom, saffron, lavender, or jasmine—in a familiar, crowd-pleasing confection like caramel. I revisited recipes that call for a whole chorus of spices, like linzer torte, gingersnaps, and panforte, and tuned up the flavors to suit a less timid, contemporary palate. An exotic trio of Indian flavors—saffron, cardamom, and cinnamon—is breathtaking and sensuous in a western panna cotta. Because aromatic ingredients infuse beautifully into rich cream, a cold infusion of mint or lemon verbena or rose geranium leaves makes stunningly simple ice creams, just as delicate but tannic (thus potentially bitter) jasmine tea makes divinely aromatic jasmine cream for Bittersweet Citrus Tart (page 163). I hope you will use and adapt these recipes using even more herbs, spices, teas, flavors, and aromas. For more recipes with herbs and spices, see Iced Citron Vodka Chocolates with Fresh Mint (page 243), Corn Tuiles with Salt and Pepper (page 90), Bourbon and Nutmeg Pound Cake (page 66), and Vanilla Bean Ice Cream (page 55), as well as the recipes with cinnamon that are listed in the index.

coffee-walnut cookies

PHOTOGRAPH ON PAGE 96

Ground walnuts and freshly ground coffee beans make delicately flavored cookies. Coffee lovers might enjoy them with a dish of coffee ice cream and cup of espresso, but they are very good with grilled fresh pineapple slices and vanilla ice cream.

makes about forty-five 2-inch cookies

2 cups (9 ounces) all-purpose flour

1 cup (4 ounces) walnut halves or pieces

¾ cup sugar

¼ teaspoon salt

2 teaspoons fresh finely ground medium-roast (not espresso-roast) coffee beans, plus about 45 whole beans

14 tablespoons (1¾ sticks) unsalted butter

1 tablespoon plus 1 teaspoon brandy

1½ teaspoons pure vanilla extract

EQUIPMENT

Baking sheets

Offset spatula

COMBINE THE FLOUR, walnuts, sugar, and salt in the bowl of a food processor and pulse until the walnuts are finely ground. Add the ground coffee and pulse to mix. Add the butter (cut in several pieces if firm) and pulse until the mixture looks damp and crumbly. Drizzle in the brandy and pure vanilla extract and pulse until the dough begins to clump up around the blade. Remove the dough, press it into a ball, and knead it by hand a few times to complete the mixing.

For slice-and-bake cookies, form the dough into a 12-inch-long log about 2 inches in diameter. (For more petite cookies, make a longer, thinner log.) *For rolled-and-cut cookies,* divide the dough in half and form into 2 flat patties. Wrap the dough and refrigerate for at least 2 hours, or preferably, overnight, or up to 3 days. The dough can also be frozen for up to 3 months.

Position the racks in the upper and lower thirds of the oven and preheat the oven to 350°F. *For slice-and-bake cookies,* use a sharp knife to cut the cold dough log into ¼-inch-thick slices. (If the dough crumbles when you cut into it, let it soften for several minutes.) Place the cookies at least 1 inch apart on the ungreased baking sheets. Press a coffee bean into the center of each cookie.

For rolled-and-cut cookies, remove one dough patty from the refrigerator and let it stand at room temperature until supple enough to roll, but still quite firm; it will continue to soften as you work. Roll the dough between two pieces of wax paper or between plastic sheets (from a heavy plastic bag) to a thickness of ¼ inch. Flip the dough over once or twice while you are rolling it out to check for deep wrinkles; if necessary, peel off and smooth the paper or plastic over the dough before continuing to roll it out. When the dough is thin enough, peel off the top sheet of paper or plastic and place it next to the dough. Invert the dough onto the sheet and peel off the second sheet. Using cookie cutters, cut out cookies, as close together as possible to minimize scraps, dipping the edges of the cutters in flour as necessary to prevent sticking. Use the point of a paring knife to lift and remove the scraps as you transfer cookies to the baking sheets, placing them at least 1 inch apart. Press a coffee bean into the center of each. If the dough gets too soft at any time while rolling, cutting, removing scraps between cookies, or transferring the cookies, slide a cookie sheet underneath the paper or plastic and refrigerate the dough for a few minutes, until firm. Repeat with the second piece of dough. Then press all of the dough scraps together gently (without working or kneading them more than necessary), reroll, and cut out more cookies.

Bake the cookies until light golden brown at the edges, 12 to 14 minutes, rotating the sheets from top to bottom and front to back halfway through the baking.

Let the cookies firm up on the pans for about 1 minute, then transfer them to a rack with an offset spatula. Cook completely. These cookies are delicious fresh but are even better the next day. They can be stored in an airtight container for at least a month.

NOTE: If you prefer to bake on lined baking sheets, use foil rather than parchment paper for better browning.

spicy linzer torte

A good linzer torte recipe is a treasure. The linzer we made in my shop decades ago won kudos from admiring German and Austrian customers, who said they'd never tasted one better, and this spicier version is even more enticing than its predecessor. The heady aroma and rich flavors of toasted nuts and spices heralds a perfect holiday dish. Wrapped in cellophane, linzers make lovely gifts. Both vanilla ice cream and the traditional whipped cream *(schlag)* are decadent, worthy partners, but I just as often enjoy linzer torte all by itself.

serves 12 to 16

¾ cup (3.75 ounces) unblanched whole almonds

1 cup (4.5 ounces) all-purpose flour

¾ cup sugar

¼ teaspoon salt

1½ teaspoons ground cinnamon

Scant ½ teaspoon ground cloves

11 tablespoons unsalted butter, cut into chunks, slightly softened

1 large egg yolk

Grated zest of ½ lemon, preferably organic or unsprayed

Grated zest of ½ orange, preferably organic or unsprayed

Scant ¼ teaspoon pure almond extract

⅔ cup raspberry preserves

Powdered sugar for dusting (optional)

EQUIPMENT

A 9½-inch fluted tart pan with removable bottom or a 9-inch round cake pan (see Note)

COMBINE THE ALMONDS, flour, sugar, salt, cinnamon, and cloves in the bowl of a food processor and pulse until the almonds are finely ground. Add the butter, egg yolk, grated zests, and almond extract. Pulse just until blended.

To make the lattice first, trace a 9-inch circle on a piece of parchment paper. Pinch off about 1 tablespoon of dough. On a floured surface, with well-floured hands, roll the piece of dough into a pencil-thin rope (the lattice expands in the oven, so it must be very thin to start with) about 9 inches long. If the rope is too delicate to lift, roll it onto the edge of a cookie sheet or a piece of stiff paper to transfer it. Position it across the center of the traced circle. Repeat with 4 more pieces of dough, placing 2 on each side of the first, parallel and 1 inch apart. Make 5 more ropes and lay them across (perpendicular or at a slant) the first 5. Trim any lattice that extends beyond the circle, and add the trimmings to the remaining dough. Slide the paper with the lattice onto a plate and freeze until needed.

Grease the sides of the tart or cake pan and line the bottom (even if removable) with a circle of parchment paper. Press the remaining dough evenly over the bottom and up the sides of the tart pan. If using a cake pan, simply press all of the pastry evenly across the bottom. Chill for at least 1 hour.

Position a rack in the lower third of the oven and preheat the oven to 350°F.

Spread the preserves evenly over the pastry in the tart pan. If using a cake pan, leave a ½-inch border of pastry showing around the edges; the bare pastry will puff and form a raised edge as it bakes. Top with the lattice, pressing it in place.

Set the pan on a baking sheet and bake until golden brown, about 30 to 35 minutes. Tent the torte loosely with foil and continue baking to a deep golden brown, 10 to 15 minutes. (If your tart pan is blue steel or dark metal, this torte may be done a little earlier.) Cool in the pan on a rack for 10 minutes.

Loosen the rim of the tart pan all around by pushing the pan bottom up gently (you will need pot holders to do this). Or, if using a solid cake pan, run a slim knife or spatula around the inside to detach the cake.

When the torte is completely cool, remove the tart pan sides. Invert the torte onto a plate, remove the pan bottom or cake pan and the parchment liner, and turn the torte right side up, sprinkling with powdered sugar, if desired.

Store the torte at room temperature. It is most delicious served within 3 to 4 days, but it is still remarkably good after a week (or even two).

NOTE: I love to bake my linzer torte in a tart pan, but my linzer torte loves to stick around the fluted edges. So I grease the flutes meticulously, and loosen the rim, as noted, while the torte is still quite hot. If the possibility of a little sticking makes you anxious, choose the cake pan instead.

caramel-glazed cardamom palmiers

These fancy cardamom-scented cookies are made with a fast food-processor cream cheese dough instead of the classic, time-consuming puff pastry. The results are impressively flaky, crunchy, and caramelized . . . and worth the little extra time it takes to shape the cookies. *makes about forty-eight 3-inch cookies*

FOR THE DOUGH

2½ cups (11.25 ounces) all-purpose flour

2 tablespoons sugar

¼ teaspoon salt

½ pound (2 sticks) cold unsalted butter

8 ounces cold cream cheese

FOR THE CARDAMOM SUGAR

1 cup sugar

Scant 1 teaspoon ground cardamom

2 pinches of salt

EQUIPMENT

Baking sheets

TO MAKE THE DOUGH, combine the flour, sugar, and salt in the bowl of a food processor and pulse a few times to mix. Cut the butter into 8 pieces and add to the flour mixture. Pulse until the butter pieces are about the size of coarse bread crumbs. Cut the cream cheese into several pieces and add to the mixture. Process until the dough begins to clump together, about 30 seconds.

Divide the dough in half and shape into 2 square patties. Wrap and chill until firm, about 4 hours.

Remove 1 square of dough from the refrigerator and let it rest on the counter to soften slightly, 15 to 20 minutes. *Meanwhile, make the cardamom sugar:* Mix the sugar with the cardamom. Transfer 2 tablespoons of the sugar mixture to a small cup and add the salt. Mix thoroughly and set aside for baking the cookies.

Set aside half of the unsalted cardamom sugar for the second piece of dough. Sprinkle the work surface liberally with some of the remaining cardamom sugar. Set the dough on the sugared surface and sprinkle it with more cardamom sugar. Turn the dough frequently and resugar it and the work surface as you roll it into a rectangle 24 by 8 inches and less than ⅛ inch thick. Use the cardamom sugar generously both to prevent sticking and to ensure that the cookies will caramelize properly in the oven.

Trim the edges of the rectangle to even them. Turn the dough, if necessary, so one long side faces you and mark the center of the dough with a small indentation. Starting at one short edge, fold about 2½ inches of dough over, almost to one-third of the distance to the center mark. Without stretching or pulling, loosely fold the dough over two more times, leaving a scant ¼ inch before the center mark. Fold the other end of the dough over three times in the same way, leaving a tiny space at the center.

The dough should now resemble a tall, skinny, open book. Fold one side of the dough over the other side, as though closing the book. You will have an 8-layer strip of dough about 2½ inches wide and 8 inches long. Sprinkle cardamom sugar under and over the dough, and roll gently from one end of the dough to the other to compress the layers and lengthen the strip to about 9 inches. Wrap the dough loosely in wax paper (plastic wrap causes moisture to form on the outside of the dough and dissolve the sugar); set aside. Roll out, fold, and wrap the second piece of dough with the remaining cardamom sugar.

Chill the dough for at least 30 minutes.

Position the racks in the upper and lower thirds of the oven and preheat the oven to 375°F. Leave the baking sheets ungreased or line them with aluminum foil.

Remove one piece of dough from the refrigerator. Use a sharp knife to trim one short end evenly, then cut into 3-inch slices (I mark the dough at 1-inch intervals and cut 3 slices from each inch) and lay them 1½ inches apart on the baking sheets.

Bake until the cookies are golden brown on the undersides, 8 to 10 minutes, rotating the pans from back to front and top to bottom about halfway through the baking.

Remove the pans from the oven. Using a spatula, turn the cookies over and sprinkle each one with a pinch or two of the salted cardamom sugar. Return the sheets to the oven for 3 to 5 minutes more, until the cookies are deep golden brown on both sides. Watch the cookies carefully at this stage to avoid burning. Remove the pans from the oven and transfer the cookies to a rack to cool completely.

Remove the second piece of dough from the refrigerator, cut, and bake. Let cool.

The cookies keep in an airtight container for at least a week.

ginger florentines

Dressy caramel-almond cookies studded with crystallized ginger and drizzled with chocolate are an exotic alternative to the traditional orange and almond Florentine combination. The key to success with these very delicate cookies is to cool them completely before removing them from the foil, and then to pack them airtight as soon as possible.

makes about sixty 3-inch cookies or 30 sandwich cookies

½ cup sugar

¼ cup heavy cream

1 tablespoon honey

5 tablespoons unsalted butter, cut into pieces

Pinch of salt

1 tablespoon plus 1 teaspoon all-purpose flour

1 cup (3.5 ounces) sliced almonds

½ cup (2.5 ounces) minced crystallized ginger

3 ounces semisweet or bittersweet chocolate, finely chopped

EQUIPMENT

Candy thermometer

Baking sheets

Heavy-duty aluminum foil

POSITION A RACK in the center of the oven and preheat the oven to 350°F. Line the baking sheets with heavy-duty aluminum foil, smoothing any wrinkles (which would distort the cookies).

In a small saucepan, combine the sugar, cream, honey, butter, and salt. Stir over low heat until the butter is melted and the mixture comes to a simmer. Brush the sides of the pan with a wet pastry brush or wet wad of paper towel to remove any sugar crystals, and to prevent the sugar from crystallizing. Attach the candy thermometer to the pan and cook, without stirring, until the mixture reaches 238°F. Remove the pan from the heat and stir in the flour, almonds, and ginger.

Drop level teaspoons (no more) of batter about 3 inches apart onto one of the foil-lined baking sheets. With the back of a moistened spoon, flatten the cookies to a diameter of about 1½ inches. Bake until the cookies are a deep mahogany brown all over (if the cookies are not baked until deeply brown, they will be soft and sticky between your teeth rather than crisp and tender and they will stick to the foil), 6 to 8 minutes, reversing the sheet from front to back about halfway through the baking. The cookies should be baked one sheet at a time, but while the first batch bakes, you can continue to drop and flatten the batter on sheets of foil. Slide the foil onto a cool cookie sheet each time before baking. When each batch is done, slide the foil sheet of cookies onto a rack to cool completely before removing the cookies.

To remove the cookies without breakage, slide a thin metal spatula completely under each cookie, or peel the foil gently from under the cookie. (If you try to lift the edge of a cookie to detach it from the foil, it is likely to break.) The cookies are very fragile at first, less so several hours later. If you are not planning to drizzle them with chocolate immediately, store the cookies in an airtight container as soon as they are cooled.

Place the chocolate in a heatproof bowl (preferably stainless steel) in a skillet of hot but not even simmering water. Stir constantly until two-thirds of the chocolate is melted. Remove the bowl from the water and stir patiently until the remaining chocolate is melted.

Drizzle the tops of the cookies with the chocolate, or spread the backs of the cookies with chocolate and then sandwich them together. Let the chocolate set, then store the cookies airtight.

my gingersnaps

PHOTOGRAPH ON PAGE 96

With crunchy edges and a chewy center, beautifully crackled on top, spicy, and loaded with diced crystallized ginger, this is my favorite spice cookie. When no one is around, I dip these into a carton of quark for a grand, if inelegant, snack—the contrast of tangy cheese with spicy ginger reminds me of gingerbread with sour cream.

makes fifty-six 2¼-inch cookies

2 cups (9 ounces) all-purpose flour

2 teaspoons baking soda

2 teaspoons ground ginger

1½ teaspoons ground cinnamon

½ teaspoon ground allspice

¼ teaspoon salt

8 tablespoons (1 stick) unsalted butter, melted and just warm

¼ cup unsulphured mild or full-flavored molasses

½ cup sugar

⅓ cup (2.3 ounces) firmly packed brown sugar or light muscovado sugar

2 tablespoons finely minced or grated fresh ginger root

1 large egg

¾ cup (4 ounces) ginger chips or crystallized ginger, cut into ¼-inch dice

About ½ cup Demerara or turbinado or ¼ cup granulated sugar for rolling

EQUIPMENT

Baking sheets

POSITION THE RACKS in the upper and lower thirds of the oven and preheat the oven to 350°F. Line the baking sheets with parchment paper.

In a medium bowl, combine the flour, baking soda, ginger, cinnamon, allspice, and salt and mix thoroughly with a whisk. Set aside.

Combine the warm butter, molasses, both sugars, fresh ginger, and the egg in a large bowl and mix thoroughly. Add the flour mixture and ginger chips and stir until incorporated. The dough will be soft.

Form the dough into 1-inch balls (½ ounce of dough for each). Roll balls in the Demerara sugar and place them 2 inches apart on the baking sheets. Bake, rotating the sheets from back to front and top to bottom about halfway through the baking, for 10 to 12 minutes, or until they puff up and crack on the surface and then begin to deflate in the oven. For chewier cookies, remove them from the oven when at least half or more of the cookies have begun to deflate; for crunchier edges with chewy centers, bake a minute or so longer.

Slide the parchment sheets of cookies onto cooling racks or use an offset spatula to transfer the cookies, and cool completely. Stored in an airtight container, gingersnaps keep for several days.

aniseed and almond shortbread

This shortbread is sweet enough to be cookies, but not too sweet to nibble with a great glass of red wine. Whole wheat flour adds an extra toasted nutty flavor to the classic almond and anise combination. Serve alongside Strawberries with Rose Cream (page 103), or add them to your holiday cookie tray. They are also very nice with a little single-malt Scotch.

makes twenty-five 1½-inch squares

12 tablespoons (1½ sticks) unsalted butter, melted and still warm

4½ tablespoons sugar

1 tablespoon plus 1 teaspoon aniseed, slightly crushed to release the flavor

½ teaspoon pure vanilla extract

¼ teaspoon salt

¾ cup (3.4 ounces) all-purpose flour

¾ cup (3.4 ounces) whole wheat flour

½ cup (2.5 ounces) chopped (easiest) or slivered (great looking but trickier to use) almonds

Turbinado, Demerara, or granulated sugar for sprinkling

EQUIPMENT

An 8-inch square baking pan

LINE THE BOTTOM and all four sides of the baking pan with aluminum foil. In a medium bowl, combine the melted butter with the sugar, aniseed, vanilla, and salt. Add the flours and mix just until incorporated. Pat and spread the dough evenly in the prepared pan. Let stand for at least 2 hours, or overnight (no need to refrigerate).

Position a rack in the lower third of the oven and preheat the oven to 300°F.

Sprinkle the almonds evenly over the top of the shortbread and press them gently into the dough. Bake for 45 minutes.

Remove the pan from the oven, leaving the oven on. Sprinkle the shortbread with pinches of turbinado sugar. Let the shortbread cool for 10 minutes.

Using the foil, remove the shortbread from the pan, being careful to avoid breaking it. Use a thin sharp knife to cut into squares (cutting through slivered almonds may produce slightly ragged—rustic—edges). Place the pieces slightly apart on a parchment-lined baking sheet and return to the oven for 15 minutes. Cool on a rack.

Shortbread keeps for several weeks in an airtight container.

panforte nero

panpepato

I love the dense, sweet, chewy dried-fruit-and-nut confection called *panforte*. It's a splendid rich partner for coffee, dessert wines, or spirits, but it is also an inspired addition to a cheese platter. My first *panforte* was made in California by Mendocino food celebrity Margaret Fox, when we were both in our twenties and about to launch our respective businesses (my chocolate dessert shop, her restaurant). Margaret's *panforte* rivaled (topped!) the original Italian specialty from Siena. By the time we were in our thirties, I was buying oodles of *panforte* "di Mendocino" for my Cocolat shops. I finally visited Siena a few years ago, and I fell hard for the "other" *panforte*, the dark, spicy medieval rendition called *panpepato* ("pepper bread') or *panforte nero* ("black strong bread"). It's easy to make, is filled with tasty, healthy ingredients, and keeps forever.   serves 12 to 16

1 cup (4.75 ounces) hazelnuts, toasted and loose skins rubbed off

¾ cup (3.75 ounces) whole unblanched almonds, toasted

⅔ cup (3 ounces) all-purpose flour

2 tablespoons natural (nonalkalized) cocoa powder

2¼ teaspoons slightly crushed fennel seeds

Slightly rounded ½ teaspoon ground cinnamon

Slightly rounded ⅛ teaspoon ground cloves

Slightly rounded ¼ teaspoon finely ground white pepper

Slightly rounded ¼ teaspoon ground ginger

Slightly rounded ¼ teaspoon finely crushed coriander seeds

Slightly rounded ¼ teaspoon freshly grated nutmeg

Grated zest of 1 orange, preferably from an organic or unsprayed fruit

8 ounces dried Mission or other figs (see Note), tough stems cut off and sliced about ¼-inch thick

⅔ cup honey

⅔ cup sugar

Powdered sugar for dusting (optional)

EQUIPMENT

An 8-inch cake round pan

POSITION A RACK in the lower third of the oven and preheat the oven to 300°F. Grease the pan or spray it with vegetable oil spray. Line the bottom with a circle of parchment and the sides with a 2-inch-wide band of parchment. Grease the parchment, bottom and sides, liberally.

In a large bowl, mix the hazelnuts, almonds, flour, cocoa, spices, orange zest, and figs.

In a 3- to 4-quart saucepan, bring the honey and sugar to a full rolling boil. Boil for 15 seconds. Off the heat pour in the dry ingredients and mix well, working quickly, before the syrup cools.

Scrape the mixture into the prepared pan and spread it evenly. Bake until the batter bubbles in the center as well as at the edges, 40 to 45 minutes. Cool the *panforte* in the pan on a rack.

Invert the *panforte* onto a plate and remove the pan. Peel off the parchment and turn the *panforte* right side up. If desired, dust the top with powdered sugar. Serve in thin slices.

Panforte keeps for months, well wrapped, at room temperature.

NOTE: Good-quality figs are available in the bulk food sections of good groceries and in gourmet markets; those packaged by commercial dried fruit companies are generally not nearly as good.

vanilla bean tuiles

Plain vanilla? Out of the oven, the deep fragrance of ground vanilla beans may stir a memory from vanilla childhood: sweet cream-filled vanilla wafers, giant scoops of vanilla ice cream, vanilla-custard-filled éclairs. . . . *makes about forty 2½-inch tuiles*

3 tablespoons unsalted butter, melted and still warm

⅔ cup sugar

3 large egg whites

¼ cup plus 3 tablespoons (2 ounces) all-purpose flour (see Note)

¾ teaspoon ground vanilla beans (purchased or ground in a coffee or spice grinder)

⅛ teaspoon salt

EQUIPMENT

Baking sheets

Silicone baking mats or heavy-duty foil (see page 91 for a discussion of foil versus silicone mats)

Small cups or a rolling pin for shaping the cookies (optional)

PLACE A RACK in the center of the oven and preheat oven to 300°F. Line the baking sheets with foil dull side facing up, and smooth the foil to remove any wrinkles (which would distort the cookies). Or line with silicone mats. Lightly butter the foil or the silicone mats.

In a small bowl, whisk together all of the ingredients until blended.

If using silicone mats, drop level teaspoons of batter 2 inches apart onto a baking sheet (bake only one sheet at a time). Using a small offset spatula, spread the batter into rounds, ovals, or elongated shapes less than ⅛ inch thick. Bake, watching carefully, until the tuiles are golden brown half to three-quarters of the way to the center but still pale in the center, 10 to 15 minutes. If the cookies are not baked long enough, they will not be completely crisp when cool. As soon as you can coax a thin metal spatula under a tuile without destroying the cookie, transfer it to a rack to cool flat. Or shape it by draping it over a rolling pin, nestling it into a little cup, or twisting it with your fingers. Working fast, remove the remaining tuiles. Repeat until all of the tuiles are baked.

If using foil, drop level teaspoons of batter 2 inches apart onto a baking sheet (bake only one sheet at a time). Bake, watching carefully, until the batter spreads and the cookies are golden brown half to three-quarters of the way to the center, but still pale in the center, 10 to 15 minutes. If the cookies are not baked long enough, they will not be completely crisp when cool. For flat tuiles, slide the foil sheet of cookies onto a rack to cool. For curved tuiles, grasp the edges of the foil when the sheet comes from the oven (without touching the hot pan or the cookies) and roll it into a fat cylinder, gently curving the attached cookies like potato chips. Crimp or secure the foil with a paper clip and set aside. When cool, unroll the foil carefully and remove the tuiles.

Alternatively, as described above, remove individual tuiles from the foil while they are hot and shape them in small cups or with your fingers. Flat or curved, tuiles are easiest to remove from the foil when completely cool. Repeat until all of the tuiles are baked.

Store the cooled tuiles in an airtight container, where they will keep for at least a week.

NOTE: Even a little too much flour may result in a thick and tough, rather than thin and crisp, tuile. Review how to measure flour (page 3), or if you have a digital scale, use it here.

cinnamon stick tuiles

Fussy bakers know that freshly grated nutmeg is superior to ground nutmeg. But what about cinnamon? I was astonished at the flavor and aroma to be had from simply grating stick cinnamon with a Microplane grater—and at how easy it was.

Substitute 1½ teaspoons freshly grated stick cinnamon (or a slightly rounded ½ teaspoon ground cinnamon) for the ground vanilla beans.

lavender tuiles

Lavender can taste soapy or medicinal in food if it is dosed with a heavy hand. Here, a little finesse produces a pretty cookie with a lovely scent and flavor. You will enjoy it with tea or Heavenly Honey Ice Cream (page 177) or with fresh berries. Dried lavender can be found in the spice section of a good supermarket or gourmet shop or by mail order (see Resources, page 249). If you grow your own, make sure it is culinary lavender—the variety *L. x intermedia,* also called Provence lavender—as other varieties can be unpleasantly pungent and resinous.

makes about forty 2½-inch tuiles

3 tablespoons unsalted butter

⅜ teaspoon crushed dried culinary lavender

⅔ cup sugar

3 large egg whites

¼ cup plus 3 tablespoons (2 ounces) all-purpose flour (see Note)

⅛ teaspoon salt

EQUIPMENT

Baking sheets

Silicone baking mats or heavy-duty foil (see page 91 for a discussion of foil versus silicone mats)

Small cups or a rolling pin for shaping the cookies (optional)

PLACE A RACK in the center of the oven and preheat the oven to 300°F. Line the baking sheets with foil dull side facing up, and smooth the foil to remove any wrinkles (which would distort the cookies). Or line with silicone mats. Lightly butter the foil or the silicone mats.

In a small saucepan, gently heat the butter until it is melted and very warm (not hot). Off the heat, stir in the lavender. Cover and allow to infuse for 5 minutes.

In a small bowl, whisk the butter and lavender together with the rest of the ingredients until blended.

If using silicone mats, drop level teaspoons of batter 2 inches apart onto a baking sheet (bake only one sheet at a time). Using a small offset spatula, spread the batter into rounds, ovals, or elongated shapes less than ⅛ inch thick. Bake, watching carefully, until the tuiles are golden brown, half to three-quarters of the way to the center, but still pale in the center, 10 to 15 minutes. If the cookies are not baked long enough, they will not be completely crisp when cool. As soon as you can coax a thin metal spatula under a tuile without destroying it, transfer it to a rack to cool flat. Or shape it by draping it over a rolling pin, nestling it into a little cup, or twisting it with your fingers. Working fast, remove the remaining tuiles. Repeat until all of the tuiles are baked.

If using foil, drop level teaspoons of batter 2 inches apart onto a baking sheet (bake only one sheet at a time). Bake, watching carefully, until the batter spreads and the cookies are golden brown half to three-quarters of the way to the center but still pale

in the center, 10 to 15 minutes. If the cookies are not baked long enough, they will not be completely crisp when cool. For flat tuiles, slide the foil sheet of cookies onto a rack to cool. For curved tuiles, grasp the edges of the foil when the sheet comes from the oven (without touching the hot pan or the cookies) and roll it into a fat cylinder, gently curving the attached cookies like potato chips. Crimp or secure the foil with a paper clip and set aside. When cool, unroll the foil carefully and remove the tuiles. Alternatively, as described above, remove individual tuiles from the foil while they are hot and shape them in small cups or with your fingers. Flat or curved, tuiles are easiest to remove from the foil when completely cool. Repeat until all of the tuiles are baked.

Store the cooled tuiles in an airtight container, where they will keep for at least a week.

NOTE: Even a little too much flour may result in a thick and tough, rather than thin and crisp tuile. Review how to measure flour (page 3), or if you have a digital scale, use it here.

jasmine tuiles

The flavor of jasmine is sultry and floral. It begins very slowly—you may hardly taste it at first—but it builds and lasts on your palate for a long time, like great wine or chocolate. Jasmine tuiles are a compelling partner for citrus, for example, or Heavenly Honey Ice Cream (page 177).

Substitute ¾ teaspoon crushed jasmine tea for the lavender.

rose tuiles

These have a pretty multicolored confetti effect from the tea and rose petals.

Substitute ¾ teaspoon crushed rose tea for the lavender.

saffron tuiles

These are exotic and impressively aromatic. Serve them with Saffron and Cardamom Panna Cotta (page 221), or a bowl of fresh sweet strawberries, or nibble with tea.

Substitute a scant ⅜ teaspoon crushed saffron threads for the crushed lavender.

fresh thyme or tarragon tuiles

Substitute 2¼ teaspoons finely chopped fresh thyme, lemon thyme or tarragon leaves for the lavender. You may also substitute olive oil for the butter, if desired.

jasmine panna cotta

This delicate, sensual dessert is flavored and scented with an infusion of jasmine green tea. Serve it unadorned with a bowl of mandarin oranges on the table. Or accompany with crisp Lemon Tuiles (page 118) or sliced sweet strawberries. The finest panna cotta is tender and quivering, just barely holding a shape. To avoid a texture like Jell-O, measure gelatin carefully or use sheet gelatin. Start the recipe one day ahead to allow the flavor of the jasmine tea to infuse into the cream.

serves 6

¼ cup plus 1 tablespoon good-quality jasmine tea leaves

3 cups heavy cream, or more as needed

¼ cups whole milk

2½ teaspoons unflavored gelatin (see Note)

¼ cup plus 2 tablespoons sugar

⅛ teaspoon salt

EQUIPMENT

Instant-read thermometer

6 wide margarita glasses or six 6-ounce ramekins or dessert dishes

THE DAY BEFORE you plan to serve, in a medium bowl, stir the tea into the cream. Cover and refrigerate for 8 to 12 hours to infuse. Strain out and discard the tea. Measure the cream and add extra if necessary to make 3 cups. If you are not ready to make the dessert, refrigerate the infused cream until you need it.

Pour the milk into a small bowl and sprinkle the gelatin over it. Set aside (without stirring) for 5 to 10 minutes to let the gelatin soften.

Meanwhile, in a small saucepan, heat the cream, sugar, and salt until steaming hot, stirring from time to time to dissolve the sugar. Off the heat, add the milk and gelatin and stir well to dissolve the gelatin. Transfer to a bowl, preferably stainless steel, set the bowl in a larger bowl of water and ice cubes, and stir frequently until the mixture thickens and registers 50°F on the instant-read thermometer.

Divide the mixture evenly among the glasses or ramekins. Cover with plastic wrap and chill for at least 4 but preferably 12 hours, or overnight.

Serve the panna cotta in the glasses or ramekins. Or wrap each ramekin briefly in a wrung-out hot wet towel and unmold the panna cotta onto dessert plates.

NOTE: You can substitute 3 leaves of sheet gelatin for the granulated gelatin. Soak the leaves in the cold milk to soften them, then fish the softened sheets from the milk and stir them into the hot cream until dissolved. Stir in the milk, and proceed as directed.

saffron and cardamom
panna cotta

I conjured this dessert from the memory of an exotic Indian rice dish scented with saffron, cardamom, and cinnamon. The spices accentuate the rich flavors of the milk, cream, (and pistachios if you like them), and freshly grated stick cinnamon pulls the whole thing together with a heady top note of flavor and perfume. *serves 6*

3¼ cups heavy cream

⅓ cup sugar

Pinch of salt

5 cardamom pods

Slightly rounded ⅛ teaspoon crushed saffron threads

1 cup whole milk

2½ teaspoons unflavored gelatin (see Note)

1 cinnamon stick

Finely chopped or grated pistachios for garnish (optional)

EQUIPMENT

Instant-read thermometer

Six 6-ounce ramekins or dessert dishes

IN A SMALL SAUCEPAN, heat the cream, sugar, and salt until steaming hot, stirring from time to time to dissolve the sugar. Off the heat, add the cardamom pods and saffron. Cover and allow to steep for 25 minutes. Meanwhile, pour the milk into a small bowl and sprinkle the gelatin over it. Set aside (without stirring) for 5 to 10 minutes to let the gelatin soften.

Add the milk and gelatin to the cream mixture and reheat to steaming, stirring well to dissolve the gelatin. Strain the mixture into a bowl, preferably stainless steel; discard the cardamom pods. Set the bowl in a larger bowl of water and ice cubes and stir frequently until the mixture thickens and registers 50°F on the instant-read thermometer.

Divide the mixture evenly among the ramekins or dessert dishes. Cover with plastic wrap and chill for at least 4 but preferably 12 hours. Serve the individual panna cottas in their ramekins or dishes, or unmold the ramekins: wrap each one briefly in a wrung-out hot wet towel and unmold them onto dessert plates. Use a Microplane zester to grate a little stick cinnamon over each one. Sprinkle with chopped or grated pistachios, if desired.

NOTE: You can substitute 3 leaves of sheet gelatin for the granulated gelatin. Soak the leaves in the cold milk to soften them, then fish the softened sheets from the milk and stir them into the hot cream (after steeping) until completely dissolved. Stir in the milk, and proceed as directed.

fresh mint and lemon
verbena ice cream

A cold infusion of mint and lemon verbena makes a fragrant and refreshing ice cream—a good reason to plant peppermint and lemon verbena in your garden.

makes 4 cups

1½ cups heavy cream

1½ cups whole milk

⅓ cup sugar

⅛ teaspoon salt

¼ cup lightly packed coarsely chopped
fresh peppermint

¼ cup lightly packed coarsely chopped
fresh lemon verbena

EQUIPMENT

Instant-read thermometer

Ice cream machine

COMBINE THE CREAM, milk, sugar, and salt in a bowl and stir to dissolve the sugar. Stir in the mint and lemon verbena leaves, cover the bowl, and refrigerate for 8 to 12 hours to infuse.

Strain the mixture into a medium bowl, pressing gently on the leaves to extract as much of the liquid as you can without bruising them; discard the leaves. For an extra-cold start, chill the mixture in the freezer for 20 minutes, stirring once or twice to prevent freezing. Freeze according to the instructions for your ice cream maker.

Serve soft or transfer to an airtight container and freeze until hard enough to scoop, at least 3 to 4 hours. If the ice cream gets too hard, before serving let it stand for a few minutes, put it in the refrigerator for 15 minutes or longer, or microwave it on low (defrost) for a few seconds at a time until scoopable.

rose geranium ice cream

Substitute ½ cup coarsely chopped unsprayed, preferably organic, rose geranium leaves for the mint and lemon verbena.

rose water and mint
ice cream

A delicate, fresh-flavored ice cream to serve with white peaches, white nectarines, or sweet strawberries.   makes about 3½ cups

½ cup whole milk

6 fresh mint leaves

½ cup sugar

Slightly rounded ⅛ teaspoon salt

2¼ cups heavy cream

¼ teaspoon rose water, or more to taste

EQUIPMENT

Ice cream machine

COMBINE THE MILK and mint leaves in the bowl of a food processor and pulse until the leaves are finely chopped.

Set a fine strainer over a bowl and strain the milk, pressing on the mint to extract all the liquid; discard the mint. Add the sugar and salt, stirring until the sugar is dissolved. Stir in the cream and rose water.

Taste and adjust the rosewater (depending on the brand and your own sensitivity to this flavor, you may have to increase the amount to as much as 2 teaspoons, or even more). For an extra-cold start, chill the mixture in the freezer for 20 minutes, stirring once or twice to prevent freezing. Freeze according to the instructions for your ice cream machine.

Serve soft or transfer to an airtight container and freeze until hard enough to scoop, at least 3 to 4 hours. If the ice cream gets too hard, before serving let it stand for a few minutes, put it in the refrigerator for 15 minutes or longer, or microwave it on low (defrost) for a few seconds at a time until scoopable.

If you are going to play with ice cream, here are a few rules that affect flavor and texture. Before they are frozen, ice cream and sorbet mixes should taste a tad sweeter than you want the final product to be, as freezing dulls our perception of sweetness. With practice, you will be able to taste and adjust sweetness fairly accurately before you freeze your mixes. When making fruit sorbets and sherbets, adjust the balance of sweetness and tanginess (acidity) by adding drops of lemon juice and/or tiny pinches of salt along with sugar until the fruit flavor is as clear and bright as possible.

Homemade ice creams and sorbets freeze harder and icier than commercial products because they don't use stabilizers or invert sugars to keep them creamy and smooth. Deal with hardness by putting the container in the refrigerator to soften the ice cream gently before scooping, or carefully microwave for a few seconds on low, just as you would for ultrarich super-premium ice creams from the supermarket. Also, absent commercial stabilizers, homemade ice creams are best consumed within a day or so, as they get icier and sometimes grainy after that—though sorbets are a little more forgiving because they are icy to begin with. For maximum smoothness, your ice cream base should be as cold as possible (between 27° and 35°F according to food scientist Shirley Corriher) before you put it in the ice cream machine. If the base contains cooked milk, at least 4 and preferably 12 hours of chilling alters the proteins in the milk and makes the ice cream smoother. Even after chilling overnight, you can improve the results by putting the base in the freezer for 15 to 20 minutes and stirring a couple of times to be sure it doesn't actually freeze around the edges. If your ice cream machine has its own freezing unit, turn it on to pre-chill for a few minutes before using it.

Sugar and alcohol make sorbets and ice creams softer and creamier, to a point, by raising the temperature at which they freeze and by actually preventing the mixtures from becoming entirely frozen. Many cooks also use a tablespoon of corn syrup in place of sugar for more smoothness and softness; or you can use honey if the flavor complements the ice cream. When it comes to sweeteners, though, I want only the amount that tastes right for the ice cream or sorbet—I see no point in adding extra sugar just to get a softer texture. One to three teaspoons of alcohol can be used to soften and smooth the texture of sorbets in particular. Use spirits that have a relatively neutral flavor, such as vodka, or choose something that complements the sorbet or ice cream you are making, such as kirsch or framboise in red fruit sorbets. A variety of spirits, including brandy, bourbon, and rum, can enhance ice creams.

Be advised, however, that too much sugar or alcohol will prevent freezing. So, if your sorbet looks slushy and melted even after hours in the freezer, you've probably gone way overboard with sugar and/or alcohol. Ice cream making is more like cooking than baking in that you can taste and adjust the flavor and "seasoning" along the way. If you have a disappointing batch of sorbet, you can even let it melt and correct the flavors—adding more fruit, or more water, or alcohol or sugar, or what have you—and refreeze it!

Finally, be aware that the fanciest or most expensive ice cream machines do not necessarily produce the best ice cream. Machines that churn quickly pump air into the ice cream, which may be acceptable for super-rich mixes but not for the most flavorful sherbets and sorbets or for the leaner mixtures of milk and cream that I prefer. For anyone willing (not me!), old-fashioned hand-crank machines that require rock salt and ice certainly make fabulous ice cream, because no one can churn them fast enough to overaerate. More practical are machines with canisters that are placed in the freezer for several hours before the ice cream is made. Of these, I continue to prefer the very basic Donvier machine, with its easy hand crank, to those with speedy electric churns. If you want a more costly machine with a self-contained freezer unit, check out the churn speed, even if you have to contact the manufacturer to do so, then choose the one that churns at the slowest rate—or hope that by the time this book is published there will be a machine with adjustable speed. I use the Lello Gelato machine with an integral refrigeration unit and a relatively slow agitator.

golden vanilla bean caramels

Vanilla caramels made with ground whole vanilla beans (or pure extract) and golden syrup, instead of the usual corn syrup, are irresistible. A candy thermometer is essential for this recipe.   *makes eighty-one 1-inch caramels*

1 cup golden syrup

2 cups sugar

⅜ teaspoon fine sea salt

2 cups heavy cream

1½ teaspoons pure ground vanilla beans, purchased or ground in a coffee or spice grinders, or 1 tablespoon plus 1 teaspoon pure vanilla extract

3 tablespoons unsalted butter, cut into chunks, softened

EQUIPMENT

A 9-inch square baking pan

Candy thermometer

LINE THE BOTTOM and sides of the baking pan with aluminum foil and grease the foil. Combine the golden syrup, sugar, and salt in a heavy 3-quart saucepan and cook over medium heat, stirring with a silicone spatula or wooden spoon, until the mixture begins to simmer around the edges. Wash the sugar and syrup from the sides of the pan with a pastry brush dipped in water. Cover and cook for about 3 minutes. (Meanwhile, rinse the spatula or spoon before using it again later.) Uncover the pan and wash down the sides once more. Attach the candy thermometer to the pan, without letting it touch the bottom of the pan, and cook, uncovered (without stirring) until the mixture reaches 305°F. Meanwhile, combine the cream and ground vanilla beans (not the extract) in a small saucepan and heat until tiny bubbles form around the edges of the pan. Turn off the heat and cover the pan to keep the cream hot.

When the sugar mixture reaches 305°F, turn off the heat and stir in the butter chunks. Gradually stir in the hot cream; it will bubble up and steam dramatically, so be careful. Turn the burner back on and adjust it so that the mixture boils energetically but not violently. Stir until any thickened syrup at the bottom of the pan is dissolved and the mixture is smooth. Continue to cook, stirring occasionally, to about 245°F. Then cook, stirring constantly, to 260°F for soft, chewy caramels or 265°F for firmer chewy caramels.

Remove the pan from the heat and stir in the vanilla extract, if using it. Pour the caramel into the lined pan. Let set for 4 to 5 hours, or overnight, until firm.

Lift the pan liner from the pan and invert the sheet of caramel onto a sheet of parchment paper. Peel off the liner. Cut the caramels with an oiled knife. Wrap each caramel individually in wax paper or cellophane.

fleur de sel caramels

Extra salt, in the form of fleur de sel or another coarse flaked salt, brings out the flavor of the caramel and offers a little ying to the yang. Add an extra scant ¼ teaspoon of coarse sea salt to the recipe. Or, to keep the salt crunchy, let the caramel cool and firm. Then sprinkle with two pinches of flaky salt and press it in. Invert, remove the pan liner, sprinkle with more salt. Then cut and wrap the caramels in wax paper or cellophane.

nutmeg and vanilla bean caramels

Add ½ teaspoon freshly grated nutmeg to the cream before you heat it.

cardamom caramels

Use the Golden Vanilla Bean Caramels or Honey Caramels (page 180) recipe to make these.

Omit the vanilla. Add ½ teaspoon slightly crushed cardamom seeds (from about 15 cardamom pods) to the cream before heating it. Strain the cream when you add it to the caramel; discard the seeds.

■ CARAMEL SAUCE

Homemade is much better than store-bought caramel sauce over ice cream, poached pears, rice pudding—or you name it.

Stop cooking any caramel recipe or variation when it reaches 225°F or, for a sauce that thickens like hot fudge over ice cream, 228°F. Pour it into a sauceboat to serve or into a heatproof jar for storage. The sauce can be stored in the refrigerator for ages and reheated gently in the microwave or a saucepan just until hot and flowing before use. You can stir in rum or brandy to taste. If the sauce is too thick or stiff to serve over ice cream, it can always be thinned with a little water or cream. Or, if you like a sauce that thickens more over ice cream, simmer it for a few minutes longer.

lavender caramel sauce

Pour this perfumed caramel sauce over Vanilla Bean (page 55) or Crema Ice Cream (page 54), and sprinkle with chopped pistachios. This makes a big batch of sauce, but it keeps almost indefinitely in the refrigerator and makes a perfect gift.　　　makes 3½ cups

2 cups heavy cream

1 tablespoon dried culinary lavender

¾ cup golden syrup or light corn syrup

¼ cup honey

2 cups sugar

¼ teaspoon fine sea salt

3 tablespoons unsalted butter, cut into chunks

EQUIPMENT

Candy thermometer

Silicone spatula or wooden spoon

ONE DAY BEFORE serving, in a small bowl, combine the cream and the lavender. Cover and refrigerate for 8 to 12 hours.

Strain the cream into a small saucepan, pressing on the lavender to extract all the liquid; discard the lavender. Heat the cream until small bubbles form around the edges of the pan. Cover and set aside.

Combine the golden syrup or corn syrup, honey, sugar, and salt in a heavy 3 quart saucepan and cook over medium heat, stirring with a silicone spatula or wooden spoon, until the mixture begins to simmer around the edges. Wash the sugar and syrup from the sides of the pan with a pastry brush dipped in water. Cover and cook for about 3 minutes. (Meanwhile, rinse the spatula or spoon for use again later.) Uncover the pan and wash down the sides once more. Attach the thermometer to the pan without letting it touch the bottom and cook, uncovered (without stirring), until the mixture reaches 305°F.

When the sugar mixture is at 305°F, turn off the heat and stir in the butter chunks. Gradually stir in the hot cream, taking care, as the mixture will bubble up and steam dramatically. Turn the burner back on and adjust it so that the mixture boils energetically but not violently. Stir, scraping the bottom and sides of the pan, until the cream is completely incorporated and the sauce is smooth. Continue to cook, stirring occasionally, until the mixture reaches 225°F or, for a sauce that thickens like hot fudge over ice cream, 228°F.

Pour the caramel sauce into a sauceboat to serve or into a heatproof jar for storage. The sauce can be stored in the refrigerator indefinitely; before using reheat gently in the microwave or a saucepan, just until warm and flowing.

Ice cream sundae with pistachios and Lavender Caramel Sauce

the flavors of wine,
beer,
and spirits

There is no more cooking sherry in the cupboard. And long gone are the days when we uncorked a bottle of wine only for company. Today microbreweries have groupies, and cocktails are fashionable again. The liquor cabinet has become a playground for the creative cook and may hold some pretty interesting or exotic bottles, including handcrafted "artisan" spirits, flavored vodkas, single-malt Scotch, as well as one or a variety of sherries, Ports, or dessert wines from Italy, Hungary, or France. We now drink with an appreciation for the flavor as well as the alcohol content in our glass.

We also aren't afraid to pour good wine, beer, or spirits into sweet or savory dishes. Ironically, in light of our greater comfort with alcohol in a daily context, cooking and baking with these beverages lets us taste them sans alcohol, which also adds to our knowledge of their true flavors! The taste of real Spanish sherry in an olive-oil-laced pound cake, or Italian vin santo in a sponge cake will make you smile. Our growing taste for bitter flavors—signaled by our Europeanized coffee drinking habits, more sophisticated taste in cheeses, and love of wine and microbrews—makes Guinness Ice Cream (page 235) a delectable possibility, along with edgy, icily appealing granitas made with beer or wine. And why not lace chocolates with infused vodka instead of the usual cognac or rum?

Marlena's wine bath with figs, peaches, and raspberries

Marlena Spieler writes one of my favorite columns in the *San Francisco Chronicle* food section, while living in London and working for the BBC and writing cookbooks too. With her blessing, I am sharing this fabulously versatile, slurpily good way to revel in ripe summer fruit with wine—complete with my own editorial commentary.

Certainly you should open a bottle expressly to make this, but remember the recipe also when you have wine open that might spoil before you can finish it. I've set up the recipe to highlight the wine bath, which can be used separately and in different ways. If you have no fruit immediately on hand, you can make the wine bath and find the fruit later—just reheat the bath and douse the fruit when you get it. Peaches, figs, and raspberries are fabulous, but other combinations that you dream up will also be wonderful. Or, say it's winter: forget the fruit. Reduce the wine a bit more, add extra sugar to taste, and voilà: a perfect sweet and tangy sauce for ice cream. Or serve it in wide shallow bowls (with or without the fruit) with a little island of ice cream and some cookies alongside and call it soup. Interestingly, the wine reduction coaxes appealing notes from the vanilla bean, low sexy flavors reminiscent of sap or wood that round the sharp edges of the wine and accentuate its own fruit. White wine is good too.

serves 4 to 6

FOR THE BATH

4 cups dry red wine (or white wine, if desired)

¼ to ½ cup sugar

½ vanilla bean

8 ripe figs, stemmed and cut lengthwise in half

4 ripe peaches, peeled, pitted, and sliced

1 to 1½ pints (2 to 3 cups) Vanilla Bean Ice Cream (page 55), Heavenly Honey Ice Cream (page 177), or Sour Cream Ice Cream (page 49) or store-bought ice cream

½ pint fresh raspberries

TO MAKE THE BATH, in a large saucepan, combine the wine, ¼ cup of the sugar, and the vanilla bean. Slowly bring the wine to a boil, taking care that it does not catch fire. (If it does, simply let the flames die away, which will take a minute or two.) Continue to cook over medium heat until the wine is reduced by half. Taste and add more sugar if necessary, depending on the wine, your taste, and the ripeness and flavor of the fruit. (You can further correct the sweetness even after you've combined the hot wine and fruit.)

If the fruit is very ripe, put it into a bowl and pour the wine over it. If it is firm, add it to the saucepan and simmer briefly in the wine to soften it slightly, but not to cook it through, then pour the wine and fruit into the bowl.

Cool and refrigerate until well chilled. The mixture will look dark and winey.

Serve the chilled fruit and wine syrup over the ice cream, and scatter the fresh raspberries on top.

Guinness ice cream

Ice cream made of beer was the logical outcome of my thinking that most ice creams are too sweet. If you love bitter flavors and beer, you will love ice cream made with beer. Even if you don't love beer, you might like how the sweetness and custard base affects the beer. I started with a base of cream and then tried a light custard before settling on an even richer custard to complement the flavor of the Guinness. This ice cream is delicious with ripe strawberries.

makes about 3 cups

1 cup heavy cream
¼ cup plus 3 tablespoons sugar
⅛ teaspoon salt
4 large egg yolks
One 11- to 12-ounce bottle Guinness

EQUIPMENT
Instant-read thermometer
Ice cream machine

PLACE A STRAINER over a medium bowl and set it near the stove, for the finished ice cream base.

In a medium saucepan, combine the cream, sugar, and salt and bring to a simmer over medium heat.

Meanwhile, in a medium bowl, whisk the egg yolks to break them up. Whisking constantly, pour the hot cream mixture slowly over the egg yolks. Scrape the mixture back into the saucepan and cook over medium heat, stirring constantly, until the mixture thickens slightly and registers 175° to 180°F on the thermometer. Strain the custard, to remove any bits of cooked egg, into the clean bowl.

Stir the Guinness into the custard mixture. Refrigerate at least 4, preferably 12 hours. For an extra cold start, put the mixture in the freezer for 20 minutes, stirring once or twice to prevent freezing. Freeze according to the instructions for your ice cream machine.

Serve soft or transfer to an airtight container and freeze until the ice cream is hard enough to scoop, at least 3 to 4 hours. If the ice cream gets too hard, before serving let it stand for a few minutes, put it in the refrigerator for 15 minutes or longer, or microwave it on low (defrost) for a few seconds at a time until scoopable.

microbrew ice cream

Substitute a malty or rich or light-flavored beer such as pale ales, pilsners, lagers, wheat beers, or brown ales for the Guinness. Even if you love to sip them, India pale ales and other extra-hoppy brews are too bitter for ice cream.

vin santo chiffon cake

Adapted from an exquisite recipe in Lindsay Shere's book *Chez Panisse Desserts*, this is a light, moist chiffon-style sponge cake with a golden brown top and the flavor and fragrance of vin santo—or any other sweet white wine—and a nuance of olive oil. Serve with whipped cream and peaches or nectarines splashed with the same wine used in the cake, or with sliced oranges drizzled with honey and wine.   serves 10

⅔ cup sugar

7 large eggs, separated, at room temperature

¼ teaspoon salt

¼ teaspoon finely grated orange zest, preferably from an organic or unsprayed fruit

¼ teaspoon finely grated lemon zest, preferably from an organic or unsprayed fruit

2 tablespoons extra virgin olive oil

½ cup vin santo or other sweet white wine, at room temperature

½ teaspoon cream of tartar

1 cup (3.5 ounces) sifted (before measuring) cake flour

EQUIPMENT

A 9-inch springform pan or a 9 by 3-inch round pan with a removable bottom

POSITION A RACK in the lower third of the oven and preheat the oven to 325°F. Grease the sides of the springform pan and line the bottom with parchment.

To make the batter with a hand-held mixer (see Note), combine ¼ cup of sugar, the egg yolks, salt, and both zests in a medium or small bowl and beat at high speed until thick and light in color. Gradually beat in the olive oil, followed by the vin santo.

Wash the beaters and dry them. Put the egg whites and cream of tartar in a large bowl and beat at high speed until soft peaks form when the beaters are lifted. Gradually beat in the remaining ⅓ cup sugar and continue to beat until the egg whites are **stiff** but still moist when the beaters are lifted.

To make the batter with a stand mixer (see Note), combine ⅓ cup of the sugar, the egg yolks, salt, and both zests in the mixer bowl and beat at high speed until thick and light in color. Gradually beat in the olive oil, followed by the vin santo. Scrape the mixture into another bowl.

Wash the beaters and bowl and dry them. Add the egg whites and cream of tartar to the bowl and beat at medium speed until soft peaks form when the beaters are lifted. On high speed, gradually add the remaining sugar and beat until the egg whites are stiff but still moist when the beaters are lifted.

Pour half of the egg mixture over the egg whites, sift half of the flour on top, and fold until nearly incorporated. Scrape the remaining egg mixture into the bowl and sift in the remaining flour. Fold just until the ingredients are blended.

Scrape the batter into the prepared pan. Bake until the cake is puffed and golden, about 30 minutes. Reduce the temperature to 300°F and bake until a thin wooden skewer inserted in the center of the cake comes out clean, 10 to 15 minutes. If the cake is browning too fast, place a piece of buttered parchment or wax paper on top. Cool the cake in the pan on a rack for at least 10 minutes, then remove it from the pan and cool on the rack.

The cake stays moist for at least 2 to 3 days if refrigerated, tightly wrapped.

NOTE: If you have both a hand-held mixer and a stand mixer, you can use the former for the egg yolks and the latter for the whites, so you don't have to wash equipment in between.

strawberries with single-malt sabayon

Strawberries in foamy sweet wine custard, made with sherry or Madeira or Sauternes, is a delicious classic. Less traditional, the flavor of single-malt Scotch with strawberries is an exciting surprise. You don't need a recipe to splash berries with Scotch and sprinkle them with sugar (which I highly recommend), but if you want to take that idea a step further, here is the foamy custard sauce with single-malt. You can serve the sauce hot, as soon as it's made—in which case, you should have your berries ready to serve, either sliced and plain, or splashed with Scotch and lightly sugared to taste—or you can chill the sauce to serve later. You can also serve the strawberries and Sabayon with wedges of sponge cake or Twice-Baked Shortbread (page 38). serves 6

SINGLE-MALT SABAYON (makes 2 cups)

6 large egg yolks

¼ cup plus 1 tablespoon sugar

⅔ cup dry white wine, such as sauvignon blanc

⅓ cup single-malt Scotch (choose one that is not too smoky or peaty; see Note)

2 pints ripe strawberries, rinsed, hulled, and sliced

Single-malt Scotch to splash the berries (optional)

Sugar to taste

To make the sabayon, in a medium stainless steel bowl, whisk the yolks and sugar. Whisk in the wine and Scotch. Put the bowl in a wide skillet with an inch of cool water in it, set the skillet over medium heat, and whisk constantly until the mixture becomes foamy and thick. This will take a few minutes—don't increase the heat to speed this up, or the sauce will not be as stable or thick as you want it to be. Continue whisking until the sauce is hot to the touch (about 160°F) and a ribbon of sauce holds a gentle shape as it falls back onto the surface. Serve immediately, or refrigerate, covered, for up to 1 day and serve it chilled.

NOTE: Choose a single malt with a honeyed, sherried, or floral character. Balvenie or a fifteen-year-old Longmoran, or any of the milder Lowlands Scotches such as Auchentoshan will do, or try the American single malt from St. George Spirits (see Resources, page 249).

cherry and kirsch gratin

Fresh, saucy cherries in kirsch are topped with a white-wine-and-kirsch-laced custard and browned quickly under the broiler. You can reinvent this recipe for other berries or sliced peaches, nectarines, plums, etc. The results are somehow both homey and sophisticated. Store-bought amaretti (Italian almond cookies) make a good accompaniment.

serves 6

FOR THE TOPPING

6 large egg yolks

¼ cup plus 1 tablespoon sugar

2½ tablespoons all-purpose flour

⅔ cup dry white wine, such as sauvignon blanc

⅓ cup kirsch

½ cup plus 3 tablespoons heavy cream

FOR THE FRUIT

3 cups (14 to 16 ounces) sweet cherries

3 tablespoons kirsch

1 tablespoon sugar, or to taste

1 teaspoon fresh lemon juice, or to taste

EQUIPMENT

An 8 by 12-inch rectangular or oval glass or ceramic baking dish

To make the topping, set a medium bowl next to the stove. In a medium nonreactive saucepan, whisk the egg yolks with the sugar and flour until well blended. Whisk in the wine and kirsch. Cook over medium heat, whisking constantly, until the mixture becomes a thick custard. Continue to whisk for 2 minutes (to cook the flour), or until the custard becomes slightly less thick and slightly translucent.

Immediately scrape the custard into the bowl. Stir in 3 tablespoons of the cream. Place a piece of wax or parchment paper on the surface of the custard to prevent a skin from forming. Refrigerate until cool, or until needed.

To prepare the fruit, pit and halve the cherries. Place them in a medium bowl, add the kirsch, sugar, and lemon juice, stir, and let macerate for at least 10 to 15 minutes or up to several hours at room temperature. Meanwhile, preheat the broiler with the rack 6 inches from the heat.

Taste the cherries and adjust the lemon juice and sugar if necessary. Scrape the cherries and juices into the baking dish and spread them evenly. Broil until the cherries are slightly tender and the juices are bubbling, 5 to 6 minutes. Remove the pan and set aside (leaving the broiler on) to cool slightly for at least 10 minutes.

Meanwhile, to finish the topping, whip the remaining ½ cup cream until almost stiff. Fold the cream into the cold custard.

Spread the mixture on top of the cherries. Slide under the broiler to brown the top, watching closely—this may take only a minute or less. Serve the gratin warm or at room temperature.

iced citron vodka chocolates
with fresh mint

Set aside the usual protocol for serving fine chocolates—these are most sensational eaten chilled. The crisp chocolate shatters between your teeth and melts instantly into soft ganache, hot spirits, icy mint . . . breathtaking. Serve on a chilled silver tray to maintain the drama. Even if this recipe seems a bit fussier than the others in this book, I can't stress how much you will enjoy the rave reviews!

The incomparable Hangar One citron vodka called Buddha's Hand inspired this recipe, but you can use unflavored vodka, or take a detour with rum, which is also splendid with the mint. Or omit the infusion and try the simpler raspberry vodka variation that follows.

This ganache must be mixed gently with a spatula rather than vigorously with a whisk to produce smooth, creamy results. And because the chocolate coating is not tempered, the chocolates must be stored in the refrigerator to prevent discoloration and blooming—which is convenient, because you are serving them cold. If you give them as a gift, though, be sure to instruct the recipient.

makes 36 or 49 chocolates

½ cup coarsely chopped fresh mint

1 cup plus 2 to 3 extra tablespoons heavy cream

9 ounces semisweet or bittersweet chocolate, either without a percentage on the label or any marked 55% through 60% (to use higher-percentage chocolates, see Note)

2 tablespoons citron vodka

12 to 16 ounces bittersweet or semisweet chocolate, chopped, for dipping

EQUIPMENT

An 8-inch square baking pan

Instant-read thermometer

Baking sheet

Dipping fork (see box, page 245)

TO MAKE THE MINT INFUSION, combine the mint and 1 cup of the cream in a small bowl or other container. Cover, and refrigerate overnight.

Strain the cream through a strainer set over a glass measuring cup, pressing on the mint leaves to extract all the cream. Discard the mint, and add enough additional cream to make 1 cup.

Line the bottom and sides of the baking pan with foil.

To make the ganache, chop the 9 ounces of chocolate into pieces no bigger than almonds and place in a medium bowl. Set aside.

In a small saucepan, bring the cream to a low boil. Pour over the chocolate and stir gently with a rubber spatula until the chocolate is completely melted and the mixture is smooth; do not whisk or splash the mixture by stirring too briskly, or the texture of the ganache will be cakey and granular instead of smooth and creamy. Stir in the vodka and mix only enough to blend. Strain the ganache (to refine the texture) into the lined baking pan, tilting it to level. Cover and freeze until hard.

Line a large baking pan with wax paper. Lift the sheet of ganache out of its pan, using the edges of the foil. Flip it over onto a sheet of parchment paper set on a cutting board and peel off the foil. Using your longest knife blade, dipped in hot water and wiped dry before each cut, cut the sheet of ganache into 6 or 7 equal strips (try not to cut though the parchment). Cut across the strips to make squares. Work quickly to prevent the ganache from thawing. Transfer the squares to the lined pan, cover the pan with foil or plastic wrap, and place it in the freezer until the chocolate centers are rock hard. Keep them frozen until the moment you are ready to dip them. (The centers may be sealed in an airtight container and kept frozen up to 2 months.)

Melt the chocolate for dipping in a thoroughly dry heatproof medium bowl set in a large skillet of barely simmering water. Be sure that all your utensils are dry, so that the chocolate does not come in contact with moisture. Stir frequently to hasten melting. When the chocolate is almost completely melted, remove the bowl from the skillet and wipe the bottom dry. Stir until the chocolate is entirely smooth and melted, then let cool to 100° to 105°F.

Place the bowl of chocolate in front of you. Set a baking sheet lined with parchment or wax paper to the right of the chocolate if you are right-handed (or to the left if you are left-handed).

Remove half of the frozen centers from the freezer and place them on a plate to the left of the chocolate (or the right if you are left-handed). Place a center in the bowl of chocolate and use the dipping fork to flip it over and push it under the surface of the chocolate. Slip the fork under the center and lift it out of the chocolate, tap the fork on the sides of the bowl to drain excess chocolate back into the bowl, and wipe the tines of the fork against the edge of the bowl before setting the chocolate onto the lined pan. Work quickly to prevent the centers from thawing before they are dipped and to prevent them from melting in the warm chocolate, and don't let the dipped center rest on the fork any longer than necessary, or it will stick to the fork. Repeat with the remaining centers on the plate. Remove the remaining centers from the freezer and dip them as before. Use the dipping fork to drizzle chocolate randomly over the chocolates.

Refrigerate the dipped chocolates at least long enough to harden the coating before removing them from the paper. Store in a covered container in the refrigerator for up to 2 weeks, or freeze for 3 months. Serve cold.

NOTE: To use chocolate marked 60% to 64%, use 7 ounces chocolate. For chocolate marked 70% to 72%, use 5½ ounces (6 if using the rum) chocolate and stir 2 tablespoons of sugar into the cream before heating it. Pour only half of the hot cream and sugar over the chocolate and stir until the chocolate is melted, then add the remaining cream and stir to blend thoroughly.

iced raspberry vodka chocolates

Omit the mint leaves (skip the infusion step) and use only 1 cup cream. Substitute raspberry vodka for the citron vodka.

■ **TO IMPROVISE A DIPPING FORK**

You can use a dinner fork with well-spaced tines or a cocktail fork with 2 or 3 well-spaced tines (too many tines too close together prevent excess chocolate from draining off the centers). Or use a sturdy plastic fork with the first and third tines broken off, or use any cheap metal fork, with the first and third tines bent back and out of the way. I have also been known to dip these chocolate with my fingers. So there is no excuse for not making these chocolates!

---

beer granita

Beer granita is a very unusual but excellent accompaniment or topping for vanilla ice cream. It accentuates the vanilla flavor, and the contrast of icy and bitter with sweet and creamy is divine. Especially hoppy or bitter beers, such as an India pale ale, are too bitter for this recipe.   makes about 2 cups

1 cup light ale or pilsner beer (see Note)   3 tablespoons sugar
¼ cup plus 2 tablespoons water

MIX THE BEER, water, and sugar together, stirring until the sugar dissolves. Pour the mixture into a shallow baking dish and put it into the freezer until partially frozen. Use a fork to scrape and break the mixture into shards and crystals. Return to the freezer to freeze completely. When frozen, scrape the mixture one more time with the fork. Keep frozen until serving.

NOTE: Beer must be measured when it's flat, unless you have a scale; a cup of beer weighs 8 ounces whether it's foamy or not!

red or white wine granita

Freezing it with a little sugar and water transforms even an ordinary wine into a very pleasing dessert. Make this light and flavorful granita with any drinkable leftover wine, or even with a bottle you've opened and found disappointing. Or, if you have a little of this and that left after a party, make your own blend. No one is looking—mix red and white to make rosé if you like.

A little whipped cream on top is lovely but not essential. Red wine granita makes a particularly good topping for vanilla ice cream. *makes about 2 cups*

1 cup red or white wine (or a mixture)

¼ cup plus 2 tablespoons water

3 tablespoons sugar

Sweetened whipped cream for topping (optional)

IN A MEDIUM bowl, mix the wine, water, and sugar together until the sugar dissolves.

Pour the mixture into a shallow baking dish and freeze until almost completely frozen, 1½ to 2 hours. Use a fork to scrape and break the mixture into shards and crystals. Return the pan to the freezer to freeze completely. Scrape and toss the granita one more time. Keep frozen until serving.

Serve in stemmed glasses, dolloped with whipped cream, if desired.

resources

■

ANSON MILLS
1922-C GERVAIS STREET
COLUMBIA, SC 29201
803-467-4122
WWW.ANSONMILLS.COM
Stone-ground organic whole grains, including
whole wheat, buckwheat, and corn.

BOB'S RED MILL
NATURAL FOODS
5209 SE INTERNATIONAL WAY
MILWAUKIE, OR 97222
800-349-2173
WWW.BOBSREDMILL.COM
An extraordinary array of stone-ground
flours, including whole wheat, graham,
kamut, and spelt flours, cornmeal and
corn flour, and much more.

CALABRO CHEESE
500 COE AVENUE
EAST HAVEN, CT 06512
866-433-7834
WWW.CALABROCHEESE.COM
Absolutely heavenly ricotta, available in
selected fine cheese stores across the
country. If you have a choice, ask for the
hand-packed version.

COWGIRL CREAMERY
80 FOURTH STREET
POINT REYES STATION, CA 94956
866-433-7834 (MAIL-ORDER)
WWW.COWGIRLCREAMERY.COM
Award-winning hand-made fresh cheeses,
including fromage blanc and cottage
cheese, crème fraîche, and paneer; also
Laura Chenel chêvre. There are retail stores
in Point Reyes Station and San Francisco,
California, and Washington, DC.

EL MOLINO MILLS
345 NORTH BALDWIN PARK BOULEVARD
CITY OF INDUSTRY, CA 91746
Stone-ground whole-grain flours.

THE IMPERIAL TEA COURT
1411 POWELL STREET
SAN FRANCISCO, CA 94133
800-567-5898
WWW.IMPERIALTEA.COM
The best tea specialist in the San Francisco
area. One other location in San Francisco
and one in Berkeley.

INDIA TREE
1421 ELLIOTT AVENUE
SEATTLE, WA 98119
800 369 4848
206-270-0293
INDIA@INDIATREE.COM
A good course for spices and muscovado
sugar. Products are available in specialty
stores and better supermarkets, but you can
also order online.

KING ARTHUR FLOUR
THE BAKER'S CATALOGUE
P.O. BOX 876
NORWICH, VT 05055-0876
800-827-6836
Everything for the baker and dessert maker,
including digital thermometers with probes.

MOZZARELLA COMPANY
2944 ELM STREET
DALLAS, TX 75226
214-741-4072
WWW.MOZZO.COM
Fresh cow's milk and goat's milk ricotta,
crème fraîche, and fresh Texas goat cheese.

PARRISH'S CAKE DECORATING SUPPLY, INC.
225 WEST 146 STREET
GARDENA, CA 90248
800-736-8443
WWW.PARRISHSMAGICLINE.COM
Everything for the baker, including Magic
Line pans with solid or removable bottoms,
in every conceivable size, 2 or 3 inches deep.

THE PASTA SHOP
5655 COLLEGE AVENUE
OAKLAND, CA 94618
888-952-4005
WWW.ROCKRIDGEMARKETHALL.COM
A fabulous gourmet store with a second
location in Berkeley. The buyers and owners
solicit advice from an impressive list of
local cookbook authors and professional
bakers, so the store has a subspecialty in
baking ingredients and chocolate. Chocolate
and cocoa from Scharffen Berger, Valrhona,
Callebaut, and Michel Cluizel, among
others; Madagascar and Tahitian vanilla
extracts and whole and ground vanilla
beans; honeys; chestnuts in a variety of
forms, including chestnut flour; nut pastes;
flavored salts; specialty sugars; fresh
cheeses; olive oils; preserves; and more.

PEETS COFFEE & TEA
P.O. BOX 12509
BERKELEY, CA 94712
800-999-2132
WWW.PEETS.COM
Fine coffee beans, freshly roasted,
and fine teas.

PENZEYS SPICES
P.O. BOX 924
19300 WEST JANACEK COURT
BROOKFIELD, WI 53008
800-741-7787
WWW.PENZEYS.COM
All kinds of spices; Madagascar, Tahitian,
and Mexican vanilla beans; several types
of cinnamon. Reading their catalog is an
education in flavor ingredients and their
uses.

ST. GEORGE SPIRITS
2601 MONARCH STREET
AT ALAMEDA POINT
ALAMEDA, CA 94501
WWW.STGEORGESPIRITS.COM and
WWW.HANGARONE.COM
America's first and finest craft distiller
makes exquisite Aqua Perfecta eaux-de-vie
(framboise, kirsch, poire, etc.) from local
fruit; grappa; the breath-taking pot-distilled
Hangar One vodkas (raspberry, Buddha's
Hand, kaffir lime, and natural); single-
malt Scotch; and heirloom apple and pear
brandies. You can visit their tasting room.

SCHARFFEN BERGER
CHOCOLATE MAKER
914 HEINZ STREET
BERKELEY, CA 94710
800-930-4528
WWW.SCHARFFENBERGER.COM
Semisweet, bittersweet, extra dark,
unsweetened, and milk chocolates; dark-
chocolate; gianduja; limited-edition special
chocolate blends; cacao nibs; and the best
natural cocoa powder.

SPUN SUGAR CHOCOLATES
1611 UNIVERSITY AVENUE
BERKELEY, CA 94703
510-843-9192
"Professional" chocolates, such as Callebaut
and Ghirardelli, which can be ordered in less
than 10-pound quantities, perfect for the
home cook; Scharffen Berger chocolates and
the Etienne Guittard line of European-style
and single-origin chocolates; and supplies
for cake decorators.

SUGAR AND SPICE
2965 JUNIPERO SERRA BOULEVARD
DALEY CITY, CA 94014
650-994-4911
Cake-decorating and candy-making supplies.

SUR LA TABLE
1765 SIXTH AVENUE SOUTH
SEATTLE, WA 98134-1608
800-243-0852
WWW.SURLATABLE.COM
Premium source for quality tools and
equipment for home bakers and cooks;
ingredients including Scharffen Berger,
Valrhona, and E. Guittard chocolates.

SWEET CELEBRATIONS
(FORMERLY MAID OF SCANDINAVIA)
7009 WASHINGTON AVENUE SOUTH
EDINA, MN 55439
800-328-6722
WWW.SWEETC.COM
Ingredients and equipment of all sorts
for the home baker.

WHOLE FOODS
WWW.WHOLEFOODSMARKET.COM
This upscale national natural food
chain is a great source of natural and
organic ingredients, including specialty
flours and sugars; fine chocolates; bulk
foods, including seeds, nuts, and grains;
unsweetened shredded, dried, and flaked
coconut; and more.

IN ADDITION

- Local cheese shops, for specialty cheeses
  and artisan cheeses.
- Local specialty coffee roasters and
  purveyors of fine teas.
- Health food and natural foods stores and
  high-end groceries, for bulk foods, grains,
  flours, seeds, and nuts.
- Restaurant supply stores, for commercial
  half-sheet pans and cake pans.

acknowledgments

I am enormously grateful to work on projects that I love, but the frosting on the cake is working with people I admire and enjoy. Thanks to Ann Bramson, my always visionary editor at Artisan books. Thanks also to Hannah Hoffman, who tested and tasted with me while getting her degree in anthropology. Thanks to culinary consultant and dear friend Maya Klein, for creative help (yet again). I loved working with photographer Leigh Beisch for the first time, and photo stylist Sara Slavin, for the sixth time. Thanks to Sandra Cook for styling the ice cream shots so beautifully and to Jan Derevjanik for her stunning book design. Thanks to Judith Sutton, for her vast experience and meticulous copyediting. Thanks to Nani Steele for assistance with food styling. Also thanks to photo assistant Lauren Grant and studio manager Shana Lopes at the Leigh Beisch Studio. Thanks to Sue Fisher King, for generously lending props. As always, thanks to my agent, Jane Dystel, and my very wise and supportive daughter, Lucy Medrich.

index